MIRROR

OF

MODERN DEMOCRACY:

A

HISTORY

OF THE

DEMOCRATIC PARTY,

FROM ITS ORGANIZATION IN 1825, TO ITS LAST GREAT ACHIEVEMENT,

THE REBELLION OF 1861.

TO WHICH IS PREFIXED A SKETCH OF

THE OLD FEDERAL AND REPUBLICAN PARTIES.

By WILLIAM D. JONES.

New-York;
N. C. MILLER, 3 PARK ROW.
1864.

J. J. Reed, Printer and Stereotyper,
43 Centre Street.

PREFACE.

THE design of this work is to expose a mischievous delusion.

Nearly forty years ago was formed a political party, styled by its projectors and leaders, "The Democratic Party." Under faithless pledges of reform it came into power, and, with the exception of a few brief intervals, has since had control of the Government. During its rule incalculable injury has been inflicted upon the country. The currency has been repeatedly deranged; these derangements having been attended with their natural concomitants, financial embarrassments, commercial revulsions, and bank suspensions; the national industry has been several times prostrated, and the general prosperity interrupted; the constitutional rights of citizens have been infringed; the faith of treaties has been violated; free territory has been conquered in aggressive wars, consigned to Slavery, and annexed to the Union; political heresies have been propagated; and corruption has, to an alarming extent, been introduced into the Government. These are a part of a long succession of evils which has marked the career of this party, and which at length culminated in this Rebellion. All this has been done in the abused name of Democracy, to which this party lays exclusive claim. It was defeated in the contest of 1860; and after having involved the nation in a most calamitous civil war, it is again making its appeals to the people for a restoration to power.

To strip from this party the guise under which it has perpetrated its evil deeds,, and is endeavoring to regain political ascendency, would be doing the country an invaluable service. And if this effort should aid any considerable number in investigating the claims of Modern Democracy, or remove the scales from the eyes of but a few of its blind devotees, the labor will not be regretted.

The present is a favorable time for the dissemination of political truth. The faith of many in the infallibility of parties is giving way; party attachments are relaxing; and many who have been deterred from investigation by the force of prejudice, are beginning to manifest a disposition for candid inquiry.

The original design of the writer was simply an exposure of the real character of the Democratic party, and its agency in the present Rebellion. But as it claims paternity in Thomas Jefferson, it was deemed proper to precede the main history by a sketch of the old Federal and Republican parties. And to render the work still more valuable, it has been made to present the leading measures of every administration under the present Constitution. This enlargement of the original plan was in a measure induced by the facility afforded for the performance of the additional labor, by the somewhat free use of the American Statesman,* granted by its obliging publisher.

---

* A work which I will take occasion here gratuitously, and without solicitation, to commend to every American citizen who wishes to procure a complete and impartial political history of the United States, at the least possible cost.

The author has not intentionally done injustice to any party or individual. Nor has he condemned, indiscriminately, the acts of the Democratic party, or impugned the motives of the mass of its members, or even of a majority of its leaders; many of whom, doubtless, have supported its most impolitic measures in good faith. But that, *on the whole*, its rule has been disastrous to the country, he fully believes.

Nor has this work been written to gratify a vindictive feeling toward political opponents. It has been prompted solely by a sense of duty arising from the conviction, that the re-establishment of the Democratic party in power, would be a calamity second only to the success of the Rebellion.

CONTENTS.

PART FIRST.

HISTORY OF THE FEDERAL AND REPUBLICAN PARTIES.

CHAPTER I.

FROM THE FORMATION OF THE CONSTITUTION TO THE CLOSE OF WASHINGTON'S ADMINISTRATION.

CHAPTER II.

ADMINISTRATION OF JOHN ADAMS.

CHAPTER III.

ADMINISTRATIONS OF JEFFERSON, MADISON AND MONROE.

PART SECOND.

CHAPTER I.

ADMINISTRATION OF JOHN QUINCY ADAMS.

CHAPTER II.

ADMINISTRATION OF JACKSON—FIRST TERM.

CHAPTER III.

ADMINISTRATION OF JACKSON—SECOND TERM.

CHAPTER IV.

ADMINISTRATION OF VAN BUREN.

CHAPTER V.

ADMINISTRATION OF HARRISON AND TYLER.

CHAPTER VI.

ADMINISTRATION OF POLK.

CHAPTER VII.

ADMINISTRATION OF TAYLOR AND FILLMORE.

CHAPTER VIII.

ADMINISTRATION OF PIERCE.

CHAPTER IX.

ADMINISTRATION OF BUCHANAN.

CHAPTER X.

ADMINISTRATION OF LINCOLN.

CHAPTER XI.

PARTIES CONTRASTED. THE DEMOCRATIC PARTY THE PARTY OF THE REBELLION.

CONCLUSION.

DEMOCRATIC MIRROR.

PART FIRST.

HISTORY OF THE FEDERAL AND REPUBLICAN PARTIES.

CHAPTER I

History of Political Parties to the close of Washington's Administration.

The date of a party organization has often a controlling influence upon the political conduct of men. They imagine themselves right in politics, because they have adopted the opinions and long followed the lead of certain statesmen and politicians. There are multitudes who, after all the changes of parties during the last fifty years, boast that they are in the regular line of the great party of which Jefferson was the head and leader. They profess to be the disciples of this great "Apostle of Liberty," while they can not tell what were the principles he taught, or the measures of public policy upon which the first two great parties were divided.

It is designed, before proceeding to the main object of this work, to present a true sketch of the Federal and Republican parties, which, though brief, will, it is believed, furnish the necessary assistance to those who desire to trace their political pedigree, and to test the claims of Modern Democracy.

These parties, as is well known, originated in the Convention that framed the Constitution of the United States. It is known, also, by every reader at all acquainted with our political history, that the States, prior to the Revolution, had no political connection; and that, for the more effective prosecution of the war of independence, a union of the States was formed. In 1777, the year after the

Declaration of Independence, Articles of Union were drawn up by the Congress, and submitted to the several States for adoption. They were styled, "Articles of Confederation and perpetual Union between the States of New Hampshire, Massachusetts, Rhode Island, Connecticut, New York, New Jersey, Pennsylvania, Delaware, Maryland, Virginia, North Carolina, South Carolina, and Georgia." These Articles were to go into effect when ratified by the Legislatures of all the States. But so slow were some of the States in adopting them, that the last State, (Maryland,) did not send in her ratification until March, 1781.

This Union was simply a *league*, or *confederation* of independent States. One of the articles expressly declared, "each State retains its sovereignty, freedom, and independence." The States were equal. Each State was entitled to any number of delegates in the Congress, not exceeding seven. Votes in that body were taken by States, each State having one vote, which was determined by a majority of its delegates. No State was entitled to a vote unless at least two of its delegates were present; nor when its delegates were equally divided.

Although the Confederation was called a Government, it had scarcely one of the essential attributes of a government. It had neither an Executive nor a Judicial department. Its grand defect was its inherent weakness. The power to execute the laws was wholly wanting. There being no national Judiciary, all suits must be tried in State courts. Indeed, the Government did not operate directly upon individuals; and as no person could be answerable to it, there was no need of national courts. There was a Legislature consisting of a single body of men, called Congress; but it did not possess the ordinary powers of legislation. As it had not the power to carry its own requisitions into effect, it possessed little more than an advisory power. It belonged to Congress to call upon the States, from time to time, to furnish their respective quotas of men and money to carry on the war; but it had not the power to compel a State to raise a man or a dollar for this purpose. It could and did borrow money on its own credit; but it had no power to make any effectual provisions for its repayment; the power of taxation being possessed exclusively by the States. Hence, this government was wholly dependent upon the good will of thirteen independent State Governments.

Another very important power of which the Confederation was destitute, was the power to regulate trade. The necessity of this power was, in fact, the more immediate cause of calling the Convention that framed the Constitution. The colonists had for more than a hundred years suffered severely from the acts of the British Parliament designed to secure a monopoly of trade. By the navigation acts of 1651 and 1663, foreign vessels were not allowed to participate in the carrying trade between Great Britain and other countries. Acts were passed also to secure the sale of her own manufactures. Some of the most necessary articles the colonists were not allowed to manufacture for themselves, under severe penalties. In short, her policy was such as to compel the people of the Colonies to sell to the mother country their raw materials and all other products which it was for her interest to buy, and to take in exchange her manufactures and whatever else she had to sell. These acts, and the oppressive duties laid from time to time upon the productions of the Colonies, were among the principal grievances which led to the Revolution.

During the war, intercourse between the two countries was suspended. But when, on the return of peace, commercial intercourse was resumed, the effects of the British policy began to be again severely felt. The country was flooded with British goods, and drained of its money to pay for them. Relief might have been obtained by countervailing duties upon British goods and vessels; but Congress had not the power thus to regulate commerce: this power, too, belonged to the States. To be effectual, the duties levied in the different States must be uniform; but the States were unable to agree upon a uniform system of duties. What was deemed for the interest of one State, might be injurious to others: hence, conflicting regulations were adopted; the spirit of rivalry and jealousy which led to this retaliatory legislation arose to such a pitch as seriously to threaten the safety of the Union.

A meeting was at length proposed, to consist of commissioners of the several States, with a view to some satisfactory arrangement. The meeting was held at Annapolis, in Maryland, in September, 1786. But as only five States were represented, no arrangement was attempted. The commissioners, however, united in recommending a gener l convention of delegates from all the States, and express d the opinion that, as there were numerous defects in the Federal Government, the powers of the deputies should be extended to other objects than those of commerce. The Convention was accordingly called by Congress, to meet at Philadelphia on the 2d Monday of June, 1787.

Very soon after the Convention was organized, an important difference of opinion began to appear. Two plans of government were presented; one by Edmund Randolph, of Virginia, the other by William Patterson, of New Jersey. A resolution also was offered, declaring, "That a National Government ought to be established, consisting of a supreme Legislative, Judiciary, and Executive." As this resolution proposed a radical change in the system of government, it met with strong opposition. Delegates were opposed to changing the Confederation of independent, sovereign States to a consolidated National Government. The Convention, they contended, had been called, not to alter the plan of government, but simply to confer upon Congress certain necessary powers which it did not possess.

To this it was replied, that other alterations had been contemplated—that some of the States had expressly suggested "the establishing of a firm *national government*," and to make such alterations as should "render the Constitution adequate to the exigencies of government and the preservation of the Union." Besides, as no plan that might be adopted by the Convention could be binding until ratified by their constituents, the Convention might propose any changes which were deemed conducive to the general welfare of the Union.

The debate upon this resolution became highly animated. Indeed, to such a height were the feelings of members raised, that the Convention was on the point of being broken up. The resolution was at length adopted; and the plan of a Constitution presented by Mr. Randolph, which, being more in accordance with that contemplated by the resolution, was taken as the basis of action by the Convention.

Defeated in their opposition to the resolution proposing a change in the plan of government, some members of the minority left the Convention long before its close, and returned to their homes. Others remained, in the hope, doubtless, of being able to restrain, in some measure, the action of the majority. Hence, the minority, being in favor of preserving the then existing *Confederation,* or *Federal Union,* the union of sovereign, independent States on the principle of State equality, were in the Convention called "*Federalists;*" and the majority, being opposed to a simple Confederation of States, and in favor of a complete Government possessing more of a *national* character, and more ample powers, were called *Anti-Federalists.* [See Luther Martin's Report to the Legislature of Maryland, in *Elliot's Debates.*] Afterward, while the proposed Constitution was before the people of the States for ratification, its friends, the Anti-Federalists, urged, as a reason for its adoption, that the States could not be held together by the Articles of Confederation; and that there was no hope of preserving the Union, but by the adoption of the Constitution. Hence they then took the name of *Federalists,* by which name one of the two great political parties was distinguished, until its dissolution after the election of Mr. Monroe.

In the State Conventions which ratified the Constitution, the same difference of sentiment prevailed. One party favored the granting of ample powers to the General Government; the other contended for the *rights of the States,* apprehensive that too much power was to be surrendered to the Federal Government, which might in time "swallow up" the State Governments. Such was the jealousy for State rights, that some of the State Conventions, though they ratified the Constitution, recommended to Congress sundry amendments to be proposed to the several States in the way provided by the Constitution. These amendments were generally in the nature of the bills of rights annexed to our State Constitutions. As the General Government possesses no powers but such as are granted by the Constitution, these express guaranties were unneces sary, and were added mainly to prevent misconstruction or abuse of constitutional powers. They are contained in the first ten articles of amendment.

Among the leading Federalists of that day, were Gen. Washington, James Madison, and John Marshall, of Va.; Rufus King and John Adams, of Mass.; Alexander Hamilton and John Jay, of N. Y.; Gouverneur Morris, of Pa.; Charles Pinckney and Charles C. Pinckney, of S. C; all of whom, except Marshall, Adams and Jay, had been members of the Convention. [Mr. King subsequently became a citizen of the State of New York.]

Notwithstanding the division of sentiment which has been noticed, there were not as yet, nor for many years afterwards, distinct, organized political parties. And General Washington, though acting with the friends of the Constitution in the Convention, was elected President without opposition. The leading measures of his administration, however, met with a strong opposition from those who were opposed to the Federalists.

The 1st Congress met in New York on the 4th of March, 1789; but a quorum of both Houses did not attend until the 6th of March. On counting the electoral votes, it appeared that Gen. Washington was unanimously elected President, and that John Adams was, by the next highest number of votes, elected Vice-President. On the 30th of April, the President took the oath of office.

Great public rejoicings had taken place on the adoption of the Constitution by mechanics and manufacturers in sundry places, because Congress had now the power to regulate commerce with foreign nations by protecting duties. Scarcely had Congress commenced its deliberations, before petitions were received from Baltimore, Charleston, New York, Boston, and other places, for the exercise of this power for the encouragement of domestic manufactures. When the first of these petitions was received, Mr. Madison had already brought forward the subject of the revenue system; and the first act passed by Congress, excepting only the law prescribing the oaths of office, was an act, the objects of which were declared in the preamble to be, "the support of the Government, the discharge of the debts of the United States, and the encouragement and protection of domestic manufactures, by duties on goods, wares, and merchandises imported." By this act, discriminating duties were laid upon both foreign goods and foreign vessels.

At this session the auxiliary Executive Departments were reörganized and adapted to the new Government. The question arose, whether the concurrence of the Senate was necessary in the removal of officers as in their appointment. The opinion of the writers of the Federalist was, that the consent of the Senate would be necessary "to *displace* as well as to appoint." This construction was supported by Mr. Sherman and Mr Gerry, who had been members of the Constitutional Convention, and opposed by Mr. Madison and Mr. Baldwin, who also had been members of the Convention. The latter view prevailed by a vote of 34 to 20.

Mr. Jefferson was appointed Secretary of State; Mr. Hamilton, Secretary of the Treasury; Gen. Knox of Mass., Secretary of War; and Edmund Randolph, Attorney-General.

The Judiciary Department also was established at this session.

Congress, having adjourned on the 29th of September, to meet again on the 1st Monday of January, 1790, met accordingly. Among the objects recommended by the President, were those of "promoting manufactures," and making "adequate provision for the support of the public credit." The latter was the great measure of the session. The Secretary of the Treasury, having been directed at the preceding session to prepare a plan, reported one accordingly.

The public credit had become so depressed, that Government paper had been sold for one-sixth to one-eighth of its nominal value. Issues of this "Continental money," as it was called, having been made to the amount of nearly 300 millions of dollars, it was not an easy task to maintain the honor and retrieve the credit of the nation, and do perfect justice to all the public creditors.

The Secretary recommended that the foreign debt should be fully paid; and in respect to the domestic debt, that no discrimination should be made between original holders of the public securities and present possessors by purchase; nor between creditors of the Union and those of the States. As the chief part of the debts of the States had been contracted on account of the Union, the same ought to be assumed by the Union. And he recommended that the debt be funded. The provision of a permanent fund for its payment would establish the public credit, and enable the Government, in any emergency, to procure means to supply the public necessity. It would prevent the fluctuation and insecurity of an unfunded debt. The debt properly funded would serve most purposes of money; and the capital thus created "would invigorate all the operations of agriculture, manufactures, and commerce."

In the measures of finance founded on this Report, originated the first regular and systematic opposition to Washington's administration. Mr. Madison, who, in convention, and for some time afterward, had been one of those called "Federalists," now joined the opposition. Some were opposed to funding systems generally. But the assumption of the State debts was a special object of denunciation. Such was the opposition to the financial measures generally, that resolutions denouncing them were passed by the Legislatures of Virginia, Pennsylvania, Maryland, and North Carolina. The plan of the Secretary was in the main adopted. Of the debts of the States, estimated at about $25,000,000, the sum of $21,500,000 was assumed in specific sums from the several States.

The opposition to these measures was to some extent increased by an act passed at the next session, (1790-1791,) in conformity to a report of the Secretary, recommending an increase of duties on imported wines, spirits, tea and coffee, and a duty on home distilled spirits. The proposed duty on domestic distilled spirits was vehemently opposed, especially by Southern and Western members, the population in that section being to a less extent the consumers of foreign goods.

It was this tax on domestic spirits which caused what was called the "Whisky insurrection," in Western Pennsylvania. An organized opposition to the law having been formed, Congress passed an act authorizing the President to call out the militia to aid in enforcing the laws. The insurrection having at length assumed an alarming aspect, the President, in the summer of 1794, ordered a military force to be raised of 15,000 men, by which the insurrection was quelled, almost without bloodshed.

But the most prominent financial measure of the session at which this tax law was enacted, (1790–1791,) was the establishment of a National Bank. This, too, had been recommended by the Secretary of the Treasury, and supported by various arguments. The Bank bill was opposed by the same party as that which had opposed other measures of the administration. Its leading opponent was Mr. Madison. The bill passed the House, 39 to 20. All who voted against the bill, except one, were from the States of Maryland, Virginia, North Carolina, South Carolina, and Georgia. All present from the other States, except one from Massachusetts, voted in the affirmative, with two from Maryland, two from North Carolina, and one from South Carolina. The President obtained the written opinions of the members of his Cabinet as to the constitutionality of the bill. They were equally divided, Hamilton and Knox affirming its constitutionality, and Jefferson and Randolph being of the contrary opinion. After mature deliberation, the President signed the bill.

Washington's foreign policy encountered scarcely less opposition than his domestic. The revolution in France, which commenced about the time when our Government under the Constitution was organized, was followed by a general war in Europe. Several European Powers had combined against France ; and the latter had made a formal declaration of war against Great Britain and Holland. It now became a question, What course should the United States pursue towards the new Government of France? During our Revolution, an alliance had been formed with that nation, which had rendered us aid in our contest with Great Britain ; and a large portion of the American people were now disposed to reciprocate the favor.

The President, though sympathizing with France, desired to maintain a neutral position, provided it should be determined that such a course was consistent with our treaties with that country. He therefore submitted a series of questions to the Cabinet, then consisting of four members.

One of these questions was, Shall a proclamation be issued enjoining non-interference by our citizens in the war between Great Britain and France? Another, Shall a minister from the French Republic be received? The members were unanimous in favor of a proclamation of neutrality, and of receiving a Minister. The Secretaries of the Treasury and of War, (Hamilton and Knox,) however, advised the reception of a Minister with a qualification; it being doubtful whether the new Government of France had been established by the general consent of the nation. The Secretary of State and Attorney-General, (Jefferson and Randolph,) favored the reception without qualification. The change of Government, they thought, did not absolve us from the obligation of preëxisting treaties. In accordance with this view, the President decided to receive the French Minister.

The grounds upon which the proclamation of neutrality was justified, were, first, that in the condition of France, as it then was, the United States could not become involved in the war without endangering their own safety; and secondly, that our obligations held only in case of a *defensive* war; whereas the present war had been commenced by France. These were the opinions of the two Secretaries first mentioned. The other two deemed it unnecessary then to decide this question. The proclamation was issued on the 22d of April, 1793. For this act, unanimously advised by the Cabinet, the President was severely censured by his political opponents. It was considered as evidence of hostility towards France.

The new French Minister had arrived at Charleston on the 8th of April, and commenced enlisting American citizens and fitting out vessels of war, by which British commerce was annoyed, and a British vessel actually captured in our waters. Yet, in these and other similar unlawful acts, he was sustained by a powerful party and its presses. He was told that the *people* would sustain him. Thus encouraged, he persisted in his warfare against the Government. A large number of British vessels, some of them within the jurisdiction of the United States, were captured by vessels fitted out by Genet, and acting under his authority. After a brief stay at Charleston, he proceeded to the seat of Government, (Philadelphia,) where he was received with loud and enthusiastic demonstrations of joy by his numerous friends. Here, too, he undertook to carry on his fillibustering scheme, and actually succeeded in fitting out at least one privateer, and getting her out to sea, during a brief absence of the President at Mount Vernon.

The conduct of Genet having at length become intolerable, it was unanimously agreed in Cabinet, that a letter should be sent to the French Government requesting his recall. This highly exasperated him. Even Mr. Jefferson, whom he regarded as a friend, became an object of displeasure; he having, as Genet alleged, used to him two languages, "one official and another confidential." He was soon after recalled. He, however, never returned to France, but remained in this country until the day of his death.

Although the Cabinet had unanimously agreed to the proclamation of neutrality, many eminent citizens and statesmen were opposed to it, and in favor of joining France. Among them was Mr. Jefferson, who considered our treaty obligations in full force, and who, though he had assented to the proclamation, regarded the question as merely reserved to the meeting of Congress.

The cause of France had been much weakened in this country by the reprehensible conduct of the French Minister. A reaction, however, was soon produced by certain impolitic measures of the British Government. A scarcity of provisions in France had induced the latter to open her ports to neutral commerce. Great Britain, hoping to reduce her enemy by famine, determined to cut off external supplies. British cruisers were instructed to stop all vessels carrying bread-stuffs to any port of France, and to bring them into a convenient port. If they were proved to be neutral property, the cargoes were to be purchased, and the ships released; or both cargoes and vessels were to be released on their masters' giving bonds that the cargoes should be disposed of in the ports of countries at peace with Great Britain. This measure Great Britain alleged to be justified by the law of nations, which made all provisions contraband and liable to confiscation, when the stopping of these supplies was intended as a means of reducing an enemy to terms of peace. It was alleged, too, that the British orders did not go to the extent allowable ; they did not prohibit all kinds of provisions, nor require forfeiture. The American Government, on the other hand, maintained that both reason and usage had established the right of a neutral nation to carry the products of their industry for exchange to all nations, belligerent or neutral, as usual, without injury or molestation. This measure greatly embarrassed American commerce, and, superadded to the supposed encouragement of Indian hostilities by the British in Canada, the continued occupation of the Western military posts, and the impressment of American seamen into the British service, awakened intense resentment in the American people toward Great Britain.

The British Government did not stop here. Orders more stringent were issued to the commanders of British vessels, under which orders American vessels engaged in the French and West India trade were seized, carried into British ports, and condemned. This new order greatly increased the excitement against Great Britain ; and a war with that country was apprehended. Although this order was subsequently modified, the excitement was not allayed. All who refused to take the side of France against Great Britain, were represented as British partisans. Nor did it avail them to urge in justification of their neutrality that France had violated her treaty with us, and that our commerce had been harassed no less by French privateers than by those of Great Britain.

Resolutions proposing preparations for war and measures of retaliation, were introduced in Congress. Before these propositions were disposed of, the President, desirous to prevent war, concluded to make an effort at negotiation, and nominated to the Senate John Jay as Envoy Extraordinary to Great Britain. The nomination, after much opposition, was confirmed. As a successful negotiation was quite doubtful, preparations for war were deemed expedient, and the measures previously reported were in part adopted. Among these measures were the requisition for 80,000 militia to be ready to march at a moment's warning, and for the levying of additional duties on imports, taxes on carriages, &c.

The chief objects of Mr. Jay's mission were, to obtain restitution for spoliations of American commerce, and the fulfillment of the treaty of peace, some of the stipulations of which had not been observed. One of them was the surrender of the Western military posts which were still occupied. These objects secured, a treaty of commerce was to be proposed.

The charge against the President of being unfriendly to France seems to have been entirely unfounded. Mr. Jay was expressly instructed to say to the British Government, "that the United States would not derogate from their treaties and engagements with France." And to Mr. Monroe, who was soon after appointed our Minister to France, the Secretary of State, Mr. Randolph, said: "The President had been an early friend of the French revolution; and whatever reasons there may have been to suspend an opinion upon some of its important transactions, yet is he immutable in his wishes for its accomplishment. * * We have pursued neutrality with faithfulness. We mean to retain the same line of conduct in future; and to remove all jealousy as to Mr. Jay's mission to London, you may say that he is positively forbidden to weaken the engagements between this country and France."

The treaty was concluded on the 19th of November, 1794, and submitted to the Senate in extra session on the 8th of June, 1795. It secured the first of the primary objects of negotiation, namely, indemnity to American merchants for the illegal capture of their property under British orders. Also the Western posts were to be surrendered, but not until the 1st of June, 1796.

Of the numerous other provisions of the treaty, some were favorable, others unfavorable. But the terms were the best that could be secured. The Senate ratified the treaty, with the exception of one provision, which related to the West India trade, and recommended the addition of a clause suspending its operation; leaving for future negotiation this question, with that of the impressment of American seamen and others, upon which the parties had been unable to agree. With this modification the ratification was advised by a vote of 20 to 10 a bare constitutional majority.

This act of the Senate produced great excitement. It was denounced in public meetings and in newspapers. The Senators were treated with indignity; and an effigy of Mr. Jay was burned in Boston. Certain causes of delay having occurred, the President did not sign the treaty until the 14th of August, 1795. He became now himself an object of the vengeance of the opposition party. Even his private character was aspersed. He was charged with having appropriated public money for his private use ; and he had violated the Constitution, and ought to be impeached. The friends of the treaty, however, appeared to increase in number, it being deemed unwise to expose the country to a war not required by the national honor.

The treaty was ratified by the British Government with the suspending clause annexed by the Senate ; and on the 1st of March, 1796, the President sent a copy to the House, with the information that it had been proclaimed the law of the land. It now remained for the House to make provision for carrying the treaty into effect. To this a determined opposition was made. A warm debate arose which involved the Constitutional question, whether the assent of the House was essential to the obligation of the treaty; and whether the President had a right to negotiate a treaty of commerce. A resolution was moved, calling upon the President for a copy of his instructions to Mr. Jay, and other documents relating to the treaty. This was opposed by the minority, who maintained that a treaty was complete when assented to by the Senate, and signed by the President. After a long debate, the resolution was adopted, 62 to 37. The President declined to comply with the call, and stated at length his reasons. They are worthy of perusal, but the want of room forbids their insertion.

On a resolution, subsequently offered, declaring it expedient to carry this treaty into effect, another long debate took place, in which Mr. Madison and Mr. Gallatin opposed the treaty. Among those in its favor was Fisher Ames, whose speech is so famed for its eloquence. At its close, calls were made for the question ; but the opposition members, fearing the immediate influence of the speech, postponed the question until the next day, (April 29th,) when it was carried in Committee of the Whole, by the casting vote of the Chairman, (Muhlenburg.) It was then reported to the House, and passed, 51 to 48.

But the history of the "Jay treaty" is not yet ended The French Government, on being informed of its ratification by the President, informed Mr. Monroe, our Minister at Paris, that the Directory considered the alliance between the United States and France terminated by the treaty; that Adet, the French Minister to the United States, would be recalled; and a special Envoy was to be sent to make the announcement to the American Government.

Among the many complaints against the United States presented to Mr. Monroe by the French Government, one was, that the United States, in their treaty with Great Britain, had abandoned the principle, that free ships should make free goods, and that naval stores were made contraband. By treaties of the United States with France and Great Britain, French property in American vessels was liable to seizure by British cruisers, while British goods were secure in American vessels. But of this France had no reason to complain. Great Britain had only reserved a right to which she was entitled by the Law of Nations; by which "the goods of a friend found in the vessels of an enemy are free; and that the goods of an enemy in the vessel of a friend are lawful prize." But France, deeming it for her interest, had, in her treaties with the United States, preferred a different principle, "that free ships should make free goods."

It was the misfortune of France that she was now suffering the unforeseen consequences of her own voluntary act. And she had the less reason to complain, from the fact that she had, in her treatment of the United States, violated her own principle. She had, in May, 1793, issued a decree authorizing the capture of an enemy's property in neutral vessels, under which decree about *fifty* American vessels had been captured and deprived of their cargoes, and a greater number had been detained.

The French Directory had determined on some retaliatory measures, which had only been delayed, in the hope that the House of Representatives would defeat the treaty with Great Britain by refusing to provide for carrying it into effect. In June, 1796, news of the decision of the

House was received at Paris; and on the 2d of July a decree was issued, that "all neutral or allied powers shall, without delay, be notified, that the flag of the French Republic *will treat neutral vessels,* either as to confiscation, as to searches, or capture, *in the same manner as they shall suffer the English to treat them.*"

Evidently the object of France was to defeat the treaty with Great Britain. Mr. John Quincy Adams, our Minister in Holland, writing to our Government, said he had intimations of such a purpose. The supposition was strengthened by a treaty made in August, between France and Spain, by which they entered into an alliance offensive and defensive, agreeing to make common cause to insure "safety to the neutral flag;" in other words, to compel the United States to protect French and Spanish property in American vessels, in contravention of our treaty stipulation with Great Britain. Spain also complained of the unequal footing upon which she had been placed by the British treaty, and made this a pretext for not delivering up the posts on the Mississippi and running the boundary line. Holland, too, then dependent upon France, joined in the complaint.

Mr. Monroe, on the alleged ground of a want of due promptitude in making to the French Government the explanations furnished him by the President in justification of the treaty with Great Britain, was recalled by the President, and Mr. Charles C. Pinckney, of S. C., appointed in his place, Sept. 9, 1796. Mr. Monroe, an ardent friend of France, had been appointed in 1794, in the place of Mr. Gouverneur Morris, in deference to his wishes, and at the request of the French Government, because the latter had manifested too little zeal for the French cause.

Mr. Pinckney arrived at Paris in December; but he was soon informed that the Directory would "no longer recognize a Minister from the United States, until after a reparation of grievances." He remained there until about the last of January, when he received from the French Government a written notice to quit the country. He proceeded to Amsterdam to wait for instructions from his Government.

We have now come to near the close of Washington's administration. Our sketch includes most of the principal measures which characterized his administration, especially those which were subjects of party controversy. The reader will have perceived, that the spirit of party then manifest was much the same as it is at the present day. We see men distinguished for their public services, whose patriotism we scarcely dare question, pursuing party ends by dishonorable means. Probably no public man ever enjoyed greater popularity than Washington; yet no administration encountered a more bitter opposition, nor were even the official acts of a statesman or public functionary more violently assailed. Even the forged letters purporting to have been written by him in 1777, in opposition to the cause of independence and favorable to Great Britain, were republished. But time has vindicated his character; and his memory will be revered by his countrymen to the latest generation.

Gen. Washington was succeeded by John Adams as President. Of the votes of the Presidential electors chosen in November, 1796, Mr. Adams received the highest number, 71, and was elected President; and Mr. Jefferson, having received 68, the next highest number, was elected Vice-President.

CHAPTER II.

From the Commencement to the Close of the Administration of John Adams.

On the 4th of March, 1797, John Adams was inaugurated as President of the United States. The personal popularity of Gen. Washington had shielded him from the open assaults of the mass of his political opponents. In this respect Mr. Adams was less fortunate. The measures of his administration, however, met with scarcely greater opposition than those of his venerated predecessor. The difficulties with France had not been settled when he came into office, but were becoming more and more aggravated. And as our controversy with France and Great Britain had become in a great measure a party question, a very peaceful administration was hardly to be expected.

Our Minister had been virtually expelled from France; and new license had been given to spoliate on our commerce. A decree had been issued, authorizing the capture of neutral vessels having on board any productions of Great Britain or her possessions. This decree was in direct violation of the rights of neutral nations, and especially of the treaty between the United States and France, which provided that "free ships should make free goods." Many of our vessels were captured under this decree and condemned; and war having become probable, the President convened Congress in special session, on the 15th of May, 1797. As there were in both Houses majorities in favor of the administration, measures were readily adopted, both for preserving peace and for providing the means of defense.

Among the acts passed for increasing the revenue, was one for "laying duties on stamped vellum, parchment, and paper." This act, probably from the similarity of its title to the British stamp act of 1765, was highly obnoxious to a large portion of the people.

Attempts at negotiation, however, were to be continued;

ana Charles Cotesworth Pinckney, Elbridge Gerry, and John Marshall, were appointed as Envoys Plenipotentiary to the French Republic, Mr. Pinckney being then in Holland. The Envoys did not receive the usual formal recognition; but a mode of correspondence with them, of a most single nature, was adopted, in which the demands of the French Government were made known. Certain passages in President Adams' Message to Congress at the extra session must be softened before the Ministers could be received; a sum of money was required for the pockets of the Directory and Ministers; and our Government must grant theirs a large loan. Our Ministers being unwilling to concede to these demands, and having no authority to negotiate a loan in any form, they proposed that one of their number should forthwith return home to consult the Government, if the Directory would suspend all further captures of American vessels, and all proceedings on those already captured: but this was refused.

The American Ministers having objected to the proposition of a loan, on the ground that it would amount to a declaration of war on our part against Great Britain, Talleyrand, the French Minister of Foreign Affairs, resorted to artifice to compass his end, but failed. At length, the Directory having intimated a disposition to treat with Mr. Gerry alone, (who had been selected from the party said to be friendly to France,) the other two Envoys returned to the United States.

On the 21st of June, 1798, the President transmitted to Congress the correspondence between Mr. Gerry and Talleyrand. In his accompanying Message, he said: "I presume that before this time he (Mr. Gerry) has received fresh instructions, (a copy of which accompanies this message,) to consent to no loans; and therefore the negotiation may be considered at an end. I will never send another Minister to France, without assurances that he will be received, respected, and honored, as the representative of a great, free, powerful, and independent nation."

At the next session, (1797–1798,) further provision was made for the public defense; and an act was passed to suspend commercial intercourse with France and her dependencies. Preparations for war having been made, Gen. Washington was appointed by the President and Senate to take command of the army ; and the appointment was accepted.

The publication of the papers relating to the attempts at negotiation, showing the unceremonious reception of our Ministers, and the degrading terms upon which the Directory would treat, placed that Government in an unfavorable light before the American people ; and, notwithstanding the opposition which the war measures received, the Federal party, instead of losing, seems rather to have gained popularity. The publication of these papers also, it is presumed, aided the passage of the bills for the national defense ; and they had so affected the public mind as to give great anxiety to Mr. Jefferson, who, in a letter to Mr. Madison, urged him to assist with his pen in defending the opposition from the effects of the publication of the dispatches. The policy of the President was also approved in numerous public meetings ; and but for those two famous acts familiarly known as the "Alien and Sedition laws," the Federal party would perhaps have retained its ascendency.

The propriety of these laws it is not my purpose to discuss. Their nature and object, however, it is proper to state for the information of those who are unacquainted with their provisions and their history. There were in this country thousands of Frenchmen, combined in organized associations, and large numbers of British subjects, who were deemed dangerous to the peace of the United States. With a view to the public safety, was passed the Act, entitled, "An Act concerning Aliens." This Act authorized the President to order out of the country all aliens whom he should suspect of any treasonable designs against the Government. Any person remaining in the country after the time mentioned for his departure, without a license from the President, was liable to imprisonment not exceeding three years, and might never be admitted to become a citizen. And the President, on satisfactory proof that the residence of such alien was not dangerous, might grant him a license to remain for a time and at a place specified. He might also require a bond with sureties for good behavior. The act, among several other provisions, secured to aliens the right to dispose of their property. It was limited to the term of two years from its passage.

The "Sedition Law" was entitled, "An Act, in addition to an Act, entitled, 'An Act for the punishment of certain crimes against the United States.'" This act provided for punishing conspiracies to oppose any measure or law of the Government, or to hinder any public officer in the performance of his duty, or to attempt to procure a riot, or an insurrection. Such offense was punishable by a fine not exceeding $5,000, and imprisonment not less than six months, nor exceeding five years; and the Court might require sureties for good behavior. The law also provided, that any person convicted of writing, printing, uttering, or publishing any false, scandalous, or malicious writing, or of aiding to do the same, against the Government, Congress, or the President, with intent to defame them or to bring them into disrepute, or to stir up sedition, or to excite any unlawful opposition to any law of the United States, or to aid or abet any hostile designs of any foreign nation against the people or Government of the United States, should be fined not exceeding $2,000, and imprisoned not exceeding two years. But, contrary to the English law of libel, then a part of the common law of this country, which did not permit the defendant to justify by proving the truth of the statement charged as libelous, this law admitted such justification, and allowed conviction only when the defendant failed to prove the truth of his statement. This provision, which had then been adopted only in the States of Pennsylvania, Delaware, and Vermont, has since been incorporated into the Constitution or the laws of every State in the Union; qualified, however, by a provision, that the statement shall have been made from good motives and justifiable ends. The act was to continue in force until the 3d of March, 1801.

These laws, now so generally regarded with disfavor, were, by many great and good men, among whom were Washington and Patrick Henry, considered good and wholesome laws, justified by the state of things.

These laws were denounced by the leaders of the opposition party as infractions of the Constitutional guaranties of personal liberty, and freedom of speech and of the press. The Sedition Act, especially, was held up to public opprobrium as the "gag law."

To array public sentiment the more effectually against these laws, appeals were made to the Legislatures of the States, soliciting their action upon the subject. Here originated the famed Virginia and Kentucky Resolutions of 1798 and 1799, which were for a long time referred to as containing the essence of the old Republican or Democratic creed. Resolutions, drawn up by Mr. Jefferson for that purpose, were introduced in the Kentucky Legislature, and passed in November, 1798. As these resolutions have been so often cited by the advocates of the Southern doctrine of State Rights, or Nullification, in support of that heresy, they deserve particular attention. They declare, that the Union is a compact between the States, *as States;* that, as in other cases of compact *between parties having no common judge, each party has an equal right to judge for itself, as well of infractions, as of the mode and measure of redress;*" that the Alien and Sedition Laws were "not law, but altogether void, and of no force;" that, "in cases of an abuse of delegated powers, the members of the General Government being chosen by the people, any change by the people would be the Constitutional remedy; but where powers are assumed which have not been delegated, *a nullification of the act is the right remedy:* and that every State has a natural right, in cases not within the compact, *to nullify, of their own authority,* all assumptions of power by others within their limits."

The Virginia Resolutions, drawn up by Mr. Madison, then a member of the Legislature of that State, at the request, it is said, of Mr. Jefferson, were adopted the 21st of December, 1798. They declared, that the Constitution was a compact to which the States were parties, granting limited powers; that in case of a deliberate, palpable, and dangerous exercise of other powers not granted by the compact, the States had the right to *interpose* for arresting the progress of the evils, and for maintaining the rights of the States within their respective limits; and that the Alien and Sedition Laws were palpable infractions of the Constitution. They also solicited the concurrence of other States in these declarations, and requested the Governor to transmit them for this purpose to the several State Executives to be communicated to the several State Legislatures, and to each of the Senators and Representatives of Virginia in Congress. No State, it is believed, responded favorably to the solicitation ; some of the States expressly disapproved the Resolutions.

At their next sessions, the Legislatures of Virginia and Kentucky, in reply to the answers of the State Legislatures, reässerted the doctrines of the Resolutions. The Report on the subject by Mr. Madison concluded with a resolution declaring their adherence to the Resolutions of 1798, and renewing their protest against the Alien and Sedition Laws as palpable and alarming infractions of the Constitution. The Report and resolution were adopted in February, 1800. On the 25th of June of that year, the Alien Law expired by its own limitation ; the Sedition Act on the 4th of March, 1801.

The Virginia and Kentucky Resolutions involve Constitutional principles which have been the subject of much discussion. Though once the grand article of the creed of a dominant party, they are now generally repudiated as disorganizing and revolutionary. They will require further notice in a subsequent part of this work.

But Mr. Adams, before the close of his term of office, found other opposition than that of the Republican party. He had lost the confidence and support of many of his own party. This alienation of his friends had been caused, in a great measure, by his course on the French question. He had declared, as the reader will recollect, that he would "never send another Minister to France, without assurances that he would be received, respected, and honored, as the representative of a great, free, powerful, and independent nation." Believing that there was not sufficient evidence of a disposition on the part of the French Government to enter upon an honorable negotiation, many of his political friends highly disapproved of his determination to send other Ministers to that country. The principal evidence upon which the President acted, was, that France, induced, probably, by the war measures which Congress had adopted, had indicated a willingness to relinquish her demand as a preliminary to negotiation, and to treat on reasonable terms. Knowing that a majority of his Cabinet, Messrs. Pickering, Wolcott, and M'Henry, were opposed to renewing the mission under existing circumstances, the nominations were made to the Senate without consulting his Cabinet or any of his friends. The gentlemen selected for the mission were Oliver Ellsworth, Chief Justice of the United States, Patrick Henry, and William Vans Murray, then Minister Resident in the Netherlands. Mr. Henry, though friendly to the administration, declined the appointment from "absolute necessity." William Davie, of N. C., was appointed in his place.

The willingness, on the part of the Directory, to receive a Minister from our Government, had been communicated to Mr. Murray; and it was intimated to him that he would be acceptable to the French Government. The name of Mr. Murray alone was accordingly sent to the Senate. The Committee of the Senate to whom the nomination had been referred, being unfriendly to a renewal of the negotiation without further assurance from the French Government, and having intimated an intention to report against the nomination, the President sent the names of Ellsworth and Henry, who were to be added to the mission. But none of the Ministers were to proceed to France until more direct assurances should be given that they would be duly received. With this understanding, the Senate consented to the appointment.

The former friends of the President, who had been for some time disaffected towards him, and whom his course had now entirely estranged—among whom were Mr. Hamilton, Gouverneur Morris, and other distinguished and influential men—doubted the sincerity of the French Government; and they considered it derogatory to the national honor to accept an offer to negotiate, until the decrees against our commerce should be repealed. The principal motive which is supposed to have dictated the course of the President, was his desire to avoid a war which he had reason to believe would have met with the opposition of the party opposed to him, and which, he feared, would be rendered the more unpopular by the large increase of taxation which it would require.

Mr. Murray, pursuant to instructions, informed the French Government that our Ministers waited for positive assurances of a favorable reception, and received an answer from the Directory, through Talleyrand, assuring him that the Envoys would be received and "should enjoy all the prerogatives which are attached to their official character by the Law of Nations, and that one or more Ministers should be duly authorized to treat with them."

On the receipt of this assurance, the President, against the wishes of a majority of his Cabinet, ordered the Envoys to prepare for their departure, and directed the Secretary of State to make a draft of instructions to them. But before their departure, intelligence was received of another revolution in France, and a consequent change of the Directory, with a single exception, which rendered it doubtful whether the Envoys would be received; and the Cabinet unanimously advised the President to suspend the mission. The President, notwithstanding, ordered the embarkation of the two Envoys, who sailed on the 3d of November, 1799. By this act of the President, the separation between himself and a majority of his Cabinet, and many of his party friends, was rendered complete.

Congress met in December, 1799. The President in his address alluded to his having received the assurances required by the French Government in relation to the reception of our Envoys, and of their having proceeded on their mission. The two Houses, in their answers to his speech, expressed their approbation of his course towards France. A majority of the Cabinet officers being no longer his friends, the President, near the close of the session, (May, 1800,) requested Mr. Pickering and Mr. M'Henry, Secretaries of State and of War, to resign. The latter complied; the former, preferring a dismissal, refused. John Marshall, of Virginia, and Samuel Dexter, of Massachusetts, were appointed in their places.

The Envoys, in consequence of detentions on the way, did not reach Paris until the 2d of March, 1800. Mr. Murray had arrived the day before. They were duly received; and three Plenipotentiaries were appointed to negotiate with them.

There was great difficulty in agreeing upon the terms of

treaty. According to the instructions to our Ministers, the old treaties were not to be renewed. They had been declared void by Congress, having been dissolved by the aggressions of France upon our commerce. Being so considered, our Government had, in the Jay treaty with Great Britain, agreed, that the ships of war and privateers of both parties should be permitted to enter each other's ports with prizes ; and no shelter was to be given in their ports to such as had made prizes upon our citizens or subjects of either of the parties. A revival of the old treaties would therefore interfere with our engagements with Great Britain. The French Ministers were unwilling to admit the nullity of the old treaty of 1778, as to do so would exclude French privateers and prizes from the ports of the United States.

An arrangement seemed for a long time impracticable. Yet a settlement of the difficulties between the two countries was to this country very desirable. There was danger of a war with France. The successes of Bonaparte rendered a general peace in Europe a probable event, which would leave us alone in a contest with that power. We wished to relieve our commerce from further exposure to depredations from the French. And we wished to save a large amount of captured property not yet condemned; there being more than forty ships and cargoes awaiting decision before the French council of prizes.

A treaty was at length concluded the 30th of September, 1800. Its principal provisions were the following: The binding force of the old treaties, and the mutual claims for indemnities, were reserved for future negotiation. All public ships, and all property captured by either party, and not yet condemned, were to be restored. All government and individual debts due were to be paid. The vessels of either party were to enjoy in the ports of the other, equal privileges with those of the most favored nation. The provision of the old treaty, that free ships should make free goods, was retained. And provision was made for the future security of American commerce. The article allowing French privateers and prizes equal privileges with those of the most favored nation, was inserted by the French Ministers, after repeated declarations from our Ministers, that this stipulation could have no effect as against our treaty with Great Britain. Mr. King, our Minister at London, presented this matter to the British Government, and was told that they saw in it no cause of complaint.

The treaty was laid before the Senate at the next session of Congress, which met this year, (Nov. 17, 1800,) at Washington. The Federal Senators opposed to Mr. Adams and the new mission, disapproved the treaty, because it did not provide for the payment of indemnities, and for the renunciation of the old treaties; and an article was adopted limiting the term of the convention to eight years, as a substitute for that which referred the question of indemnity and the old treaties to future negotiation. The President, though he considered the alteration as being for the worse, ratified it, and appointed James A. Bayard, of Delaware, as Minister to carry the treaty with the Amendment to France for ratification by that Government. Mr. Bayard declined that appointment; and the Presidential term of Mr. Adams being near to a close, he left the matter to his successor.

The event showed the mistake of the Senate. When the amended treaty was submitted to Bonaparte, he added a proviso, that the expunging of the article relating to indemnity and old treaties, should be considered as a relinquishment of claims for indemnity. With this amendment, it was ratified by our Government. Thus did France succeed in obtaining what she had proposed to our Ministers—*a new treaty without indemnities.*

Among the acts passed during Mr. Adams' administration, was a naturalization law, by which the term of residence of an alien, in order to become a citizen, was changed from five years to fourteen; and the time of making the application previous to admission, which was three years, was changed to five years. This act was passed in 1798, the year in which the Alien and Sedition laws were enacted.

An act was passed near the close of the last session of Congress under his administration, which gave great dissatisfaction to his opponents. To prevent delays in the administration of justice, caused by the great extent of the circuits and districts in which the courts were held, the number of judicial dtstricts, thirteen, composing three circuits, was increased to twenty-three, and the numbers of circuits to six. The objection to the passage of the act was, that it gave to the President., less than three weeks before the expiration of his term of office, the appointment of a large number of judges, attorneys, and marshals.

A Presidential election was approaching. The Federal candidates were John Adams and C. C. Pinckney. The Federal opponents of Mr. Adams, preferring Mr. Pinckney for President, endeavored, by secret efforts, to secure him the largest number of electoral votes. This would, by the then existing mode of election, in case the Federal party were still in the majority, make Mr. Pinckney the President. [See Cons., original Article.] Mr. Adams, apprised of their scheme, and supposing the opposition to him had arisen from their partialities for England and his desire to avoid a war with France, stigmatized them as a British faction. Mr. Hamilton was among the most active in this attempt to defeat Mr. Adams. Mr. Adams received all the Federal votes, 65; Mr. Pinckney received 64, and John Jay 1. Jefferson and Burr, the Republican candidates, received each 73. Neither of the two latter having a majority, the election devolved upon the House of Representatives, voting by States. After a week's unsuccessful balloting, Mr. Jefferson received the votes of *eight* States; Mr. Burr received the votes of *six* States; and *two* States were equally divided. Mr. Jefferson then, on the 36th ballot, received the votes of *ten* States. This result was effected by the casting of blank ballots by three Federal members who preferred Mr. Jefferson to Mr. Burr.

The design was charged upon the Federalists in the House of standing out and preventing an election, and of passing an act to vest the Executive authority in some high officer of the Government. But the charge has been disproved. James A. Bayard, member of the House from Delaware, afterwards Senator in Congress, and one of the Commissioners who negotiated the peace with Great Britain, was implicated in the charge. But in a deposition, April 3, 1806, he denied the charge, and stated the reasons for holding out so long. This deposition was confirmed by George Baer, one of the Federal members from Maryland, who, in a letter to a friend, in 1830, solemnly declared, that a proposition to prevent an election and to usurp the legislative power was not made; but they were pledged to each other to elect a President before the close of the session. Mr. Bayard, in his deposition, assigned as a reason for the delay, an attempt, on their part, to obtain from Mr. Jefferson, through his friends, assurances that he would, if elected, sustain the public credit; maintain the naval system; and not remove the subordinate officers; and that these assurances having been made, the opposition of Vermont, Maryland and Delaware was withdrawn.

CHAPTER III.

From the Commencement of Mr. Jefferson's Administration to the Close of the Administration of John Quincy Adams.

Thomas Jefferson was inaugurated on the 4th of March, 1801. The general policy of the Government having been established, few measures of great importance claimed the attention of the new administration.

Mr. Adams had made a considerable number of appointments just before the close of his term of office. Mr. Jefferson considered this an infringement of his prerogative. The commissions of some of them having not yet been delivered, he suppressed these commissions, and made new appointments. Great objection was also made to the appointments of judges and other officers in conformity with the provisions of the new Judiciary act, which has been noticed. The judges holding their offices during good behavior, they could be removed only by repealing the act, which was accordingly done at the next session of Congress.

An act was also passed repealing the duty on stills, domestic distilled spirits, refined sugars, licenses to retailers, sales at auction, carriages, stamped paper, &c.; also an act to repeal the naturalization law of the preceding administration which had prolonged the term of residence required of aliens previous to their admission as citizens.

The great measure of Mr. Jefferson's administration, was the purchase of Louisiana. The negotiation was an interesting one. Our Government had contemplated merely an arrangement by which, for the security and convenience of our commerce, territory on the East side of the Mississippi, including New Orleans, might be ceded to the United States, and the Mississippi made a common boundary, with a common use of its navigation for them and Spain—the latter being supposed to be in possession of Louisiana and the Floridas. It was ascertained, however, that by a secret treaty, Louisiana had been ceded to France. Bonaparte, being in want of money, proposed to our Minister in that country, (R. R. Livingston,) to sell the whole of Louisiana. Although our Minister, (Mr. Monroe having been sent to aid Mr. Livingston,) were not authorized to buy the whole territory; yet, as no treaty could bind the United States until ratified by our Government, terms for the whole were agreed upon by the parties; and the treaty was ratified by both Governments. Mr. Jefferson, though he admitted the purchase and annexation to be unauthorized by the Constitution, thought the acquisition too valuable to be lost, signed the treaty, and proposed an *ex post facto* amendment of the Constitution to give sanction to the measure; but it was never attempted. It was, however, argued by some, and is believed by many at the present day, that the power to acquire territory by war, purchase, or treaty, properly and naturally belongs to every independent sovereignty. It was stipulated in the treaty, that the inhabitants of the ceded territory should be incorporated into the Union, and admitted as soon as possible, according to the principles of the Federal Constitution, to the enjoyment of all the rights, advantages, and immunities of citizens; and that, in the mean time, they should be protected in the free enjoyment of their liberty, property, and religion.

In 1804, the territory was divided; the South part of it being called Orleans, the residue, the District of Louisiana. The act prohibited the bringing of slaves into the Territory of Orleans from beyond the limits of the United States, or from any of the States such as had been imported since the 1st of May, 1798. Thus early was recognized the power of the General Government over Slavery in the Territories of the United States.

It had been the policy of Mr. Jefferson's predecessors to encourage an effective fortification of our harbors, and the maintenance of an efficient navy. Mr. Jefferson recommended a less expensive system of defense, which was adopted, and which came to be called the "gun-boat system." In 1803, an act was passed, authorizing the President to procure the building of fifteen small vessels, called gun-boats, for which $50,000 were appropriated. His plan was to build about two hundred and fifty of these boats, twenty-five every year. The aggregate cost was estimated at about one million of dollars. A substitute was also to be provided for the usual expensive fortifications. This plan of defense, however, proved a failure. Before it was completed, Congress refused to make further appropriations for building gun-boats ; and the measure was abandoned.

During the new war between France and Great Britain, which commenced in 1803, and in which most of the powers of Europe became involved, the merchant vessels of the belligerent nations, from their exposure to capture, were withdrawn from the ocean. This gave to the United States and other neutral maritime nations an unusually profitable carrying trade with the belligerent countries, on established principles of national law recognized by Great Britain herself: that the goods of a neutral, consisting of articles not contraband of war, in neutral vessels, employed in a direct trade between a neutral and a belligerent country, are protected, except in ports invested or blockaded. A large portion of this trade consisted in carrying goods from colonies of the enemies of Great Britain to their parent countries. Great Britain alleged that this trade was unlawful, on the principle that a trade from a colony to its parent country, not being permitted to other nations in time of peace, can not be made lawful in time of war ; and an order was issued for the capture of our vessels ; and a large number were captured. One object of this measure was to distress Napoleon and his allies.

The President, January, 1806, laid the subject before Congress ; and he also noticed the impressment of our seamen by Great Britain. It had been her practice—and she claimed it as her right—to search American vessels in pursuit of British seamen ; and, in so doing, had taken many of our own native citizens, and forcibly impressed them into her service.

In May, 1806, were issued the celebrated British orders in council, declaring the principal ports on the Western coast of the continent of Europe in a state of blockade. These orders were soon followed, on the part of Napoleon, by the Berlin decree, (so called from its having been issued by him while in that city on his way northward,) declaring the British Islands in a state of blockade, and prohibiting all commerce with them. It was his purpose to stop all trade between Great Britain and the continent. A more stringent order than the first was then issued by the British Government, which was followed by the Milan decree of Napoleon. Both Governments carried their restrictive measures to the greatest extremes, to the destruction of American commerce. These blockades were unlawful, not being maintained by adequate force. Hence they were, as they were termed, mere "paper blockades." It was by some supposed to be the object of both parties to drive the Americans from their neutral position.

The seizure of our ships, cargoes, and men, induced Congress, in December, 1807, on recommendation of President Jefferson, to pass the famous Embargo law, which prohibited American vessels, in order to their safety, from leaving our ports. Perhaps another object of the measure was a preparation for war.

This controversy had become a party question in this country. The Federalists, from certain facts which had been elicited, suspected that the object of the Embargo was to aid Bonaparte in crippling the commerce of Great Britain. France having a comparatively limited foreign commerce, the blow would fall with greater weight upon her enemy, whose foreign trade was very extensive. The suspicion of Mr. Jefferson's subserviency to France was strengthened by certain letters; one Mr. Armstrong, our Minister in France, to Mr. Madison, our Secretary of State, stating that Napoleon had declared, that "the Americans should be compelled to take the positive character of either allies or enemies." The letter also stated, that several of our ships and cargoes had been confiscated, contrary to previous assurances given. Another of these letters was from Mr. Canning, the British Minister of Foreign Affairs, to Mr. Pinkney, our Minister in London, giving assurance of a friendly disposition towards this country, and expressing a strong desire "to accommodate the orders in council, as far as was consistent with their object, to the feelings and interests of the American Government and people." These two documents, so different in their character, the President did not see fit to publish; and their suppression was attributed to the fear that the people, seeing the contrast between them, would disapprove the course of the Government toward the two countries. And since the death of Mr. Jefferson, and the publication of his correspondence, reference has been made to a letter from him to a friend in 1808, in which he pronounces the condemnation of our vessels taken by the French privateers *piracy*, which, the Federalists thought, rendered her equally deserving of retaliatory legislation.

The embargo affected very seriously the shipping of New England; and the complaints in that quarter were loud and unceasing during its continuance. It was repealed in March, 1809, by the *non-intercourse* law, which prohibited all intercourse with France and Great Britain; but provided, that, if either nation should so revoke or modify her edicts as that they should cease to violate our neutral commerce, trade with that nation should be renewed.

In August, 1810, Mr. Madison being President, our Minister in Paris was informed, that the Berlin and Milan decrees were revoked, and would cease to have effect after the 1st of November following; stating as a reason for the revocation, that our Congress had retraced its steps, and had engaged to oppose Great Britain, which had refused to acknowledge the rights of neutrals; and stating, also, as a condition of the repeal of the decrees, that "the English shall revoke their orders in council, and renounce the new principles of blockade which they have wished to establish; or that the United States shall cause their rights to be respected by the English." Considering this as sufficient evidence of the repeal of the decrees, the President, by proclamation, declared the restrictions imposed by the act of May to be removed as against France; and Congress passed an act declaring them in force against Great Britain.

The British Government did not consider this *conditional* repeal such as to justify the repeal of the orders in council. A long correspondence between our Government and that of Great Britain ensued, for which the reader is referred to our larger histories.

There being so much doubt as to the revocation of the French decrees, Mr. Smith, Secretary of State, prepared a letter to the French Minister at Washington, in which, among a long list of questions, he inquired whether the decrees had been revoked; or whether he could give any assurance in relation to their revocation or modification. But the President interdicted the sending of the letter.

War was declared the 18th of June, 1812. The vote in the Senate was 19 to 13; in the House, 79 to 49. Of those who voted against the war, 15 were Republicans. Before the adjournment, the Federal members of the House, with the exception of 2, joined in an address to their constituents, in which they reviewed the controversy between the three Governments, with the view of showing the impropriety and injustice of declaring war, and of making a distinction between France and Great Britain. On the latter point, they say: "If honor demands a war with England, what opiate lulls that honor to sleep over the wrongs done us by France? On land, robberies, seizures, imprisonments by French authority; at sea, pillage, sinkings, burnings under French orders. These are notorious. Are they unfelt because they are French? Is any alleviation to be found in the correspondence and humiliations of the present Minister Plenipotentiary of the United States at the French court? In his communications to our Government, as before the public, where is the cause for selecting France as the friend of our country, and England the enemy?"

Nearly the whole of the Federal party was opposed to the declaration of war; but many gave it their support as a measure of the Government. Among the men of distinction of this latter class, was John Adams.

A few days after the declaration, a copy of the decree of Napoleon, dated April 28, 1811, was received, repealing the Berlin and Milan decrees. The British Minister soon took his departure, bearing a letter proposing to the British Government a suspension of hostilities with a view to an adjustment. Among the conditions of the proposed armistice, one was, that the impressment of our seamen should be discontinued. But before the British Minister, (Mr. Foster,) reached home, our Government was informed that *the orders in council had been revoked*, the revocation to take effect the 1st of August next. The only remaining grievance then to be redressed by war, was that of impressment—a grievance, however, of great magnitude

The number of seamen impressed, though never actually ascertained, must have been great. More than 6,000 cases were recorded in the State Department; but probably a much greater number were impressed. No arrangement for a suspension of hostilities being practicable, the war was prosecuted by both parties.

In November, 1812, Mr. Madison was reëlected President. He was known to have been reluctant to engage in a war; and his nomination had been delayed, as the war party were unwilling to support him, unless he should determine to favor the war. Notwithstanding his nomination, De Witt Clinton, a more zealous friend of the war, was nominated by the Republican members of the New York Legislature. The Federalists, having made no nomination, supported Mr. Clinton, who received 89 electoral votes, and Mr. Madison 128.

Brief, and necessarily imperfect, as is this sketch of the controversy which terminated in the war of 1812, more space has been given to it than was intended. But as our difficulties with Great Britain and France were so long a subject of contention between the two political parties, it was deemed proper to give the reader an intelligible view of the question.

The war continued until February, 1815. Commissioners had been appointed by both Governments, who met at Ghent, in Belgium, and concluded a treaty of peace in ——— 1814, which was received at Washington in February following, ratified by the British Government. After the news of the abdication of Napoleon had been received, new instructions were sent to our Commissioners, authorizing them, if peace could not otherwise be had, to waive the question of impressment, and leave it for future negotiation. So this question remained unsettled. The treaty was ratified the 17th of February, 1815.

Among the measures of Mr. Madison's administration which deserve notice, is the incorporation of the second Bank of the United States. The establishment of the first, in 1791, was a part of the financial policy of Mr. Hamilton, and was opposed by Mr. Madison and other opponents of Washington's administration.

In 1810, the year before the expiration of the charter,

application was made for its renewal; and a favorable report was made by Mr. Gallatin, Secretary of the Treasury, but at too late a period of the session to be acted upon. The application was renewed the next year; and a bill was introduced into each House; but both bills were lost; that of the House having been indefinitely postponed, 65 to 64; and that of the Senate having had its enacting clause struck out by the casting vote of the Vice-President, George Clinton, on the ground of its supposed unconstitutionality. Among the prominent Republicans who supported it, were Mr. Crawford and Mr. Giles—Mr. Clay opposed it.

At the session of 1814–1815, Secretary Dallas reported a plan of a Bank. It was supported mainly by Republicans. It was opposed, however, by some Republicans, among whom was Mr. Calhoun, who proposed a counter project, which allowed the Government no control in the direction of the Bank, nor a right to demand loans from it. The Federalists supporting this plan, it was carried by a large majority. Secretary Dallas having, at the request of the House, given his opinion as to the effect of Mr. Calhoun's project, the bill, on the question being taken on its third reading, was lost, 45 to 107; the Federalists now voting against it. A bill on Mr. Dallas' plan was then introduced in the Senate, and passed. The vote in the House stood, 81 in its favor, and 80 against it, without the vote of the Speaker, who, after giving his reasons for opposing the bill, voted against it, producing a *tie;* and then declared the bill to be lost. A reconsideration was carried, and a compromise bill was reported and adopted, but was vetoed by the President, not because he considered it unconstitutional; its constitutionality "having been recognized by the Legislative, Executive and Judicial branches of the Government, accompanied by the concurrence of the general will of the nation;" but because it did not appear to him to be calculated to answer the purposes for which it was desired.

Still another bill, on the principles of Mr. Dallas' plan, was originated in the Senate, and passed that body, but was indefinitely postponed in the House, by a majority of one vote.

The next year, 1816, a bank bill was passed, and approved by the President. Mr. Clay, who, with many other leading statesmen, had changed his views since 1811, now a member of the House, and its Speaker, made an able speech in its favor. It was believed that a Bank was necessary to restore a healthy currency, and to facilitate the financial operations of the Government. It passed the House, 80 to 71. Its capital was $35,000,000 ; one-fifth to be subscribed by the Government, and one-fifth to be paid in specie. It was entitled to the deposit of the public moneys, and was required to disburse them in any part of the Union without charge to the Government. It was also to pay $1,500,000 as a bonus for its charter. Of the twenty-five directors, five were to be appointed by the President and Senate. The deposits were removable by the Secretary of the Treasury for sufficient reasons, to be laid before Congress.

At the same session, (1816,) was passed a new tariff act. The European wars, which had existed during most of the time since the organization of our Government, had furnished a good market for agricultural products, with which our people had been enabled to procure supplies of manufactured goods. Hence, high duties for the encouragement of manufactures were comparatively unnecessary. The interruption of our trade with Great Britain during our war with that country, and the double duties on imported goods imposed at the commencement of the war, which were to continue until its close, and for a year thereafter, had given an impetus to home manufactures. But on the return of peace, large importations of foreign goods were again made, to the injury of our manufactures ; and as the double duties were about to cease, and as the foreign market for our bread-stuffs would also cease, or be greatly diminished, in consequence of the return of those composing the vast armies of Europe to their usual employments in home production, it now became necessary to adapt our tariff of duties to a state of peace. Provision must be made to pay the public debt ; and the war had shown the importance of being independent of foreign nations for necessaries.

Accordingly, Mr. Madison, in his Message, recommended

a "tariff on manufactures," and urged it for the purposes, both of revenue, and of making us "safe against competitions from abroad." A tariff of duties on imports was reported to Congress by Secretary Dallas, and, with some modifications, became a law. Mr. Calhoun was one of its most zealous advocates. It was supported by Mr. Clay also, and opposed by Mr. Webster. The bill passed the House, 88 to 54 ; the Senate, 15 to 11.

A protective tariff was not at this time, nor was it for many years after, a party question. It was supported and opposed according to its supposed effects upon the leading industrial interests of the States respectively. Nor was its constitutionality to any great extent, if at all, disputed. The tariff of 1816, was voted for by a majority of the members of the House from the New England States, where manufactures had made considerable progress. From the agricultural States, New York, Pennsylvania, New Jersey, &c., the vote was nearly unanimous in its favor, protection to manufactures being deemed equally favorable to the agricultural interest. Its strongest opposition was from the planting States, though it was proportionably less than later tariffs have received from those States.

From the protection afforded by this tariff, manufactures of several kinds were greatly promoted, of which the principal was that of coarse cotton cloths. In the main, however, it proved inadequate ; and the prosperity of the country was for a long time retarded. Foreign goods were imported in large quantities ; and the country was drained of its money to pay for them, our agricultural products, especially bread-stuffs, being, to any considerable extent, no longer wanted in exchange ; the industry of the country was prostrated ; and general distress prevailed. Several attempts were made in Congress to revise the tariff, but without success, until 1824. A bill passed the House in 1820, 91 to 78 ; but it was defeated in the Senate, 22 to 21. Of the votes in the House from the New England States, 18 were for, and 17 against the bill. New York, New Jersey, Pennsylvania, and Delaware, were unanimous in favor of it, except 1 in Penn. The Southern States proper, or planting States, were nearly unanimous against it. The Western States, with Louisiana, were unanimous in its favor. Kentucky, in favor of it, 5 ; against it, 3.

In 1824, after a most arduous effort, a bill for a general revision of the tariff was passed. On this bill, Mr. Clay was opposed by Mr. Webster, both being then members of the House. The bill was passed to a third reading, 105 to 102. The votes of the several States were as follows :

Maine: Yea, 1; nays, 6. *New Hampshire:* Yea, 1; nays, 5. *Massachusetts:* Yea, 1; nays, 11. *Rhode Island:* Yeas, 2. *Connecticut:* Yeas, 5; nay, 1. *Vermont:* Yeas, 5. *New York:* Yeas, 26; nays, 8. *New Jersey:* Yeas, 6. *Pennsylvania:* Yeas, 24; nay, 1. *Delaware:* Yea, 1. *Maryland:* Yeas, 3; nays, 6. *Virginia:* Yea, 1; nays, 21. *North Carolina:* Yeas, 13. *South Carolina:* Nays, 9. *Georgia:* Nays, 7. *Kentucky:* Yeas, 11. *Tennessee:* Yeas, 2; nays, 7. *Ohio:* Yeas, 14. *Indiana:* Yeas, 2. *Illinois:* Yea, 1. *Louisiana:* Nays, 3. *Mississippi:* Nay, 1. *Alabama:* Nays, 3. *Missouri:* Yea, 1.

From this record of votes, it appears, that Maine, New Hampshire, and Massachusetts, which were fishing and navigating States, were almost unanimous against the tariff. Rhode Island and Connecticut, manufacturing States, were in favor of it, *one* from the latter excepted. Also the grain producing States, Vermont, New York, New Jersey, Pennsylvania, Delaware, Kentucky, Ohio, Indiana, Illinois, and Missouri, were nearly three to one in favor of protection, from its supposed benefit to agriculture. The planting States generally, having an unfailing market abroad for their great staples, were united with the shipping and fishing States against the tariff. By this act, Eastern capital was directed more to manufactures; and since that time, the Eastern and Southern States have taken opposite sides on this question.

In the Senate, the vote was 25 to 21, as follows:

Maine: Yeas, 2. *New Hampshire:* Yea, 1; nay, 1. *Massachusetts:* Nays, 2. *Rhode Island:* Yeas, 2. *Connecticut:* Yeas, 2. *Vermont:* Yeas, 2. *New York:* Yea, 1; nay, 1. *New Jersey:* Yeas, 2. *Pennsylvania:* Yeas, 2. *Delaware:* Nays, 2. *Maryland:* Nay, 1. *Virginia:* Nays, 2. *North Carolina:* Nays, 2. *South Carolina:* Nays, 2. *Georgia:* Nays, 2. *Kentucky:* Yeas, 2. *Tennessee:* Yeas, 2. *Ohio:* Yeas, 2. *Indiana:* Yeas, 2. *Illinois:* Yea, 1. *Louisiana:* Nays, 2. *Mississippi:* Nays, 2. *Alabama:* Yeas, 2. *Missouri:* Yeas, 2.

By the restoration of peace, the asperity of party feeling was greatly mitigated. Many of the Federalists no longer kept up their opposition to the administration. Mr. Monroe was elected in 1816, against a feeble opposition; 183 Republican electors being chosen, and 34 Federal. The latter gave their votes for Rufus King. After this election, a large number of Federalists, conceiving an organized opposition to the Republican party no longer necessary or expedient, publicly disclaimed any further connection with the Federal party, which, before the next Presidential election, ceased to have an organized existence. Mr. Monroe was reëlected in 1820, without opposition, no Federal candidate having been nominated. And as *party* generally implies the opposition of a part of the community to another part, it is questionable whether even the Republican, perhaps neither party can properly be said to have had existence at that time.

It had been the practice, from the time of the nomination of Mr. Jefferson, of the Republican members of Congress to meet in caucus while in attendance at the last session before each Presidential election, to nominate candidates. This mode of nomination had become so unpopular, that out of the 216 Republican members, only 68 attended the meeting; of whom 64 voted for William H. Crawford; 2 for John Quincy Adams; 1 for Andrew Jackson; and 1 for Nathaniel Macon. Albert Gallatin received 57 votes as candidate for Vice-President. Mr. Crawford and Mr. Gallatin were declared nominated.

The great body of the Republican electors did not consider themselves bound by this nomination. The Republicans in the Legislatures of the New England States, recommended Mr. Adams; and the friends of Gen. Jackson and Mr. Clay respectively, in the Western States, nominated them also. Thus four candidates, all acknowledged Republicans, were before the people for their suffrages. Of the Presidential electors chosen in November, 99 gave their votes for Gen. Jackson; 84 for Mr. Adams; 41 for Mr. Crawford; and 37 for Mr. Clay. There being no choice by the electors, the election devolved upon the House of Representatives, where the votes are given by States. Mr. Adams received the votes of 13 States; Gen. Jackson of 7; and Mr. Crawford of 4 States. Mr. Adams having the votes of a majority of the States, was elected.

From the foregoing sketch of old parties, it would seem difficult to trace the existence of either to a later period. Attempts have been made, however, to identify modern parties with the old ones. Democrats have founded their claim to popular favor in their pretension to be in the regular line of descent from Jefferson; and have been wont, for party effect, to stigmatize their opponents as Federalists. And among the opponents of the Democratic party are some who have undertaken to establish their connection with the old Republican party, through the National Republican party which supported John Quincy Adams, in 1828, and the late Whig party. In the character and creeds of different parties the most dissimilar, there are some points of coïncidence. This, however, is insufficient to determine the paternity of any party.

But what if the line of succession were thus conclusively established? No man or party is infallible or immutable. Great as was the popularity of Mr. Jefferson and his administration, there were in them some things to be condemned as well as some to be approved. For his advocacy of the equal and inalienable rights of men; his endeavors to guard the constitutional rights of the people; and many of the measures of his administration, he is entitled to the gratitude of his countrymen, and is worthy of imitation. On the other hand, his secret opposition to Washington; his encouragement of Genet in fitting out privateers in our ports; his patronage, by money and personal influence, bestowed upon presses established to calumniate Washington and his administration; his charging him with being leagued with conspirators against our Government, whose design was to substitute for it one formed after the British model; his nullifying sentiments declared in the Kentucky Resolutions; and some of his measures of public policy, few candid men, at the present day, will presume to defend. Why, then, should men be so anxious about the pedigree of their parties? The validity of the claims of a party to the public confidence and support should be determined, not by the antiquity of its organization, nor by its numerical strength; but by the soundness of its principles and the expediency of its measures.

PART SECOND.

HISTORY OF THE DEMOCRATIC PARTY.

CHAPTER I.

Administration of John Quincy Adams.

JOHN QUINCY ADAMS was inducted into the Presidential office on the 4th of March, 1825. Familiar with public affairs, having spent the whole previous period of his manhood in the public business; a Republican, who had supported Mr. Jefferson from the time of the Embargo, and his successors, Madison and Monroe; immediately succeeding the latter, with whose views, except those on the Constitutional power to make internal improvements, (of which Mr. Monroe had some doubts,) and to the continuance of whose general policy he had pledged himself in his Inaugural Address; it was natural to presume that his administration would be peaceful and prosperous. But scarcely had he been seated in office—not a measure of public policy having been enacted—before he found himself in the midst of a powerful opposition. The chief cause of this early opposition was his appointment of Mr. Clay as Secretary of State.

At the time of the election, Mr. Clay was a member of the House of Representatives. As the election of President was to be made from the three candidates having the three highest numbers of electoral votes, (Mr. Clay not being one of them,) he must participate in the election. Possessing great influence, especially with the Western members, whose votes he could probably control, deep anxiety was felt as to which of the candidates, Adams or Jackson, he would vote for. It was rumored that Mr. Clay and other Western members were to vote for Mr. Adams, who, in consideration of their support, was to appoint Mr. Clay Secretary of State. The election of the former and the appointment of the latter were considered as evidence of the alleged "bargain." The dissatisfaction among the friends of the defeated candidates, especially those of Gen. Jackson, was very great; and the charge of "corrupt coalition" was rung throughout the Union. And it must be confessed, that the verification of the rumored appointment; Mr. Clay's non-compliance with the request of the Legislature of Kentucky to vote for Gen. Jackson; and certain other circumstances, gave ground for the belief that the election of Mr. Adams and the appointment of Mr. Clay, were the result of a previous agreement. But the united testimony of all the Western members implicated; letters from Gen. La Fayette, (then on a visit to this country,) Mr. Benton, and others, to all of whom Mr. Clay had stated his intention, should an election by the House of Representatives become necessary, to vote for Mr. Adams; the confessions of others who had given countenance to the charge; and two solemn denials by Mr. Adams himself, publicly made since the close of his Presidental term, in one of which he said: "Before you, my fellow-citizens, in the presence of our country and of Heaven, I pronounce that charge totally unfounded;" all these are deemed sufficient to justify the verdict of acquittal which has been rendered by the public judgment.

But, although the charge of corruption has been disproved, the appointment of Mr. Clay after the charge had been made, is one of the numerous indiscretions committed by Mr. Adams during his long public life. It confirmed the suspicion of the alledged bargain, and strengthened the opposition early formed to effect his overthrow.

The determined purpose of the opponents of Mr. Adams, and the nature of the means to be employed for its accomplishment, may be inferred from a declaration of Richard M. Johnson, of Kentucky, made in the presence of Mr. Seaton, one of the Editors of the National Intelligencer, as Mr. Seaton alleged, that "Mr. Adams' administration shall come down, though pure as the angels at the right hand of the throne of God." Col. Johnson, in reply, gave to this statement no direct and total denial, but disclaimed having used so strong and exceptionable language as that ascribed to him, in expressing his opposition to the new administration. Mr. Seaton, however, reiterated, substantially, his former statement; and his high moral and social standing leaves little doubt of its correctness.

An opposition party was soon formed by the union of the friends of the defeated candidates. Although Gen. Jackson had been peculiarly obnoxious to the friends of Mr. Crawford, having been denounced in the most bitter terms, as a "Federalist," whose "doctrines were food and raiment for the Federalists and no-party men," as a "Dictator" in temper and spirit, and fit only to be the chief ruler in an arbitrary government; yet, the parties having a common object, a union was readily formed. Mr. Calhoun, who had just been elected Vice-President, having many friends, these also joined the opposition. The great object—to "overthrow the administration"—is thus alluded to in a certain letter published in the opposition papers: "To the friends of Jackson and Crawford, those of Mr. Calhoun are added; and the union forms such a force of numbers, talents, and influence, that it seems improbable that this can be effectively met by Mr. Adams and Mr. Clay and their friends, aided by their united experience, ability, patronage, and official advantages, great as they are. Men are so very sincere in their dislikes, that the most opposite natures will coalesce to diminish the power of an object of a higher common aversion, and will surrender the strongest personal competition to unite for mutual safety."

To effect the "chief end" of this combination, every act or measure of the administration which could, by misrepresentation or distortion, be turned to the advantage of the opposition, was seized upon for this purpose. Several important measures suggested in Mr. Adams' first annual Message, were made to give way to numerous propositions for "retrenchment and reform," which were introduced for political effect.

Mr. Benton, who seems to have acted a prominent part in these early assaults upon the administration, introduced a proposition to amend the Constitution; the object of which was to secure the election of President in all cases by the people. He proposed another amendment, making members of Congress ineligible to any civil office under the General Government during the Presidential term in which they are to serve. Mr. Clay and a few other members having received appointments from Mr. Adams, the amendment was designed to take from the President the power to appoint to office members of Congress upon whose votes he might be dependent for his election. Mr. Benton also reported on the expediency of reducing the patronage of the Executive, and presented six bills for that purpose. One of them was "a bill to regulate the laws of the United States, and of public advertisements." The withdrawing of the patronage of the printing of the laws from a few of the newspapers opposed to the administration, and bestowing it upon others that supported it, explain the object of this last report.

One of the subjects alluded to in his first annual Message, (December, 1825,) was the "Panama Mission." A Congress of Commissioners from the Spanish American Republics of Colombia, Peru, Chili, Buenos Ayres, and Mexico, was to assemble at Panama, to deliberate upon objects of common interest, and, as some supposed, for the purpose of providing for a successful resistance to Spain, and for giving security to their independence. Our Government had been invited to be also represented in the Congress; and the invitation had been accepted. On the 26th of December, the President nominated to the Senate Richard C. Anderson, of Kentucky, and John Sergeant, of Pennsylvania, as Commissioners, and William B. Rochester, of New York, as Secretary of the Mission, and again disclaimed, as in his annual Message, the intention either "to contract alliances, or to engage in any undertaking or project of hostility to any other nation." He believed the meeting would afford a favorable occasion for establishing a more liberal as well as a more stable commercial intercourse than had been enjoyed, and principles which should govern their conduct as belligerents and neutrals in time of war. It might also be advisable to settle the question, whether the security of Republican Institutions did not require the parties to prevent any European power from establishing a colony within the borders of the parties—a principle announced by Mr. Adams' predecessor, and generally denominated the "Monroe doctrine."

To some readers an explanation may be here necessary. An alliance of European monarchies had been formed to check the progress of liberty. And it was believed that their designs were not restricted to Europe, but that they meditated interference between Spain and her revolted provinces in America. The establishing of a colony on this side of the Atlantic by any European power being regarded as dangerous to our own peace and happiness, Mr. Monroe promulgated the declaration, that "any attempt of the Allied Powers to extend their system to any portion of this hemisphere, would be considered as dangerous to our peace and safety," and would be opposed. This principle is at present recognized by most of our eminent statesmen. It is, however, the opinion of some, that the declaration of Mr. Monroe was not intended to establish a principle for all future time. One object of Mr. Monroe was, to prevent the occupation of Cuba by any other European Power; an event then not altogether improbable which might endanger the safety of the United States.

The Committees of the Senate having been appointed by Mr. Calhoun, the Vice-President, as President of that body, and a majority of the Committee on Foreign Relations, to whom the subject was referred, being opposed to the mission, reported against it. The resolution, declaring it inexpedient to send Ministers to the Congress, was, however, negatived, 24 to 19; and the nominations were confirmed.

In the House, whose concurrence was necessary in an act appropriating the money for carrying the mission into effect, a favorable report was made, and, after much discussion, the money was appropriated.

The debate in the Senate was much protracted by the discussion of the Slavery question which had been introduced. There might be colored delegates in the Congress. To associate with them would be a tacit admission of their political equality. This might have an unfavorable effect upon the "peculiar institution." Cuba might be invaded by the South American States, the slaves emancipated, and a colored Republic established. A conquest of the island by England or France was preferable to the erection of such a Republic so near our Slave States. The latter would be, in effect, a direct interference with Slavery in the South. The President had said to Europe that we could not allow Cuba and Porto Rico to be transferred to any European Power; the same must be said to the Spanish American States. We could not allow their principle of universal emancipation to be called into activity where its contagion in our neighborhood would be dangerous to our quiet and safety. The safety of the Southern portion of our Union must not be sacrificed to a passion for diplomacy.

So soon do we see this self-styled, misnamed Democratic party identifying itself with Slavery, of which it has since been its main defense and support. Better, in the view of these men, that Cuba should remain a Monarchical dependency, with the mass of its people groaning under a tyranny worse than monarchs exercise, than that, by their deliverance, the Slave Power should be in the least endangered. There was but a slight probability that Slavery would be at all affected by the contemplated meeting. Slight as it was, however, it was sufficient to alarm these Southern Democrats, who were sustained by the votes of their Northern allies, with whom the "putting down of the administration," right or wrong, had become a paramount object.

The United States were not represented in the Congress. Mr. Anderson, one of the Commissioners, then our Minister to Colombia, died on his way to Panama; and the protracted debates in both Houses of Congress, prevented the attendance of Mr. Sergeant. The Congress met on the 22d of June, and, having closed its session there on the 15th of July, adjourned to meet again in February, at Tacubaya, near the city of Mexico, to give opportunity for the States not represented at Panama, to join in the treaty of league and perpetual friendship which had been concluded at Panama. Mr. Poinsett, our Minister to Mexico, was appointed Commissioner in the place of Mr. Anderson; and Mr. Sergeant, with Mr. Rochester, departed for Tacubaya in November. But, owing to some internal commotions in some of the Republics, the Congress did not assemble.

So the Mission failed. Though well intended, and perhaps wise and proper if the Congress had been fully attended, it was by the opponents of Mr. Adams turned to the disadvantage of his administration.

In the early part of Mr. Adams' administration, a controversy arose between the General Government and the State of Georgia, in which the latter took initiatory steps toward nullification. A treaty was made in February, 1825, between the United States and Gen. M'Intosh, a chief of the Creek Indians, and a few other chiefs of the nation, who ceded to the United States their lands in Georgia, for which they were to take lands West of the Mississippi, to which they were to remove in September, 1826. The treaty having been made without the consent of the representatives of the nation, it gave great dissatisfaction. Having made considerable progress in civilization and agriculture, they were averse to any further sales, and had enacted the punishment of death against any chief who should sanction such a measure. Accordingly M'Intosh and one or two others were executed for their unauthorized and fraudulent transaction.

The Indians were unwilling to leave their lands; and the attempt of the agents of the State to survey the territory was resisted by the Creeks. The President ordered the survey to be abandoned until the time prescribed for their removal; and Gen. Gaines was sent to quell disturbances, if any should arise, and by force, if necessary. This exasperated Gov. Troup, who said it was his duty to execute the law of the State which authorized the survey and appropriation of the lands; and repeated his determination to proceed in the survey, "cost what it will;" adding, "The Government of Georgia will not retire from the position it occupies to gratify the agent of the hostile Indians; nor will it do so, I trust, because it knows that, in consequence of disobedience to an unlawful mandate, it may soon be recorded, that 'Georgia was.'"

Soon after, he was informed by the War Department, that if Georgia "should undertake the project of surveying the lands before the time specified for removal, it would be wholly upon its own responsibility." To which the Governor replied, that if the General Government intended to interpose its power to prevent the survey, "the President may rest content that the Government of Georgia cares for no responsibilities in the exercise of its right, but those which belong to conscience and to God, who, thanks to Him, is equally our God, as the God of the United States."

But there was another objection to the proceedings of Georgia. The sovereignty of the soil was ceded to the United States; therefore Georgia could not lawfully bargain with the chiefs for the right of survey without the assent of the United States. Nor could the Government itself grant the right until the time for the removal, as it was bound to protect the Indians "against the encroachments, hostilities, and impositions of the whites and all others." And Gen. Gaines was informed by the Secretary of War, (Mr. Barbour,) that if the Governor should persist in his purpose, "it will present one of the most unfortunate events which have yet occurred in our history." The insolence of the Governor is seen in a letter to the President, in which he said: "You stand on the insulated eminence, an almost solitary advocate for making and breaking treaties." On being informed, however, of the President's intention to prevent intrusions upon the Indian territory, and to refer the treaty to Congress, the Governor concluded to defer the execution of his purpose.

In April, 1826. a new treaty was made and ratified by the Government, by which nearly all the land of the Indians in Georgia was obtained. Gov. Troup, dissatisfied with the treaty, ordered the surveys to commence the 1st of September, 1826. Being apprised of the President's determination to employ force in executing the laws, the Governor declared his purpose to resist, and said measures for resistance were in progress. On the same day, he ordered officers to liberate surveyors that had been or might be arrested by the General Government; and the military were ordered to be in readiness to repel any invasion of the territory of the State. He concluded, however, not to persist in his determination to oppose the General Government by force, having learned that it was the President's intention to negotiate with the Indians for the remaining strip of land not ceded; which was effected about the first of January, 1828.

With respect to a reference of the subject to the Supreme Court which had been suggested, the Governor said: "It will be for the Government of Georgia ultimately to submit, or not, to the decision of that tribunal." He did not consider the Supreme Court the constitutional arbiter in controversies involving rights of sovereignty between a State and the United States.

Mr. Monroe had recommended an attempt to effect the removal of the Indian tribes beyond the Mississippi; and for this purpose Secretary Barbour, in February, 1826, transmitted to Congress a bill. But no definitive action was taken upon it.

Bent on the one great object, the "overthrow of the administration," the opposition left unemployed no means which could be devised for this purpose. A resolution was offered, calling upon the Secretary of State for a list of the newspapers in which the laws were directed to be published since he came into office, designating the changes which had been made, and the reasons for each change. It was alleged that he had made changes from personal and political motives. To employ eighty-two presses in the service of the administration was alarming to the liberties of the people.

On the other hand, the right to call upon a public officer for the *reasons* of his acts was denied. Such a call was believed to be without precedent. Out of the eighty or more presses in which the laws had been published, only sixteen had been changed—some from geographical considerations; and in four instances, the persons displaced and those appointed were of the same political party. The resolution was debated at great length; but no definitive action was had upon it. The course pursued by the next administration in respect to appointments, will soon appear.

Before the excitement caused by the alleged "coalition" of Messrs. Adams and Clay had subsided, a new impulse was given to it by a direct charge made by Gen. Jackson himself, occasioned on this wise: An anonymous letter appeared in the Fayetteville (N. C.) Observer, stating that the writer had been told at the Hermitage, by Gen. Jackson, "that Mr. Clay's friends made a proposition to his friends, that if they would promise, for him, not to put Mr.

Adams into the seat of Secretary of State, Clay and his friends would, in one hour, make him, Jackson, the President. He indignantly rejected the proposition." It soon became known, that Carter Beverly, of Wheeling, Va., was the author of the letter. His veracity being impeached, he requested of Gen. Jackson a confirmation of the statements in his published letter. The General, in his answer, said he had been called on, in January, 1825, by a member of Congress, who said, that he had been informed by the friends of Mr. Clay, that the friends of Mr. Adams had made overtures to them, saying, if Mr. Clay and his friends would unite in aid of the election of Mr. Adams, Mr. Clay should be Secretary of State. And he was of opinion it was right to fight such intriguers with their own weapons, &c., &c.

Mr. Clay, in a letter to the public, challenged Gen. Jackson to the proof. The General replied in an address to the public, and named James Buchanan as the member of Congress alluded to. Mr. Buchanan, in a public letter, through the Lancaster Journal, disclaimed having come to Gen. Jackson as an agent for any one. He says: "I called on Gen. Jackson solely as his friend, upon my individual responsibility. Until I saw Gen. Jackson's letter to Mr. Beverly, and at the same time was informed by a letter from the Editor of the U. S. Telegraph, that I was the person to whom he alluded, the conception never once entered my mind that he believed me to have been the agent of Mr. Clay, or of his friends, or that I had intended to propose to him terms of any kind for them, or that he could have supposed me capable of expressing the opinion, that it was right to 'fight them with their own weapons.'" Mr. Buchanan then suggests how Gen. Jackson may have been led into the mistake.

Here, then, is presented a question of veracity between the General and Mr. Buchanan, as the former would not confess to a "mistake." Many readers will recollect the publication, in 1856, of what purported to be an original letter from Gen. Jackson to Mr. Polk, in which he advised him not to appoint Mr. B. to a seat in his Cabinet, for the reason that he was a deceitful man, or unworthy of confidence, and referred to the denial above mentioned, saying: "He did propose to fight them with their own weapons." The reader will form his own opinion as to which of the two gentlemen is the more worthy of credence.

In 1828, the tariff was again modified. The protection afforded by the act of 1824, was generally satisfactory. A means, however, had been devised of evading in a measure the intentions of the act. Woolen goods were subject to an *ad valorem* duty of 33⅓ per cent. on the price at the place whence imported. False invoices of these goods were made out at prices below their actual value, and the duties paid accordingly. By this means, the treasury was defrauded of a part of the revenue, and the manufacturer of a part of the protection to which he was entitled. To remedy this evil, and a few others, a bill was introduced in 1827, usually called the "woolens bill," and was passed by the House, 106 to 95, but defeated in the Senate by the casting vote of Vice-President Calhoun, to the great dissatisfaction of the manufacturers. Public meetings were held in some States, and a National Convention, composed of delegates from 13 States, met at Harrisburg, Pa., to consult on measures to promote the interests of agriculture and manufactures: and at the next session of Congress, (1827–1828,) numerous petitions were received praying for relief. An act was passed, increasing the duties on iron and some other articles; changing the duties on others from *ad valorem* to specific duties, laying those upon woolens according to the *minimum* principle.*

---

* To some readers, perhaps, this term may need an explanation. *Minimum* signifies the least quantity or value assignable in a given case. By the act of 1824, woolen cloths costing in the foreign market over 33⅓ cents the square yard, were charged with a duty of 33⅓ per cent. But as many were imported with invoices at prices one-fourth or one-third less than those really charged, this act provided that all woolen cloths costing abroad under 33⅓ cents, must be charged with a specific duty of 14 cents a yard. Costing over 33⅓ cents, and under 50, they must *be deemed* to have cost 50, and charged 40 per cent. duty; that is, 50 cents is *the least value* upon which the duty was to be charged. Costing over 50 cents, and not exceeding $1, they must be considered as having cost $1, and be charged accordingly; one dollar being the *minimum*, or *least price* upon which the duty was to be estimated. The next minimum was $2,50, and the next and last $4. The benefit of this principle is

By the act of 1824, many articles previously charged with *ad valorem* duties, were made subject to specific duties; and by the act of 1828, the duties on an additional number of articles were altered from *ad valorem* to specific, as by specific duties, and duties by the *minimum* rule, (which are *in effect* the same as specific duties,) the intended measure of duties is secured.

This tariff was, on the whole, probably, the highest that had ever been enacted. Among its most prominent supporters were Silas Wright, Barnard, Martin Hoffman, Martindale, and Strong, of N. Y.; Mallory, of Vt.; Bates, of Mass.; Ingersoll, of Conn.; Buchanan, Forward, and Ingham, of Pa.; Vinton and Wright, of Ohio. Among its opponents were Anderson and Sprague, of Maine; Cambreleng, of N. Y.; Alexander, Gilmer, and Randolph, of Va.; Hamilton and M'Duffie, of S. C.; Wickliffe, of Ky.; Wilde, of Ga. It passed the House, 105 to 94, as follows:

Maine: Nays, 7. *New Hampshire:* Yeas, 4; nays, 2. *Massachusetts:* Yeas, 2; nays, 11. *Rhode Island:* Yea, 1; nay, 1. *Connecticut:* Yeas, 4; nays, 2. *Vermont:* Yeas, 5. *New York:* Yeas, 27; nays, 6. *New Jersey:* Yeas, 5. *Pennsylvania:* Yeas, 23. *Delaware:* Yea, 1. *Maryland:* Yea, 1; nays, 5. *Virginia:* Yeas, 3; nays, 15. *North Carolina:* Nays, 13. *South Carolina:* Nays, 9. *Georgia:* Nays, 7. *Kentucky:* Yeas, 12. *Tennessee:* Nays, 9. *Ohio:* Yeas, 13. *Indiana:* Yeas, 3. *Illinois:* Yea, 1. *Louisiana:* Nays, 3. *Mississippi:* Nay, 1. *Alabama:* Nays, 3. *Missouri:* Nay, 1.

The bill, somewhat amended, passed the Senate, 26 to 21, as follows:

Maine: Nays, 2. *New Hampshire:* Nay, 1. *Massachusetts:* Yea, 1, (Webster;) nay, 1, (Silsbee.) *Rhode Island:* Yea, 1; nay, 1. *Connecticut:* Yeas, 2. *Vermont:* Yeas, 2. *New York:* Yeas, 2, (Sanford

---

readily seen. For instance: If an importer should present an invoice of cloth at 50 cents a yard which is worth 75 cents, the fraud would be readily discovered, and the article would be deemed to have cost $1, and charged accordingly. This would compel the foreign manufacturer to make all goods costing over 50 cents, intended for our market, worth, as near as possible, $1, and not exceeding that price. And so of the other *minima*, $2,50 and $4. The duties on woolens were, after the first year, to be increased 5 per cent.

and Van Buren.) *New Jersey:* Yeas, 2. *Pennsylvania:* Yeas, 2 *Delaware:* Yeas, 2. *Maryland:* Nays, 2. *Virginia:* Nays, 2. *North Carolina:* Nays, 2. *South Carolina:* Nays, 2. *Georgia:* Nays, 2. *Kentucky:* Yeas, 2. *Tennessee:* Yea, 1; nay, 1. *Ohio:* Yeas, 2. *Louisiana:* Yea, 1; nay, 1. *Indiana:* Yeas, 2. *Illinois:* Yea, 2. *Mississippi:* Nays, 2. *Alabama:* Nays, 2. *Missouri:* Yeas, 2, (Benton and Barton.)

The indignation of the South excited by the passage of this act, was not allayed until after the enactment of the Compromise act of 1833.

One year remained of Mr. Adams' Presidential term; and, lest the load of unprincipled opposition under which it was staggering should prove insufficient to crush it, another attempt was made to effect the object.

In January, 1828, Mr. Chilton, of Kentucky, moved resolutions declaring the expediency of the speedy discharge of the public debt, and, in order to effect it, the necessity of a general system of retrenchment, the discontinuance of needless offices, the reduction of salaries; and instructing the Committee of Ways and Means to report such means of retrenchment as might be deemed necessary. The friends of the administration, although aware that the resolutions had been introduced for party effect, yet, concurring in the measure proposed, and believing that the Government had been economically administered, made no serious opposition to their reference.

Among the list of alleged abuses, the *navy list* was said to be crowded; cadets had been educated at West Point who were out of employment; a fifth auditor had been appointed for a time which had expired, and his services were no longer necessary; too many clerks were employed; the contingent fund had been improperly used; many salaries might be reduced; and the reduction should begin with the compensation and mileage of members of Congress; and there was an unnecessary expenditure for printed documents.

Opposition members were not unanimous upon all points. Messrs. Buchanan, Randolph, and M'Duffie, although they believed in the necessity of reform, did not think the present a favorable time, nor the manner proposed a proper one. Mr. Buchanan said also that the duties of the fifth auditor had been doubled, and the office was necessary.

Several members of the opposition also opposed a reduction of their compensation. Mr. M'Duffie said, he would say nothing that would have a bearing upon the administration one way or another. The question was not what the Government had done ; that was past ; but this was a practical resolution which had reference to future reforms. Whether there were abuses or not—whether the Panama Mission was expedient or not, was not now before the House ; it was at an end ; why was it brought up here, and at this time ? As bearing upon the administration, these things had no business here. In reference to the public debt, and the mode of its discharge, he said, all the means which the country possessed of paying it were, by existing laws, to be applied to that object ; and no resolution would either hasten or retard its payment.

The President was censured by some for his having rewarded with office members of Congress who had aided in his election, and accused of having claimed for the General Government powers unauthorized by the Constitution, and incompatible with the rights of the States and the liberties of the people. Having, by a lawless construction, extended the powers of the Government, he had threatened a sovereign State (Georgia) with the military force of the nation.

Members on the other side were willing to institute the inquiry. The President had himself, in 1826, and again in 1827, recommended "the most vigilant economy and all honorable expedients, for the total discharge of the public debt." No new offices had been created by this administration ; nor had any salaries been raised except that of the Postmaster-General, whose business had been largely increased. The $10,000,000 annually reserved as a sinking fund must inevitably pay the debt ; and the present administration had paid, not only the ten millions annually, but a part of the deficiencies of the preceding administration. The Academy at West Point was also defended against the attack of opposition members, Mr. Buchanan assisting in the defense. The Panama Mission had received the sanction of both Houses, and been approved by the nation. What would not have been said against the administration if the invitation to attend the meeting had not been accepted? The administration was not responsible for the failure of the meeting. The charge that the West India trade had been lost by the administration, was also replied to. [This will receive proper notice in our sketch of Gen. Jackson's administration.] Numerous other charges were preferred and replied to; but for want of room, they must be passed over without notice.

The resolutions were referred to a Select Committee; but probably because the object of their mover and supporters had been attained, no bill to carry them into effect was ever reported.

At this session, (1827–1828,) a petition from citizens of the District of Columbia was presented to Congress for the prospective abolition of slavery in the District, and for the repeal of those laws which authorized the selling of supposed runaways for their prison fees or maintenance. The petitioners declared slavery among them to be "an evil of serious magnitude, which greatly impaired the prosperity and happiness of the District, and to cast the reproach of inconsistency upon the free institutions established among us." They represented the domestic slave trade there as "scarcely less disgraceful, and even more demoralizing in its influence," than the foreign slave trade which is declared piracy, and punishable with death. "Husbands and wives are separated; children are taken from their parents without regard to the ties of nature, and the most endearing bonds of affection are broken forever." A stronger anti-slavery document has not, in later times, been presented to Congress. It did not, however, meet with a favorable reception.

At the next session, (1828–1829,) the last under the administration of Mr. Adams, protests against the tariff act of the preceding session from the Legislatures of Georgia and South Carolina, were presented to the Senate. The act was entitled, "An act in alteration of the several acts imposing duties on imports." The Georgia protest pronounced it "deceptive in its title, fraudulent in its pretexts, oppressive in its exactions, partial and unjust in its operations, unconstitutional in its well known objects, ruinous to commerce and agriculture—to secure a hateful monopoly to a combination of importunate manufacturers." The protestors, in temper and language similar to that in which the General Government was addressed in the Indian case, "demanded the repeal of the act," and asked that this expression of the opinion of the State of Georgia might "be carefully preserved among the archives of the Senate." The protest savored strongly of nullification. It was presented by Mr. Berrien. In the course of his remarks, he adverted to the efficiency with which the Government had sustained itself during so many trials, and expressed the opinion, that it was yet to undergo a more fearful trial in questions affecting our internal peace; an event which, he hoped, might be far off. Little, however, could he have expected *such* a trial as that through which it is now passing! Little, too, did he think that, before his death, he would himself become the advocate, as he really did, of a protective tariff.

The protest of South Carolina was presented by Mr. Smith, a Senator from that State. It assigned at length the reasons for protesting against the system of protecting duties, pronouncing it "unconstitutional, oppressive, and unjust;" and, lest opparent acquiescence in the system should be drawn into precedent, the Legislature, in the name of the commonwealth, claim to enter their protest on the journals of the Senate.

The Presidential election had taken place, with the expected result, the election of Gen. Jackson, who had received 178 electoral votes, and Mr. Adams 83. Mr. Calhoun was reëlected Vice-President against Richard Rush.

The more the causes of Mr. Adams' defeat are considered, the less strange does it appear. Gen. Jackson having, in 1824, received a greater number of the electoral votes than Mr. Adams, the election of the latter by the House was by many considered a violation of the Democratic principle; and he was called the "minority President." True, this argument was not entitled to any weight, but it turned many into the support of his competitor. Let us consider this argument. In the first place, a plurality of electoral votes does not prove a majority of the popular vote. There were, in 1824, four candidates; and it is impossible to say what would have been the popular vote if Mr. Crawford and

Mr. Clay had not been candidates. It was well known that the friends of Mr. Crawford, in some of the Northern States, especially in New York, decidedly preferred Mr. Adams to Gen. Jackson. But the electors were chosen in that State by the Legislature. The Albany Argus, the potent organ of the Crawford party, most bitterly denounced Gen. Jackson, pronouncing him the least fit of all the candidates for President, and branding him with the opprobious epithet of "Federal." Sometimes, too, a large State chooses Presidental electors by a bare majority of its voters, while a small State elects its few electors by a marority of many thousands. Not having the statistics at hand, I cannot say how far this was the case in 1824. But I have before me a history of parties in which I find the follwing statements, founded, it is presumed, on correct date :

Mr. Adams had the greatest number of popular votes at the polls. Gen. Jackson did not receive a plurality in North Carolina ; and it was by a coalition with the friends of Crawford that he received the electoral vote of that State. Mr. Crawford, on the plurality principle, was entitled to the credit of the 15 electoral votes, which, in the electoral college were cast for Gen. Jackson. This reduction would have left him 84, the number cast for Mr. Adams. New York, on the same principle, would have given Mr. Adams 36 electoral votes instead of the 26 he received in the Legislature, by which the electors were then chosen. These 10 additional votes would have made his aggregate 94 against the General's 84. In the New England States, his popular majorities greatly exceeded those in the eight States whose electors voted for the General. In the electoral colleges of the Slave States, moreever, which voted for Gen. Jackson, the votes cast for slaves, not by them, and which may be termed popular, though constitutional, were of course, included. These subtracted from the canvass, the relative strength of Mr. Adams is further augmented ; so that he was the choice, as well of a large plurality of the voters, as of a majority of the States.

But it should be deemed sufficient that he was elected in a manner prescribed in the Constitution. The framers did not think proper to require an election to be made by a majority of an aggregate popular vote cast directly for candidates ; but preferred an election through the intervention of electors ; and provided for an election by the House of Representatives by States, in case no election should be made by the electoral colleges. The people have approved this mode by the adoption of the Constitution. The election of Mr. Adams was, therefore, *in accordance with the will of the people,* and no violation of the Democratic principle.

The charge of corruption, too, in the election of Mr. Adams, had a powerful influence against his reëlection. It had, indeed, been disproved to the satisfaction of candid and intelligent men ; but the evidence had been carefully concealed from the readers of Democratic papers. In not a single paper of that party, have I ever seen one of the numerous facts exculpating the gentlemen charged. And it may be stated as a trait in the character of the Democratic presses generally, that they never correct injurious or slanderous statements. There are doubtless exceptions ; but it is believed they are few. Respecting the case in question, it may probably be said in truth, that not one Democrat in ten of those to whom the charge had become familiar by repetition, has to this day read or heard any part of the evidence by which it was so triumphantly refuted.

Several other causes, not mentioned, contributed to the success of Gen. Jackson ; not the least powerful of which was the prestege of military fame. The simple fact of his having the well-earned title of the "Hero of New Orleans," was sufficient to counterbalance, in the estimation of many minds, the most important qualifications of his competitor.

CHAPTER II.

Administration of Andrew Jackson.—First Term.

ANDREW JACKSON was inaugurated President of the United States oc the 4th of March, 1829. His promises in his In. augural Address were numerous and proper. He should regard the limitations of the Executive power ; respect the rights of the States ; observe strict economy to facilitate the payment of the public debt ; show equal favor to agriculture, commerce and manufactures ; commend idternal improvement, so far as it could be promoted constitutionally ; and, omong other things, would observe toward the Indian tribes within our limits, a just and liberal policy. And he mentioned as one of his prominent duties, "*the task of reform*; which will require, particularly, the correction of those abuses that have brought the General Government into conflict with the freedom of elections, and the counteraction of those causes which have disturbed the rightful course of appointment, and have placed or continued power in unfaithful or incompetent hands."

The reader who does not understand the *nature* of the "reform" here alluded to, or "abuses" committed by his predecessor which needed "correction," will soon find an explanation in the manner and extent of the exercise of the appointing power by the new President.

The persons selected for Cabinet officers, were, Martin Van Buren, of N. Y., Secretary of State ; Samuel D. Ingham, of Pa., Secretary of the Treasury ; John H. Eaton, of Tenn., Secretary of War ; John Branch, of N. C., Secretary of the Navy ; John M. Berrien, of Ga., Attorney-General ; and Wm. T. Barry, of Ky., Postmaster-General. Until this time, the Postmaster-General was not a Cabinet officer. John M'Lean, of Ohio, the incumbent of that office, was appointed an associate Justice of the Supreme Court.

To enable us to judge of the consistency, if not the propriety, of the President's conduct, it is necessary to know what were his "antecedents." Although he had never attained great distinction as a civilian, his sentiments on many political subjects had been publicly expressed. On the questions of the tariff and internal improvements, he was among those who were strongly committed in their favor. In 1823, he was in the Senate of the United States, advocating the highest protective duties, while Mr. Clay was in the House engaged so assiduously in pressing through that body the protective tariff of that year. It was then that Gen. Jackson wrote his notable letter to Dr. Coleman, in favor of what was called the "American system;" and to which he had committed himself anew just before his election. The people of Indiana and other Western States, were in favor of the protective system and internal improvements; but as Gen. Jackson had been adopted as a candidate by the people of the Southern States, who were so strongly opposed to these measures, the Senate of Indiana, in January, 1828, requested the Governor to address to Gen. Jackson a letter, "inviting him to state explicitly whether he favors that construction of the Constitution which authorizes Congress to appropriate money for making iuternal improvements in the several States; and whether he is in favor of a system of protective duties; and whether, if he is elected President, he will, in his public capacity, recommend, foster, and support the American system."

In his answer, the General reässerts his principles as declared in the Coleman letter to which he referred Gov. Ray, sending him a copy, and to which the reader also is referred. The letter is an epitome of the great arguments by which the system is maintained, and is worthy of perusal by every American citizen. The want of space alone forbids its insertion here. [For the letter, see American Statesman, pp. 402, 403.] On this question, his views were the same as those of Mr. Adams.

But there were other principles than those of political economy to which Gen. Jackson was committed, or which he had avowed. In his correspondence with Mr. Monroe, after the election of the latter had been ascertained, he recommended the appointment of men to o&ce without reference to their party attachments. In other words, he was opposed to proscription for opinion's sake.

Mr. Adams having appointed to office several members of Congress who had voted for him as President, Gen. Jackson, in an address to the Tennessee Legislature, in October, 1825, said, in reference to such appointments, that he was in favor of a provision in the Constitution rendering any member of Congress ineligible to office under the General Government during the term for which he was elected, and for two years thereafter. One of the reasons for such prohibition was, that "members, instead of being liable to be withdrawn from legislating upon the great interests of the nation, through prospects of Executive patronage, would be more liberally confided in by their constituents; while their vigilance would be less interrupted by party feelings and party excitements." And he adds, "*if important offices continue to devolve on the Representatives in Congress, . . . corruption will become the order of the day.*"

Before his election, Gen. Jackson had also declared himself opposed to the eligibility of a President to the office for the next term. The object of this restriction was to remove all inducement to use the power of patronage in his hands to secure a reëlection.

How nearly the *practice* of the President corresponded to his previously avowed principles, is well known by those who are familiar with the politics of those times. His "no-party" principle was immediately illustrated in his appointments; in which he adopted a new rule of action, not practiced by any of his predecessors. They had, as was proper, selected for members of the Cabinet, as their political advisers, and as assistants, men who would coöperate with them in executing the laws and in carrying out the general policy of the administration. Gen. Jackson did the same. But immediately after the appointment of his Cabinet, he commenced the removal of incumbents, a considerable number of whose places were filled before the Senate adjourned, (the 17th of March.) During the recess of the Senate, district marshals and attorneys; surveyors, inspectors, and collectors of ports; naval officers; appraisers of goods; receivers of public moneys; auditors, controllers, and clerks in the Executive Departments, were displaced, and political adherents appointed in their places. And of Postmasters, nearly five hundred were removed during the first year of the administration.

This general removal of political opponents, though severely reprehended and condemned by the opposition party, and referred to as inconsistent with his professed sentiments before his election, was to some no matter of surprise. It had been announced before his election, that he would, if elected, "reward his friends and punish his enemies." Clerks who had held places during successive administrations and changes of parties since the time of Washington, and at a period of life too late to engage in new pursuits, were dismissed to make place for others who, according to the rule, were entitled to "rewards" for party services. The seat of Government swarmed with hungry partisans claiming a share of the crumbs of Executive patronage. Thus early had the public a practical exposition of the promised "reform"—the "correction of those abuses that had brought the General Government into conflict with the freedom of elections." Here was the beginning of the "reward and punishment" system, which has probably done more to corrupt the Government, than all other influences combined. Had Mr. Adams adopted this means to strengthen his party, it is not improbable, he might have secured a reëlection. He had made only *two* removals, both for cause, during his whole Presidential term. Jefferson, after the Government had been, during its entire previous existence, in the hands of his opponents, removed only *thirty-nine*, in eight years; and no other President removed more than ten, of whom some were for cause.

Some, to relieve the President from the charge of corruption, have ascribed this contradiction of a professed principle to a certain extraneous influence. The removal system had long prevailed in the State from which he had selected his Secretary of State, who had for many years directed the politics of his State. That an "oily" tactician of a long and successful experience, should obtain a controlling influence over a confiding, unsuspecting chief, is not strange; or that, as was believed, he had become "a power behind the throne greater than the throne itself."

From the horror expressed by Gen. Jackson and his

friends at the appointment, by Mr. Adams, of a few members of Congress to office, which had led Congress to call for a list of such appointments "since the foundation of the Government," for the alleged object of enabling Congress to remove an evil said to exist and to be growing, one would suppose this practice would have been scrupulously avoided. But the list transmitted showed, that Mr. Adams had, in thirteen months, to the time of the report, appointed *five* members of Congress. Gen. Jackson, during the first three months of his term, appointed *twelve*, and during his administration, about double the number of such appointments made by any of his predecessors, of whom Mr. Monroe had made the highest number, *thirty-five*. Yet, while pursuing practices so contrary to his professions, he recommended in his first annual Message, an amendment of the Constitution, bringing the election of President directly to the people, prohibiting the appointment of members of Congress, and restricting the service of the President to one term of four or six years. But, objectionable as he seemed to think a reëlection to be, he had not been long in office before he consented to be again a candidate.

Among the subjects noticed in this Message was that of the rechartering of the Bank of the United States. He said, its Constitutionality and its expediency were both questioned, and it had failed in the great end of establishing a uniform and sound currency. And he suggested in its stead one founded upon the credit of the Government and its revenues which should "avoid all constitutional difficulties, and secure all the advantages expected from the present Bank." This attack upon the Bank took the country by surprise. The reasons for agitating the subject of its recharter *six years before the expiration of its present charter*, a period extending two years beyond the close of his official term, and during which *three new Congresses must be elected*, were for a time incomprehensible to the people. The constitutionality of the Bank, as Mr. Madison supposed when he signed the bill establishing it, had been settled by the decision of the Supreme Court, and by the acquiescence of the people in that decision for a considerable period; nor were the people aware of its failure to create a uniform and sound currency, as its notes were current in all parts of the country.

The subject was referred, in the House, to the Committee of Ways and Means, Mr. M'Duffie, of S. C., Chairman, who, with a majority of the Committee, were political friends of the President. The Committee, in their Report, pronounced the Bank constitutional and expedient, and disapproved the President's project of a new Bank. They controverted his statement that the Bank had "failed to establish a uniform and sound currency."

In the Senate, the Committee on Finance, Mr. Smith, of Md., Chairman, a majority being friends of the administration, made a report on "the expediency of establishing a uniform currency," which maintained that a sound and uniform currency existed, furnished by the Bank of the United States ; and they declared the President's scheme "impracticable."

At the same session, a bill to authorize the General Government to subscribe to the stock of the Maysville and Lexington Turnpike Road in Kentucky, was vetoed by the President. A similar bill in relation to the Washington Turnpike Company, was also negatived by the President. Two other bills for internal improvements, one of them appropriating money for light-houses, improving harbors, directing surveys, &c., were retained until the next session, when in his annual Message, he gave his objections to the bills, and to the system of internal improvements. How far these vetoes were consistent with his pledge to Governor Ray and the Legislature of Indiana before his election, let the reader judge. A bill was passed, however, providing for the improvement of harbors, and clearing certain rivers, having passed the House, 136 to 53 ; and the Senate, 28 to 6 ; and another providing for surveys, &c. ; both of which were approved by the President. The application of the veto to so many bills displeased many of the President's friends.

Gen. Jackson had in his Inaugural promised "to observe toward the Indian tribes a just and liberal policy." His sense of justice and liberality toward these tribes, a few facts will suffice to illustrate.

The resolute purpose of Mr. Adams to protect the Creeks in the peaceable possession of their lands had provoked the bitter resentment of the Government and people of Georgia,

Having had intimations before the election, that Gen. Jackson would favor their claims to the right of soil and of jurisdiction over it, they lost no time in attempting to gain possession. A law was passed by the Legislature of Georgia extending over the Cherokee country the laws of the State. The Indians memorialized Congress for protection. The Attorney-General, Mr. Berrien, taken from that State to a seat in the Cabinet, was applied to for his opinion, which was unfavorable to the claims of the Indians, conceding to them merely the right of occupancy, the fee of the soil being in the State. It was the purpose of the President to effect the removal of the Indians West of the Mississippi ; and a bill was reported for this purpose in each House. The debate on the Senate bill was a long and an able one. The bill passed to a third reading by a vote of 28 to 19. It passed the House, 103 to 97. This bill did not in words compel the removal of the Indians. The change of policy consisted in conceding to the States the right of soil, and in subjecting the Indians to the government of the States. It was presumed, that, if reduced to the alternative of submitting to the laws of Georgia and Alabama, or of exchanging their lands, they would choose the latter.

In the course of the debates on the bill, the policy of the Government toward the Indians by former administrations, from that of Washington down, and all the treaties made from time to time, were referred to, to prove the claim of the Indians to the ownership of the lands ; and it is certainly difficult to see how, from the facts presented, both Houses could sanction the new policy.

A treaty was made with the Choctaws, who ceded their lands, and agreed to remove beyond the Mississippi within three years. Those choosing to remain as citizens of Georgia, were to have reservations of land for their use, and after residing upon them for five years, were to possess them *in fee*. They were to be governed in their Western residence by laws of their own, which, however, must not be inconsistent with those of the United States.

The Cherokees, unwilling to emigrate, soon found themselves under the operation of the laws of Georgia ; and, having failed in their appeals to the Government for protection, they took measures to have their case submitted to the Supreme Court. Their counsel, Mr. Wirt, proposed to Gov. Gilmer, of Georgia, the making of a case, by consent, before that Court; but the Governor declined.

George Tassels, an Indian, having committed a homicide in resisting the execution of the laws of Georgia, was tried, convicted of murder, and sentenced to be hanged. Before the day fixed for his execution, the State of Georgia, pursuant to a writ of error obtained from the Supreme Court of the United States, was cited to appear, and show cause why judgment against Tassels should not be corrected. The Legislature declared the interference of the Chief-Justice in the administration of the criminal laws of Georgia a flagrant violation of her rights; enjoined all State officers to disregard all such mandates of the Court; required the Governor to resist by force all invasions upon the administration of the laws; and ordered the execution of Tassels, which was done.

The act of Georgia nullifying the government and laws of the Indians and enforcing the laws of the State within the territory, made it a misdemeanor for white men to reside within the limits of the Cherokee nation without license from the Governor or his agent, and without having taken an oath to support the Constitution and laws of the State. Under this act, Rev. Mr. Worcester, a missionary, and five others, were arrested. A writ of *habeas corpus* was issued. Their discharge was demanded by their counsel, on the ground that the act under which they had been apprehended was contrary to the Constitution of the United States, and the Constitution of Georgia. The judge maintained the constitutionality of the law. But as Mr. Worcester and one of the others were missionaries, and one of them (Mr. W.) was a postmaster; as they were there by consent of the General Government for the purpose of civilizing and Christianizing the Indians; and as they were Government agents for the disbursement of the public moneys for that purpose; he discharged them under the State law which excepted all agents of the General Government from its provisions. The other four persons were bound over for trial.

Mr. Worcester was soon after removed from the office of postmaster, with the view, as was supposed, to make way for his arrest. This supposition proved true. Ten persons were indicted, convicted, and *sentenced to four years imprisonment!* Only Mr. Worcester and Dr. Butler were imprisoned; the others having been pardoned on giving assurance that they would not again violate the laws. Mr. Worcester applied to the Supreme Court for relief. The Court pronounced the laws of Georgia unconstitutional, and ordered Worcester's discharge. The mandate of the Court was disregarded, the missionaries kept in prison, without hope of liberation before another session of the Court, the next year. They therefore discontinued their suit; and were discharged by the Governor. About three years thereafter, a treaty was concluded providing for the removal of the Cherokees.

The proclamation of President Jackson against the South Carolina nullifiers was issued before the Indian difficulties were ended. This raised for a time the hopes of the Cherokees. The President having declared the supremacy of the Constitution and laws of the United States over those of State authority, and having acknowledged the Supreme Court to be the proper tribunal to decide upon the constitutionality of the laws, they hoped he would ultimately enforce the treaties and the laws made for their protection. But their hopes were vain. What was constitutional on one side of the dividing line between the States was unconstitutional on the other! In other words, nullification on one side was wrong, and on the other right.

Among the party questions during the administrations of Adams and Jackson, was that of the West India Trade. No preceding administration had been able to secure a trade with the British West India Islands on terms satisfactory to our Government. Acts of Parliament were passed soon after Mr. Adams came into office, again opening certain colonial ports upon new terms and conditions; but they provided that these ports should be closed against any nation that should not accept these terms. Mr. Adams did not accept them for reasons which he assigned. The acts had not been officially communicated; and they were so obscure that they had been differently construed by British officers in different colonies; and as Great Britain had promised to resume negotiation, it was better to await the result of that negotiation. An arrangement by treaty was preferable, because its terms could not be avoided but by mutual agreement ; whereas an act of Parliament could be altered or repealed whenever the interests of Great Britain should require a change of policy.

Mr. Gallatin was sent to England to negotiate ; but before his credentials had been presented, an order in council was issued cutting off all negotiation, and prohibiting all intercourse with her West India Colonies. In pursuance of acts of 1818 and 1820, our ports were declared closed against British vessels from any place in any British territory to which our vessels were not admitted. By a treaty concluded at London, in August, 1827, a reciprocal trade was established between the United States and the territories of Great Britain in Europe for ten years from 1828 ; but the exclusion of our vessels from her Colonies was continued. Our produce, however, still found a market in the British West India Islands by way of the Danish, Swedish, and other neutral islands ; to which it was carried in American vessels ; and thence it was reshipped to the British Islands. Hence our navigation was not very sensibly affected. The Canadians complained that the arrangement had not secured to them the advantage of supplying the West India Islands ; and the extra cost of this indirect trade fell upon British consumers.

The new administration having charged its predecessor with the *loss* of the West India trade, it was to be expected that a strenuous effort would be made to *regain* it. Mr. McLane, the new Minister to England, was directed to represent to the British Government, that the American people, in changing the administration, had testified their disapproval of the acts of the late administration, and that the claims set up by them which had caused the interruption of the trade, would not be urged : that is, what had been injudiciously asked as a *right*, we were now willing to receive as a *boon ;* and the present administration should not be held responsible for the acts of their predecessors.

An arrangement was in due time effected. It was at once announced, with great exultation, by the administration presses, as an achievement which had baffled the diplomacy of our Government for forty years. The recovery, "by the honest, high-minded, straight-forward administration of Andrew Jackson," of an unrestricted commerce, temporarily enjoyed under the act of Parliament, of July, 1825, but "unwillingly and criminally thrown away by the blundering negotiation" of Mr. Adams, was hailed as an important achievement. The opposition declared not only that the trade had not been lost, but that *nothing had been gained by the new arrangement;* and that our navigation which had enjoyed the carrying trade, *would be diminished by the British shipping*, for which loss no equivalent would be received.

The arrangement secured to our vessels and cargoes the right to enter the ports of her West India and other British Colonies, on equal terms with her own coming from the United States. But the benefits of this anticipated "reciprocal trade" had scarcely begun to be realized, when, by an act of Parliament, produce coming into the British West India ports directly from the United States, was subjected to exorbitant duties, but was admitted into the Canadian provinces, and thence *shipped to the British West India Islands in British vessels, free of duty, to the exclusion of American shipping.* The flour, also, manufactured in Canada from American wheat, was considered as having changed its character, and was admitted free into England, as *colonial* produce. The duty on a barrel of flour from the United States into the British West India Colonies, was 6s., or $1 33; but from the Canadas no duty was charged. Lumber was charged at $7 per 1000 feet; but from the British North American Colonies it was free. To evade the duties, British vessels conveyed our produce to Canadian ports, and thence, as British produce, to the islands, free of duty.

No wonder that the British papers rejoiced at the benefits derived from "the arrangement." One said: "Jonathan, after all, will not find the great boon so good a thing as he expected, under the existing restrictions." Another said: "We only allow their vessels to bring to our ports the produce and manufactures of the United States: they make their ports free to our commerce in every sense of the word."

As was predicted by the opposition, our tunnage was greatly diminished, and the British increased. So injuriously did this policy affect the lumber trade of Maine with the West Indies, in which a vast amount of shipping had been previously employed, that Congress was petitioned for relief. The adverse effects of this boasted "arrangement" were, as far as possible, concealed. The administration presses were silent in respect to its practical workings ; they rather continued to claim credit for the measure. Even Mr. Benton, in his "Thirty Years' View," after its disastrous effects had been so severely felt, lauds it in terms no less eulogistic than those in which it was first announced. Thousands of the old friends of Gen. Jackson, still speak of this measure as one that reflects the highest honor upon his administration.

In the summer of 1831, Mr. McLane was appointed Secretary of the Treasury in President Jackson's new Cabinet, and Mr. Van Buren was appointed to take his place as Minister at London. The appointment was made during the recess of the Senate, and the nomination was made to that body at the next session. The nomination, after an excited debate of several days, was rejected by the casting vote of Vice-President Calhoun. The principal objection made to the nomination, was the character of his instructions to Mr. McLane respecting the West India negotiation, by which he had humbled us in the eyes of foreign nations. He had instructed our Minister to press upon a foreign Government the misconduct of one part of the American family in the relations of our Government with that foreign power, and the more amiable and kind feelings of another division of it. Mr. Clay was opposed to the nomination also because the nominee had, as he believed, introduced the odious system of proscription into the General Government ; the system practiced in the gentleman's own State by the party of which he was the reputed head. It was a detestable system, putting up officers and honors to a scramble to be decided at every Presidential election.

Mr. Marcy, among others, replied, defending the instructions, and censuring the conduct of the previous administration, by which the colonial trade was lost. He also vindicated the politics of New York. They (the politicians) saw nothing wrong in the rule, that "to the victor belong the spoils of the enemy." The rejection was effected by the united votes of the opposition Senators, and those who, in the quarrel between the President and Mr. Calhoun, had attached themselves to the fortunes of the latter. Mr. Van Buren being suspected of some agency in the disruption of the Cabinet, and, as a political rival, an object of jealousy to Mr. Calhoun, and withal a favorite of the President, their hatred to him was not less intense than that which they entertained toward his chief. However justly Mr. Van Buren may have incurred the censure of the Senate and of the American people, his rejection, by the reäction in public sentiment, which it produced, was one of the most effective means of his promotion.

The Democratic party have been charged with holding to the Southern doctrine of State Rights, or Nullification. In the great debate in the Senate, in 1830, on Foot's resolutions relative to the public lands, in which the powers of the General Government and the State Governments, and the nature of the Union, became a prominent topic of discussion, the views of Democratic Senators appear to have coincided very nearly with those of Mr. Hayne. It is believed, that, of all the administration Senators who participated in the debate, only one, (Mr. Livingston, of Louisiana,) took the ground of Mr. Webster. Mr. Hayne maintained that the Constitution was a compact between the States, *as States;* and that there was no higher authority than that of a State, as a party to the compact, to judge of infractions of the Constitution; and that a State had the right to nullify any law of Congress which it should deem unconstitutional. This right was claimed on the authority of the Kentucky Resolutions drawn up by Mr. Jefferson. [See page 33.] And it is well recollected that the leading administration presses pronounced the speech of Mr. Hayne unanswerable—an "able, sound, democratic argument," for which the Democrats of the nation "owed him a debt of gratitude." And it was, for a time, at least, highly applauded by leading men of that party in all parts of the Union. Mr. Benton, Mr. Woodbury, Mr. Grundy, Mr. Rowan, and others took the side of Hayne, though all did not assert the right of *violent* resistance. Mr. Rowan pronounced the idea that the Supreme Court had the power to decide the question of the constitutionality of a law, a fallacy. These doctrines, he said, had been inferred from the tenor of the first message of Mr. Adams to Congress. Now, the explicit avowal of them by the honorable Senator (Mr. Webster) removed all doubt, as to the political faith of Mr. Adams. His most distinguished apostle had avowed it. "The two parties," said Mr. R., "are now clearly distinguishable by their opposite political tenets; the one headed by our illustrious chief magistrate, who is the advocate of the rights of the States; the other party is now headed by the Senator from Massachusetts." He expressly declared the right of a State to resist a law of Congress by force.

Did Mr. Rowan speak "by authority" when he claimed Gen. Jackson as a supporter of the doctrines then and there advocated by the leading Democratic Senators? Of this there may be on the public records no positive evidence. But his sanction of the nullification, by Georgia, of the treaties of the United States, and of the decision of the Supreme Court, affords strong *presumptive* evidence, that, up to the time of South Carolina nullification, of which his enemy, Mr. Calhoun, was the principal author, he favored the Southern doctrine, as defended in this debate. And had not actual resistance to the laws been determined on by that State, it is not improbable that these doctrines, now so generally odious, would have continued, to this day, a part of the Democratic creed.

At the session of 1831–1832, a new tariff act was passed, by which the duties on some articles, as iron, coarse woolens, &c., were materially reduced; though, on the whole, it was not less satisfactory to the friends of protection than the act of 1828. In South Carolina, the "Union" party considered it as a concession, while the "States rights" party regarded it as no less objectionable than former acts. It passed the House, 132 to 65; the Senate, 32 to 16. This was the act which provoked the hostility of South Carolina. Two propositions made at the same session for a large reduction of duties to meet the views of Southern members, were rejected; one of which had been reported by Mr. Verplanck, who represented the interests of the importers of the city of New York, who were opposed to restrictions upon trade; the other by Mr. M'Duffie, which required a gradual reduction to a uniform duty of 12½ per cent. on all goods imported after the 30th of June, 1834.

In October following, (1832,) the time to prepare for forcible resistance to the law, so long threatened, arrived. The Governor of South Carolina convened the Legislature, which authorized the calling of a Convention "to consider the character and extent of the usurpations of the General Government." The Convention assembled in November, and adopted an ordinance declaring the tariff act null and void, and forbidding the authorities of either the General or State Government to enforce the payment of duties within that State. Any act of Congress to authorize the employment of force against the State was declared void, and would not be submitted to; and from the time of its passage, the State would consider herself absolved from further obligations to the Union, and proceed to organize a separate government. The ordinance was to take effect the 1st of February, 1833.

On the 11th of December was issued the famous Proclamation of President Jackson against nullification. The views which it expresses of the nature of the Union, the supremacy of the laws of the United States, and the prerogative of the Supreme Court in respect to determining the validity of the laws of Congress, were similar to those expressed by Mr. Webster and Mr. Livingston in the Senate; which induced the belief that the proclamation was written by the latter, who was now Secretary of State. It very ably opposed the doctrine of secession, and defended the right of the General Government to punish those who should attempt, by force of arms, to destroy it; and he admonished the Carolinians not to incur the penalty of the laws.

The Legislature of South Carolina passed laws to give effect to the ordinance. Arms and ammunition were ordered to be purchased: and all needful preparation was made to resist the enforcement of the laws of Congress for the collection of the revenue. A bill was reported in Congress, empowering the President to employ the land and naval forces of the Union, to enforce the collection of the revenue in case of resistance. The bill was passed in the

Senate the 20th of February, 32 to 1. Mr. Tyler alone voted in the negative, other Senators opposed to the bill having withdrawn. It passed the House on the 1st of March, 148 to 48.

To prevent apprehended collision, the State of Virginia had assumed the office of mediator, and appointed a commissioner, (Benjamin Watkins Leigh,) to expostulate with the Government of South Carolina for the preservation of peace. The nullifying acts were to go into effect the 1st of February; but on being informed of the intention of Virginia to interpose, and before the arrival of Mr. Leigh, the operation of the laws was suspended until after the adjournment of Congress. Another cause contributed to this result. Mr. Verplanck had again introduced a bill similar to that of the preceding session, proposing a sudden reduction of duties, within two years, to a uniform rate of 20 per cent.; and there was, for a time, some hope of its passage, which would have pacified the rebellious State.

But while this bill was pending, and its passage having become quite improbable at this session, Mr. Clay, on the 12th of February, 1833, introduced his compromise tariff bill, which had in view two objects: one, to prevent the destruction of the tariff policy; the other, to avert civil war, and restore peace to the country. This bill, before it passed the Senate, was adopted in the House, in lieu of Mr. Verplanck's bill, and passed, (Feb. 26,) 118 to 84. It passed the Senate, 29 to 16. It was opposed by Mr. Webster and others because it gave up the principle of protection, and was insufficient to sustain the manufacturing interest. It was urged by Mr. Clay in reply, that, although Mr. Verplanck's could not pass at the present session, there was reason to fear that an attempt in the next Congress to destroy protection would be successful; and it would be better to extend the period of gradual reduction to the 30th of June, 1842, than to intrust the adjustment of the tariff to the incoming Congress. The act provided, that in all cases in which the duties exceeded 20 per cent., was to be gradually deducted, thus: one-tenth of all over and above 20 per cent., after the 31st of December, 1835; another tenth after the end of each of the years, 1837 and 1839; and of the remainder, one-half after the end of the year 1841 ; and the remainder after the 30th of June, 1842.

On the 11th of March, 1833, the nullifying ordinance of South Carolina was repealed.

With many it has been a question, whether, in 1830, President Jackson really held to the opinions ascribed to him by his nullifying friends. It is by some supposed that he did, and that the practical working of the scheme convinced him of his error, and led him to abjure the heresy. An extract from a debate in the House on the "Force Bill," may assist in solving this question.

In the course of this debate, the consistency of the President on the doctrine of State Sovereignty was called in question. Mr. Daniel, of Ky., alluded to the controversy between Georgia and the General Government in regard to the claims of the Cherokees, whose case had been carried by appeal from the Courts of Georgia to the Supreme Court of the United States. Mr. D. said it was well known that the President was in favor of the repeal of the 25th section of the Judiciary Act, which authorized the right of appeal from the Superior Courts of the States to the Supreme Court of the United States ; and this, said Mr. D., addressing the Chair, you, yourself, well know. [Mr. Polk, of Tennessee, then occupied the Chair in the absence of Speaker Stevenson.] All the members from Tennessee, he believed, with one or two exceptions, voted for the repeal of this section. But there were many more corroborative proofs of the President's opinions on this subject. A distinguished Senator (Mr. Grundy) from the President's own State, expressed the following opinion in 1830, in the debate on Foot's resolution : "If the State possesses the power to act as I have shown, the necessary consequence is, that the act of Congress must cease to operate in the State, and Congress must acquiesce by abandoning the power, or obtain an express grant from the great source from which all its powers are drawn. The General Government have no right to use force. It would be a glaring absurdity to suppose that the State had the right to judge of the constitutionality of an act of the General Government, and at the same time to say that Congress had the right to enforce submission to the act." The doctrines advocated by Mr. Hayne, said Mr. D., had at that time met with the approbation of the President, as expressed in direct terms in a letter from him to Mr. Hayne. The terms were to the effect, that the speech contained an exposition of the true principles of republicanism, and that it should be bound up and placed in his library along with the works of Thomas Jefferson.

Mr. Bell, of Tenn., here rose and inquired of Mr. Daniel, whether he had a personal knowledge of the President's approval of these principles, and of his commendation of Mr. Hayne's speech.

Before Mr. Daniel could reply, Mr. Carson, of N. C., rose with much earnestness, and said: "I, from my personal knowledge, can declare that such is the fact. The President expressed to me his approbation of that speech, in person."

Mr. Daniel proceeded, and said, what he knew of the President's opinions on this subject was from documents emanating from his own pen, and from the various statements of gentlemen whose veracity could not be impeached, independent of a host of corroborating circumstances. These nullifying doctrines had thus received the sanction of the member from Tennessee, (Mr. Grundy) who had just advocated the "Force Bill" in the Senate. They were approved by the President himself, until, in the downward path of his administration, he had thought fit to abandon every principle which had brought him into power: economy, retrenchment, State rights—all that had formed the watchword of the party—all had vanished into thin air.

Add to this testimony the fact before stated, that the leading Democratic papers of the country, among which was the Albany Argus, the acknowledged exponent of the principles of its party, commended in unqualified terms, the speech of Mr. Hayne for its "able, sound, democratic argument," and there is no room to doubt, that President Jackson, the head of the party, with the great body of its members, who were wont to boast of their adherence to the Jeffersonian republican principles of 1798, were in favor of the doctrine of Nullification. We may, however, congratulate the country, that he was compelled, by the force of circumstances, to change his position. His commanding influence might otherwise have popularized this disorganizing, revolutionary doctrine, and confirmed the Southern construction of the Constitution. For the decided stand he took against the nullifiers of 1832, he deserves high praise. Had a similar determination to enforce the laws been manifested by the late Executive in the incipient stage of the present Rebellion, it would have been promptly quelled; and the immense sacrifice of life and treasure which it will have occasioned, might have been avoided.

At the session of 1831–1832, a bill making appropriations for certain internal improvements for the year 1832, passed both Houses; and, notwithstanding his previously expressed objections to a system of internal improvement, the President approved the bill. It contained about fifty objects of appropriation, some of them of less importance than those which he had before negatived, and appropriated sums exceeding, in the aggregate, $1,200,000. Another bill, making appropriations for the improvement of harbors and rivers, passed the House 95 to 68, and was ordered engrossed in the Senate, 25 to 16. This bill, though quite as *national* in its character as the other, did not receive the President's signature. Though he received it three days before the adjournment of Congress, he retained it until Congress had adjourned, and thus prevented further action upon it. One or two other bills during this session received his veto. The frequent use of this power by Gen. Jackson obtained for him the significant title of "Veto President."

The subject of the Public Lands, which had frequently engaged the attention of Congress, was again agitated at this session, (1832.) A bill was reported by Mr. Clay. The revenue from duties on imports being sufficient for ordinary purposes, he proposed a distribution of the proceeds of the sales of public lands among the States for a limited time, subject to be resumed by the Government in case of war. To the five per cent. now reserved from the proceeds, ten per cent. was to be added for making internal improvements in the new States. This was intended to allay the complaints of the people of those States, that the public lands were exempt from taxation for five years from the time of sale. The residue of the fund derived from sales was to be divided among all the States in proportion to their federal population, to be applied to purposes of education, internal improvements, or colonization, at the pleasure of each State. The time limited for distribution was five years.

A counter report was made by another Committee, proposing to reduce the price of fresh lands to one dollar per acre, and of those which had been in market five years to fifty cents per acre ; and proposing to allow to the new States fifteen instead of ten cents in addition to the present five per cent. Mr. Clay's bill, however, was adopted, 28 to 16. It was sent to the House, where it was virtually rejected by postponing its consideration to the first Monday of December next. The bill was renewed at the next session, and with some amendments passed the Senate, 24 to 20 ; the House, 96 to 40. The bill was received by the President the day before the close of the session, but was not returned by him until the next session—which was virtually another veto. Having in his first Annual Message, (December, 1829,) recommended the distribution of the surplus revenue among the several States, as the most proper mode of disposing of it, a disapproval of the measure was to many quite unexpected, and was imputed to other reasons than those given in the Message accompanying the returned bill.

The unexpected attack on the Bank of the United States in the President's first Message, has been noticed. The ultimate destruction of this Institution against such odds as he had to encounter at the commencement of the contest, is one of the strange events which mark our political history.

The stockholders of the Bank applied at this session for a renewal of its charter. Among the reasons stated for so early an application, they said : "Unless the question is decided by the present Congress, no definitive action can be expected until within two years of the expiration of the charter ; a period before which, in the opinion of your memorialists, it is highly expedient, not merely in reference to the institution itself, but to the interests of the nation, that the determination of Congress should be known."

The memorial was referred, in the Senate, to a Select Committee; in the House, to the Committee of Ways and Means. The Chairmen, Mr. Dallas, in the Senate, and Mr. McDuffie, in the House, were both Democrats. The bill reported by Mr. Dallas was the one adopted in both Houses. It passed the Senate, 28 to 20; the House, 107 to 85; but it was vetoed by the President; for which act he was severely censured by some of his political friends, as well as nearly all his opponents. He assigned various reasons for the veto; but they failed to satisfy the friends of the Bank. The opinions of the Supreme Court, he contended, ought not to control the coördinate authorities. "The Congress, the Executive, and the Court must each for itself be guided by its own opinion of the Constitution. Each public officer swears that he will support it as he understands it, and not as it is understood by others." And he said the President was independent of both Congress and the Judges.

Nowhere was the President more severely censured for the veto than in Pennsylvania, where he had enjoyed great popularity. At a meeting in Philadelphia, it was declared, that his rejection of the Bank bill, his assaults on the principle of protection to American industry, upon the Supreme Court, and upon the independence of Congress, had "severed the ties by which the people of Pennsylvania had been connected with him;" and they declared that, "the reëlection of a President whose official path had been strewed with violated pledges, would be a national calamity."

In the House of Representatives, a Committee was appointed to inspect the books and examine into the proceedings of the Bank. Numerous acts of misconduct had been alleged against the Bank as furnishing ground for the inquiry. The majority of the Committee reported six cases of alleged wrong doing, which were designed to show that the Bank had violated its charter. But the Committee would not express their opinion as to their force. Allegations were also made of corrupt management, designed to show that the Bank was no longer entitled to public confidence. A counter report was made by the minority, in which the allegations of the majority were met and severally disposed of. A third report was made by John Quincy Adams alone, who had joined with his two colleagues of the minority, McDuffie and Watmough, in the second report above mentioned. This report of Mr. Adams discloses the cause of the first attack upon the Bank. The facts reported by Mr. A., though published among the public documents, are known to but a small portion of the American people. He says: "They are not noticed in the report of the Chairman, but in the opinion of the subscriber, are more deserving of the attention of Congress and of the nation, than any other papers commented upon in the report."

It appeared that Isaac Hill, editor of a Democratic paper in Concord, N. H., and chief director of the party in that State, who had recently been appointed a Controller of the Treasury at Washington, had, in June, 1829, three months after the Inauguration of Gen. Jackson, sent to his friends in Philadelphia two petitions, to one of which he had obtained the names of about sixty members of the New Hampshire Legislature, and which his friends were to present to the President and Directors of the Bank, asking for a change in the Board of Directors in the branch at Portsmouth. Several Jackson men were named in the petition for directors.

Soon after, the Secretary of War wrote to Mr. Mason, President of the branch at Portsmouth, directing the books, papers, and funds of the Pension Agency to be delivered to a Mr. Pickering, of Concord, for the benefit, as is evident, of a small bank, of which Mr. Hill was the president before his removal to Washington. Mr. Mason objected to this order, as contrary to law. The charter made it the duty of the Bank to disburse the public moneys for the Government; and for this purpose the pension funds were placed in its branches; and Mr. Mason denied the legality of the order and his own right to surrender the funds and papers as required.

On the 11th of July, 1829, Mr. Ingham, Secretary of the Treasury, transmitted to Mr. Biddle, President of the Bank, a confidential letter from Mr. Woodbury, of N. H., containing a complaint against the President of the branch at

Portsmouth, and charging that the influence of the Bank was used "with a view to political effect." He said also that the people desired Mr. Mason's removal, many of whom had requested him (Mr. W.) to ask his (Mr. Ingham's) influence, at the mother Bank, in producing a change. He said, further, that similar complaints had come from Kentucky, Louisiana, and other places.

In a letter to Mr. Biddle, Mr. Woodbury said that the charges against Mr. Mason "originated exclusively with his political friends." This statement Mr. Biddle thought irreconcilable with that of the same person in his letter to Mr. Ingham, that the Bank was managed "with a view to political effect." An examination was instituted; and Mr. Biddle went to New Hampshire for that purpose. After a thorough investigation, the Board found that the accusations were groundless; that the most zealous of Mr. Mason's enemies did not venture to assert that he had ever, on any occasion, been influenced by political feelings; and that what had been represented as public opinion, was nothing more than the personal hostility of a few individuals. Mr. Mason was therefore immediately reëlected.

In view of these facts, who can doubt, that it was the object of leading Democrats to get control of the Bank, "with a view," either "to political effect," or to their pecuniary advantage; and, failing in this, they invoked the aid of the President, whose popularity they well knew how to appreciate, in demolishing an institution which they could not make subservient to their selfish ends?

The defeat of the Bank bill by the veto of the President took place a few months before the Presidential election of 1832. The Bank question being one of the principal issues between the parties, the veto gave increased activity to the canvass. Mr. Clay, the candidate of the National Republican party, was a devoted friend of the Bank; and a large portion of the Democrats, especially in Pennsylvania, being in favor of its recharter, the friends of Mr. Clay hoped the veto would inure materially to his advantage. It is probable, however, that Gen. Jackson lost not a single electoral vote in consequence of his rejection of the Bank bill. He received of the electoral votes 219, and Mr. Clay 49. South Carolina gave her 11 votes to John Floyd, of Va.; and the 7 votes of Vermont were given to William Wirt, the candidate of the Anti-Masonic party.

CHAPTER III.

Administration of Andrew Jackson.—Second Term.

President Jackson entered upon his second term on the 4th of March, 1833. Considering his reëlection as a decision of the people against the Bank, he was encouraged to continue his hostility to the institution. And the next measure to be executed was *the removal of the public moneys from the Bank of the United States.* Of this the public were apprised by his last annual Message (Dec., 1832) before his second Inauguration; from which it appeared that "measures had already been taken by the Secretary of the Treasury to enable him to judge whether the public deposits in this institution were entirely safe." As this fact must be established in order to justify their removal, and as the power of the Secretary might prove inadequate to this object, the President recommended the subject to the attention of Congress. An inquiry into the transactions of the Bank and its branches, he said, was "called for by the credit which was given throughout the country to many serious charges impeaching its character, which, if true, might justly excite the apprehension, that it was no longer a safe depository of the money of the people."

The measure taken by Secretary McLane to ascertain the safety of the deposits, was the appointment of Henry Toland to make the investigation, who reported to the Secretary the 4th of December, the day of the date of the Message, that the liabilities of the Bank amounted to $37,296,590; and the fund to meet them, $79,593,870; showing an excess of $42,296,920. As all liabilities must be first paid in case of insolvency or dissolution, he considered the security of the public money unquestionable. Nor was there any doubt of the solvency of the Bank.

In the House, the subject was referred to the Committee of Ways and Means, who, after due inquiry, reported that the resources of the Bank were upwards of $43,000,000 beyond its liabilities. The report concluded with a resolution, "That the Government deposits may, in the opinion of the House, be safely continued in the Bank of the United States." The resolution was adopted, 109 to 46.

The act declared that the deposits should be made in the Bank and its branches, "unless the Secretary of the Treasury should at any time otherwise order and direct, in which case he should immediately lay before Congress, if in session, and if not, immediately after the commencement of the next session, the reason of such order and direction." Disappointed in the result of the investigation, he determined on the removal of the deposits without the reason that they were unsafe, and appointed Moses Kendall to confer with State Banks in relation to future deposits and distribution of the public revenue. He read to his Cabinet (September 18,) a manifesto, giving reasons for removing the deposits, among which were: the Bank was of a dangerous tendency; it had paid for printing and circulating articles to influence public sentiment; he desired to evince his gratitude to the people by carrying their decision into effect; they having, by electing him, decided against the rechartering of the Bank, &c., &c.

William J. Duane, was now Secretary of the Treasury, having been appointed in May, in the place of Mr. McLane, who had been transferred to the head of the State Department in the place of Mr. Livingston, appointed Minister to France. Mr. Duane was directed to remove the deposits; but he declined to obey the direction. He assigned as reasons for refusing to carry the direction into effect, that the change, without necessity, was a breach of faith; that the measure appeared vindictive and arbitrary; that, if the Bank had abused its powers, the Judiciary, and, in the last resort, the Representatives of the people were able and willing to punish; that the latter had pronounced the deposits safe; that it was hazardous to place them in the local banks, which were not, on an average, able to pay in specie one dollar in six of their paper in circulation; that it would place in the hands of a Secretary, dependent for office on the Executive will, a power to favor or punish those banks, and make them political machines; that he believed the efforts to hasten the removal of the deposits had originated in schemes to promote selfish and factious purposes; and that persons and presses in the confidence and pay of the administration, had attempted to intimidate and constrain the Secretary to execute an act in direct opposition to his own solemn convictions.

This long list of reasons, all of them of more or less weight, one would suppose, would have deterred the President from the execution of his arbitrary purpose. But the Secretary's refusal was followed by his removal, and the appointment of Roger B. Taney, then Attorney-General, in his place. Mr. Taney immediately directed the removal of the deposits to the State Banks selected as the fiscal agents of the Government. This act caused great excitement, and was condemned by many of the President's political friends, in all parts of the country. Persons and presses that had been among his most zealous supporters, expressed their decided disapproval of this arbitrary exercise of power; and not a few withdrew from him their support.

A Committee appointed by the Directors of the Bank, made a long and elaborate report, designed as a full vindication of the course of the Directors, and as a refutation of the charges brought against it. They alluded to the efforts made in the summer of 1829 to remove Mr. Mason and the public funds from the branch at Portsmouth in order to satisfy Isaac Hill, who requested a change because "the friends of Gen. Jackson had but too much reason to complain of the management of the branch at Portsmouth," manifesting thus early "a combined effort to render the institution subservient to party purposes." Hence it became necessary to come to some immediate and distinct understanding of its rights and duties. They also gave extracts from the correspondence between Mr. Biddle and the Treasury Department, (alluded to in preceding pages,) which, they said, "revealed the whole secret of the hostility to the Bank of those who, finding it impossible to bend it to their purposes, had resolved to break it." The Bank had been charged with paying, from the funds deposited, for publications containing "invectives against the officers of the Government," and designed "to operate on elections and secure a renewal of its charter." In reply the report says, that the power actually given to the President of the Bank to expend its funds, which he had exercised, and which would continue to be exercised, was for the defense of the Bank against the calumnies with which, for four years, the institution had been pursued.

In the change which was made in depositing the public funds, no money was transferred from the Bank to the State banks. Future deposits were made in the latter; and the money was drawn from the former only as it was wanted by the Government. The change took place the 1st of October, 1833. The spite of the *official* enemies of the Bank was now exhibited in an attempt to "break" it by unexpected and sudden drafts. Mr. Kendall, the Government agent, in a letter to a New York editor, a few days after the removal of the deposits, spoke of the effects of a sudden withdrawal of the public moneys, (then nearly ten millions,) from the Bank, and added: "Yes, sir, this boasting giant is but a reptile beneath the feet of the Secretary of the Treasury, which he can crush at will. It exists by his forbearance, and will, for the next forty days; and great forbearance will it require to save it from destruction."

Accordingly, a few weeks after the utterance of this threat, the Bank was surprised by the presentation of a number of large drafts: one of $100,000 at the branch in Baltimore; two others, one of $100,000, and another of $500,000, at the Bank in Philadelphia; and three others, of $500,000 each, had been drawn upon the branch in New York. These drafts were all in favor of the State Banks in these places selected to receive the deposits. It had been the practice of the Treasury to transmit to the Bank a weekly statement of drafts to be made upon it; but these large sums were drawn for without the usual previous notice.

The effects of this unprincipled war upon the Bank—the rapid withdrawal of the deposits, and the known attempt to "crush" the institution—compelled, as a measure of safety, a curtailment of its loans; and a severe money pressure soon followed. Bills of State Banks depreciated in value on account of the scarcity of money; and these banks too were compelled to reduce their discounts. Public meetings were held, and memorials to Congress were prepared, praying for the return of the deposits to the Bank. The price of public stocks declined from 10 to 30 per cent.; interest rose to ruinous rates; laborers were discharged; and the price of real estate greatly declined. All this the opponents of the Bank attributed to the panic produced by the Bank and its friends for political purposes, or with a view to the renewal of its charter.

The intensity of the excitement increased. Meetings were called irrespective of party, and the removal of the deposits unanimosuly condemned. The Legislatures of several States did the same. The House of Delegates of Virginia pronounced the removal of the federal revenue from the Bank, where Congress had required it to be deposited, "an unauthorized assumption and dangerous exercise of Executive power." The Legislatures of some States, however, approved the course of the President.

The new Congress met in December, 1833. Mr. Calhoun and his friends now acting with the opposition, the administration party in the Senate was in the minority. The subject of the deposits occupied much of the time of this session. Memorials and remonstrances were received; and the question of the return of the deposits, and the course of the Bank, were long the subjects of debate.

In the Senate, two resolutions were offered by Mr. Clay: the first declaring, that in the proceedings of the President in relation to the public revenue, he had assumed power not conferred by the Constitution and laws; the second, that the reason assigned by the Secretary for the removal of the deposits were unsatisfactory and insufficient. The first was adopted, 26 to 20; the second, 28 to 18. The President soon after sent to the Senate a Message, *protesting* against this act of the Senate, as being, in substance, an impeachment of him contrary to the form prescribed by the Constitution, and requesting that the Message and protest be entered on the journals of the Senate; but the Senate refused to receive the paper.

Several reports and counter-reports, in relation to the bank and the removal of the deposits, were made during this session; but it is impossible to give them place. Although not devoid of interest, they do not essentially affect the general aspect of the question.

Mr. Benton, at the time of the adoption of Mr. Clay's resolution, (March, 1834,) pronouncing the President's proceedings in relation to the deposits to be in derogation of the Constitution and laws, gave notice that he would from time to time move that the resolution be expunged. He accordingly made such motion at the next session, (1834–1835.) But after some discussion, it was laid upon the table, 27 to 20. Unfaltering in his purpose, he repeated the motion at each successive session until 1837, when he was successful. The motion was opposed by Messrs. Calhoun, Webster, and Clay. The two first named Senators maintained, that, as the Constitution requires the Senate to keep a journal of its proceedings, the expunging of any part of it, would be a violation of the Constitution. "A record *expunged*," said Mr. Webster, "is not a record which is kept, any more than a record *destroyed* is a record which is *preserved*. The part expunged is no longer a part of the record; it has no longer a legal existence. It can not be certified as a part of the proceedings of the Senate for any proof or evidence." He protested that they had no right to deprive him of the personal constitutional right of having his yea and nay recorded and preserved on the journal. They might as well erase the yeas and nays on all other questions as on this. Some Senators had been instructed by their State Legislatures to vote for expunging. Mr. Calhoun and Mr. Webster both believed these instructions had been obtained "by dictation from the White House;" that they had their origin in promptings from Washington; and had been brought about by the influence of the Executive branch of this Government." The vote was taken near midnight: Yeas, 24; Nays, 19; absent, 4. The Secretary of the Senate then drew a square of broad black lines around the resolution of the 28th of March, 1834, and wrote across it, "Expunged by order of the Senate, this 16th day of January, 1837."

We now come to a subject which has been productive of a more intense excitement, a more protracted and bitter controversy, and which has more deeply affected the interests of the nation, than any other political question that has ever divided the American people—the question of SLAVERY.

In 1833 was formed the American Anti-Slavery Society. Its object was, by fair and candid discussion, to produce a strong and general anti-slavery sentiment at the North, the moral influence of which, it was hoped, would be felt at the South; and to convince slaveholders that Slavery was a moral and political evil, and that both duty and the mutual interests of the slave and the master required its immediate abolition. Neither the parent Society nor any of its auxiliaries originally, or for several years afterwards, contemplated or suggested a political organization to promote the object of these associations.

Anti-Slavery Societies were soon formed throughout the Northern States. The South became alarmed. Attempts were made to suppress anti-slavery societies and their publications. The "Emancipator," published in the city of New York, was indicted by a grand jury in Alabama; and a requisition by Gov. Gayle was made upon Gov. Marcy of the State of New York for the surrender of the publisher, R. J. Williams, as a "fugitive from justice," to be tried as an offender against the laws of Alabama concerning Slavery. The requisition was, of course, disregarded. In Louisiana a reward of $50,000 was offered for the delivery of Arthur Tappan, a prominent abolitionist in the city of New York; and rewards were offered for several other persons. And the Legislature of Mississippi offered a reward of $5,000 for any person who should be convicted of having circulated the "Liberator" or any other seditious paper within that State. Public meetings were held, at which Abolitionists were denounced; and fears were expressed of a dissolution of the Union.

The South had then, as it has had ever since, hosts of sympathizers in the North, who promptly responded to the sentiments expressed in Southern meetings. In many of the principal Northern cities, meetings were held which were attended by the most prominent citizens. The strongest sympathy was expressed for the slaveholders, and the Abolitionists were stigmatized as "disturbers of the public peace," and as "disloyal to the Union." Southern papers expressed great satisfaction at this declaration of Northern sentiment. They "hailed this plighted faith to arrest, 'by all constitutional and legal means, the movements of these incendiaries," and hoped the pledge would be redeemed by legislative enactments, without which all else would be little more than "a sounding brass and a tinkling cymbal." "Up to the mark the North must come, if it would restore tranquillity and preserve the Union." Another complained that the Albany meeting did not "recommend putting down, by the strong arm of the law, discussions which [it declared] were at war with every moral duty and every suggestion of humanity." Surely, that which is declared so pernicious can and ought to be made legally *punishable.* It is *works* and not *words* we want. A meeting in South Carolina declared, that if the South should have "to choose either union without liberty, or disunion with liberty and property, be assured they will not hesitate which to take, and will make the choice promptly, unitedly, and fearlessly." And it was unanimously resolved, that "should the non-slaveholding States omit or refuse, at the ensuing meeting of their respective Legislatures, to put a final stop to the proceedings of their Abolition Societies, *by efficient penal laws,* it will then become the solemn duty of the whole South, in order to protect themselves and secure their rights and property against the unconstitutional combination of the non-slaveholding States, and the murderous designs of their Abolitionists, to withdraw from the Union."

It was proposed "to withhold the profits of Southern commerce from those engaged, either actively, or by countenance, in propagating the designs of fanaticism." "Through the purse is the surest road to the understandings of men."

The aid of the General Government was invoked in the war against free speech and a free press. The Postmaster-General was requested to prevent the transmission by mail, of Anti-Slavery papers and documents. Mr. Kendall, in answer, said "it was not in his power, by any lawful regulation, to obviate the evil." But regarding the transmission of papers "tending to promote discontent, sedition, and a servile war, from one state to another, as a violation of the spirit if not the letter of the federal compact, which would justify, on the part of the injured States, any measure necessary to effect their exclusion," he suggested that their only means of relief at present was "in responsibilities voluntarily assumed by postmasters." He hoped Congress would, at the next session, put a stop to the evil, and pledged his exertions to promote the adoption of a measure for that purpose.

The reader will be naturally disposed to inquire whether the President concurred in the suggestions and advice of his Postmaster-General. He was indeed noted for "taking responsibilities;" but that the head of a party professing the strongest repugnance to "loose construction," who, in accordance with his rule of "strict construction," had vetoed measures similar to those sanctioned by his early predecessors, should justify or connive at so palpable "a violation" not only "of the spirit" but of "the letter" of the Constitution, would be incredible, had we not good evidence of the fact. In his next annual Message, December, 1835, he said: "I must also invite your attention to the painful excitement produced in the South by attempts to circulate, through the mails, inflammatory appeals addressed to the passions of the slaves, in prints and in various sorts of publications, calculated to stimulate them to insurrection, and to produce all the horrors of a servile war." And he suggested the passage of a law to "prohibit, under severe penalties, the circulation, in the Southern States, through the mail, of incendiary publications, intended to instigate the slaves to insurrection."

If the President, in the extracts above quoted, meant to convey the ideas which the language seems clearly to express, it is difficult to say which is the more to be condemned, the untruthfulness of the one, or the recommendation contained in the other. That "inflammatory appeals" had been addressed to slaves, or that any attempts had been made to get any Anti-Slavery publications, whatever, into their hands, he had no good reason to believe. Nothing of an "incendiary" character had then, nor has since, emanated from the Anti-Slavery press; and it is quite certain that a paper of any kind could not reach slaves "through the mails." By the "incendiary publications" the prohibition of which he recommended, he evidently meant the ordinary Anti-Slavery papers and documents, such as his Postmaster-General suggested the suppression of by his deputy postmasters in the Southern States, in the Southern States, on "responsibilities voluntarily assumed." A more flagrant violation of the constitutional right of freedom of speech and of the press, can hardly be imagined than was proposed in the bill introduced in the Senate in pursuance of the recommendation. There are doubtless many of his admirers of that day still living, who regarded with favor the provisions of that bill, who are now horror-stricken by the summary suppression of papers which are endeavoring to cripple the Government in its efforts to quell the Rebellion.

The bill alluded to was reported by Mr. Calhoun, Chairman of a Select Committee, to whom this part of the Message had been referred. It prohibited postmasters from knowingly putting into the mail any printed or written paper or pictorial representation relating to Slavery, addressed to any person in a State in which their circulation was forbidden; and it prohibited postmasters in such State from delivering such papers to any person not authorized by the laws of the State to receive them. And the postmasters of the offices where such papers were deposited, were required to give notice of the same, from time to time; and if the papers were not, within one month, withdrawn by the person depositing them, they were to be burnt or otherwise destroyed.

Mr. Calhoun, in his report, reïterated his long-cherished doctrine of State Sovereignty. He claimed for a State the right to defend itself against internal dangers, and denied the right of the General Government to assist a State, even in case of domestic violence, except on application of the authorities of the State itself. It belonged to the States whose institutions were in danger, and not to Congress, as the Message supposed, to determine what papers were incendiary; and each State was bound to prevent its citizens from disturbing the peace or endangering the security of other States; and the latter, if disturbed or endangered, had a right to demand of the former the adoption of measures for their protection. And if it should neglect its duty, the States whose peace was assailed might resort to means to protect themselves, as if they were separate and independent communities.

Here we have a sample of the seed sown thirty

years ago, the bitter fruits of which we are now reaping.

When the question was taken on the engrossment of the bill, there was a tie, 18 to 18. The Vice-President, (Mr. Van Buren,) having temporarily left the chair, returned, and gave the casting vote in the affirmative. Of the Senators from the Free States, Messrs. Buchanan, Tallmadge, and Wright, voted in the affirmative. Those from Slave States who voted in the negative, were Messrs. Benton, Clay, and Kent, of Maryland.

It is but just to say, that Mr. Van Buren's casting vote, and the several votes of Mr. Wright, are not conclusive evidence of their having desired the passage of the bill. Mr. Calhoun, as Mr. Benton says, "had made the rejection of the bill a test of alliance with Northern Abolitionists, and a cause for a secession of the Southern States; and if the bill had been rejected by Mr. Van Buren's vote, the whole responsibility of its loss would have been thrown upon him and the North, and the South inflamed against those States and himself—the more so, as Mr. White, of Tennessee, the opposing Democratic candidate for tho Presidency, gave his votes for the bill. [Mr. White was supported by a branch of the party opposed to Mr. Van Buren, the regular nominee.] The several successive tie votes have been ascribed to the intention of placing Mr. Van Buren in this position. With this intent, some voted for the bill, and others absented themselves, knowing that on the final vote it would not pass. This supposition appears probable from the full vote given on the question of its passage: ayes, 19; noes, 25; only four absent; Mr. Buchanan, Mr. Tallmadge, and Mr. Wright, again voting in the affirmative; and seven from the Slave States, in the negative. The votes of Mr. Van Buren and others, though given for the reason stated, cannot be justified upon that ground.

Although this bill received but little support from Northern Senators, there was at this time a strong tendency toward a union of the interests of the Democracy and those of Slavery. This union was soon after consummated. There were for many years exhibitions of considerable strength in the Southern portion of the Whig party; but where Whig measures came into conflict with the interests of Slavery, the latter were, with many of the Southern Whigs, the controlling consideration. This gave the Democrats an advantage which has contributed largely to the predominance which they have, for most of the time, since maintained.

Petitions for the abolition of Slavery and the Slave Trade in the District of Columbia continued to be presented to Congress; and the excitement was increased by the manner in which they were treated. On the 8th of February, 1836, a resolution was adopted, to refer all petitions on this subject to a select Committee. On the 18th of May, Mr. Pinckney, from this Committee, reported three resolutions; the first denying the power of Congress over Slavery in the States; the second declaring that Congress ought not to interfere with it in the District of Columbia; the third requiring all petitions and papers relating to the subject to be at once laid upon the table, without being printed or referred, and without any further action upon them. On the 25th of May, the vote was taken on the first resolution under the pressure of the previous question. Mr. Adams said, if the House would allow him five minutes, he would prove the resolution to be false. The resolution was adopted, with only eight dissenting voices. The next day the second was adopted, 132 to 45; the third, 117 to 68.

In the Senate, a petition from the Society of the "Friends" in the State of Pennsylvania at the Caln quarterly meeting, was presented by Mr. Buchanan, who said he was in favor of giving the memorial a respectful reception; but he wished to put the question at rest. He therefore moved that the petition be read, and rejected. The question on receiving was decided in the affirmative, 36 to 10; the latter votes all from Southern Senators. The whole subject, including the rejection of the petition, was agreed to 34 to 6. The noes were from Davis and Webster, of Mass., Prentiss, of Vt., Knight, of R. I., and Southard, of N. J.

Mr. Calhoun had objected to the reception of this and all such communications, and considered it the duty of Congress to refuse a hearing to all petitions relating to negro Slavery. He again held up the terror of secession to awe the Senate into respect for the wishes of the South.

Mr. Benton wished the adoption of the most effectual method of putting down Abolition Societies. It was time that the practice of sending such petitions to Congress was discontinued and the South quieted. But to quiet the South, the North must be quieted. The South would not be at ease until Abolitionism was put down in the North; and Senators from the non-slaveholding States should lead in the matter.

Other Senators participated in the debate, in which the right of petition, and the power of Congress over Slavery in the District of Columbia and the Territories were thoroughly discussed.

Among the notable occurrences during President Jackson's administration, was a generul derangement of the currency The Bank war was not confined in its objects to the destruction of that institution. The President's hatred to paper money was scarcely less than his hatred to the "monster" Bank. We have briefly noticed the effect upon the currency of the contractiou of the Bank's circulation, caused by his attempts to "crush the reptile." The Bank had satisfactorily performed the offices contemplated by its authors, (Mr. Madison and the Republican Congress of 1816,) one of which offices was that of a "regulator" of the currency. A United States Bank note, though payable only at the Bank or branch whence it was issued, was current in any part of the United States, and was generally regarded as equivalent to specie. Hence, the most careful and prudent winding up of its affairs must, to some extent, have produced an unfavorable effect upon the currency. It had also held a salutary check upon the State Banks, which was about to cease.

It was resolved to substitute for the "bank rags" now used as a circulating medium, the "hard money." The receipt, by Government officers, of bank notes of a denomination less than five dollars, had been prohibited after the 30th of September, 1835. And an order was issued from the Treasury Department, dated 22d February, 1836, forbidding their *payment* to any public officer or creditor; and, unless otherwise prescribed by law, no such notes of a denomination less than ten dollars were to be received or paid after the 4th of July next. And the Deposit Banks were required, in payments not exceeding $500, to pay one-fifth in gold coin, if preferred by the creditor. They were requested not to issue, after the 4th of July, notes less than five dollars, nor after the 3d of March, 1837, notes less than ten dollars. The alledged object of this regulation was, "to render the currency of the country more safe, sound, and uniform."

On the 11th of July, 1836, was issued another order, thereafter generally designated the "specie circular," which produced great sensation. In anticipation of the "winding up" of the Bank of the United States, notwithstanding the efforts of the Government to check the issue of paper money, an immense increase of the number of State Banks took place. For the thirty-five millions of bank capital withdrawn from use by the expiration of the National Bank, many times that amount of State bank capital was created. And it is worthy of note, that the greatest increase was in Democratic States, where the politicians echoed most loudly the President's denunciations of paper money. The facility of obtaining bank accommodations had encouraged speculations to an unprecedented extent, especially in landed property. The receipts from sales of public lands, were, in 1834, $4,857,600; in 1836, they had risen to $24,877,179. This order was designed to prevent a monopoly of the lands by speculators, and to check the accumulation of this doubtful paper money into the Treasury. In cases of sales, except to actual settlers, or residents of the State, and in quantities not exceeding 320 acres, payment for lands sold after the 15th of August, was to be made in specie; and after the 15th of December, in gold and silver, without exception. This order was issued under an existing law, which authorized the Secretary to receive or reject bank paper at his discretion. This circular was issued only one week after the adjournment of Congress. It had been withheld, as Mr. Benton says, to avoid any interference of Congress, a majority of both Houses being known to be opposed to the measure. A majority of the Cabinet also were opposed to it.

A general revulsion soon followed the issuing of this Treasury circular. And at the next session of Congress, a joint resolution was early introduced by Mr. Ewing "to rescind the Treasury order of July 11th, 1836." In the debate on this resolution, the causes of the pecuniary distress and the objects of the order were discussed. One object, Mr. E. said, was to save the Deposit Banks from failure, by collecting specie in the land-offices to be distributed among these banks to enable them to pay over the money to the States.

Mr. Benton charged the "panic" to the Bank and its friends, who wished to get a renewal of its charter as a remedy for the evils they had themselves created. He said there was no safety for the federal revenue but in the total exclusion of local paper from every branch of the revenue—customs, lands, and post-office.

Mr. Crittenden said the operation of the order had been to derange the currency, and give it a direction inverse to the course of business. Our great commercial cities were the natural repositories where money centered and settled. It was more valuable there than in the interior. Any intelligent business man in the West would rather have money paid him in New York than at his own door. Hence, forcing the specie against the natural course of business from East to West, was beneficial to none, injurious to all. He admitted that the Deposit Banks had been strengthened by the order, as had been asserted by Mr. Benton ; but it was at the expense of all other banks in the country.

The resolution was referred to the Committee on Public Lands, who reported a bill providing that the Government should receive the paper of specie paying banks, which should thereafter issue no notes of small denominations. But the bill was so amended as merely to rescind the Treasury order, and was so passed, 41 to 5. In the House it was ordered to a third reading by a vote of 143 to 59, and passed by a large majority. It was sent to the President, who returned it to the Senate with his VETO.

In June, 1836, Michigan and Arkansas were admitted into the Union. The people of both Territories had taken measures preparatory to admission as States, without previous action of Congress ; and copies of their Constitutions accompanied their application for admission. In the case of Arkansas, whose application was first made, the Attorney General, Mr. Butler, to whom the question had been submitted, gave it as his opinion, that measures to subvert the Territorial Government, and to establish a new one without the consent of Congress, would be unlawful. This opinion, however, was disregarded by majorities in both Houses. In the Senate, the vote on the admission of Michigan was 23 to 8, many of the Senators having left their seats. The vote previously given on a motion to recommit the bill, was considered as nearly a test vote on the admission, which was 28 to 19. Two days after, (April 4,) the Arkansas bill passed the Senate, 31 to 6. The two Senators from Vermont, Swift and Prentiss, objected because the State Constitution permitted Slavery, and prohibited its abolition by the State Legislature.

In the House also objections were made for the same reason. Mr. Cushing, of Massachusetts, condemned the clause prohibiting emancipation without the consent of the owners of the slaves, "as anti-republican, as wrong on general principles of civil polity, and as unjust to the inhabitants of the non-slaveholding States." The Legislature could not emancipate, even if it should be ready to indemnify the owners. It was "to foreclose, in advance, the progress of civilization and of liberty forever." He concluded with a severe reply to a threat of Mr. Wise, that, if, contrary to the terms of the Missouri Compromise, the North should impose restrictions upon slave property at the South, the latter would be impelled "to introduce Slavery into the heart of the North."

Mr. Adams was content to receive Arkansas as one of the slaveholding States; but he was unwilling that Congress should assent to an article in her Constitution withholding from the Legislature the power of giving freedom to the slave.

The bill for admission was passed with the objectionable clause. It was ordered to the third reading, 143 to 50; and the Michigan bill, 153 to 45. A few members in each House, it is believed, voted in the negative on both bills on account of the informality of the application and the Slavery provision. A very cogent reason for pressing the passage of these bills, by Democratic Senators, against these objections, but which reason was of course not expressed in debate, was believed to be, that the admission of these

States at this session would secure to Mr. Van Buren, at the approaching election, six additional electoral votes. And it is quite probable, that the people of Arkansas purposely availed themselves of this circumstance to incorporate into their Constitution this obnoxious provision, presuming there would be in their three electoral votes an argument sufficiently potent to overcome an objection which had been successfully urged against a similar provision in the Constitution of Missouri in 1821.

A favorite measure of Mr. Clay was the distribution of the proceeds of the sales of the Public Lands among the States ; but his efforts to procure the passage of a law for this purpose had not succeeded. The public debt having been paid, and the receipts from land sales having been for a few years unusually large, the surplus revenue had accumulated in the Treasury to the amount of many millions of dollars. At the session of 1835–1836, Mr. Clay again introduced a distribution bill which passed the Senate, 25 to 20 ; but in the House it was laid on the table, 114 to 85.

A new and successful plan, however, was devised. A bill had been introduced into the Senate further to regulate the deposits of the public money, which was so amended as to provide for the distribution of the surplus public revenue among the States. As constitutional objections to distribution were known to be entertained by some, the money, instead of being distributed among, was to be *deposited with*, the States, and to be returned at the call of Congress, if it should at any time be needed by the General Government. All the surplus money in the Treasury on the 1st of January, 1837, reserving five millions, was to be thus deposited with the States in proportion to their respective representations in the Senate and House of Representatives. The sum to be distributed was about thirty millions. A few States considering the words "deposited with" a mere evasion, refused for some years to receive their shares of the money. No part of it has yet been called for, nor is it likely to be. It has been loaned by the States, and the income is appropriated to educational and other State purposes.

The recognition of the independence of Texas was proposed at this session. Independence had been declared in March, 1836 ; and after the victory of the Texans at San Jacinto in May, petitions for recognition were received by Congress from different sections of the country. These petitions were in the Senate referred to the Committee on Foreign Relations. There was no material opposition to the prayer of the petitioners ; but Senators recommended caution. Texas should first have a government *de facto.* Mr. Calhoun advocated not only immediate recognition, but immediate admission into the Union, and assigned as "powerful reasons," the peace and security of the Slave States, and the benefits to the navigating and manufacturing interests of the North and East. Mr. Niles, of Conn., said we should regard our national faith with Mexico. A hasty acknowledgment might expose our Government to a suspicion of having encouraged our citizens in volunteering to aid the Texans. And this suspicion would be greatly strengthened by annexation.

The memorials were referred ; and on the 18th of June the Committee reported in favor of acknowledging the independence of Texas "whenever satisfactory information should be received that it had in successful operation a civil government capable of performing the duties and fulfilling the obligations of an independent power." The resolution was adopted unanimously : Yeas, 39.

At the next session, December, 1836, President Jackson, in a special message, advised Congress not to recognize the independence of Texas, until there should be no longer any danger of her being subjected, as had been our policy in the cases of Mexico and the South American States. The Texans had resolved, if recognized, to seek admission into the Union ; and a too early movement might subject us to the imputation of seeking to establish the claims of our neighbors to a territory with a view to its acquisition by ourselves. The Senate, however, on the 1st of March, 1837, adopted a resolution declaring the acknowledgment expedient and proper, 23 to 19. In the House, a similar resolution was laid upon the table, 98 to 86. The object contemplated, however, was afterward attained, by an amendment of the appropriation bill, providing a "salary and outfit of a diplomatic agent to be sent to the Government of Texas, whenever the President should receive satisfactory evidence that Texas was an independent power, and that it was expedient to appoint such a Minister." The amendment was adopted, 171 to 76.

President Jackson closed his official term with an unsettled difficulty with Mexico on his hands. Since the conclusion of a treaty of amity and commerce with that country in 1831, our flag had been insulted, and injuries had been committed upon the persons and property of our citizens; and our demands for satisfaction had not been complied with. On the 7th of February, 1837, he sent to Congress a special message, in which he stated that these injuries, "independent of recent insults to the Government and people by the late extraordinary Mexican Minister," (who had suddenly taken his departure,) "would justify, in the eyes of all nations, immediate war." But "considering the present embarrassed condition of that country, we should act with wisdom and moderation, by giving to Mexico one more opportunity to atone for the past, before we take redress into our own hands." And he recommended an act authorizing reprisals, and asked the use of the naval force if she should refuse compliance with another demand.

The Message was referred in both Houses; but neither Committee reported in favor of the act asked for; but both reported in favor of another demand. Such an act, they said, would violate the treaty with Mexico, which provided, that "neither of the contracting parties will order or authorize any acts of reprisal, nor declare war against the other, on complaint of injuries or damages, until the party considering itself offended shall first have presented to the other a statement of such injuries or damages, verified by competent proofs, and demanded justice and satisfaction, and the same shall have been refused or unreasonably delayed."

A National Democratic Convention was held in Baltimore as early as May, 1835. Gen. Jackson was well known to be in favor of Mr. Van Buren as his successor; and as the Convention was composed exclusively of the friends of Gen. Jackson, the nomination was unanimous. Richard M. Johnson, of Ky., was nominated for Vice-President, having received 178 votes to 87 for Wm. C. Rives, of Va. No other candidates were nominated by a National Convention. Gen. Harrison was nominated by Whig Conventions in some of the States, and by the Anti-Masonic State Convention at Harrisburg, Pa., Francis Granger, of N. Y., was nominated at most or all of these Conventions for Vice-President. Several other candidates were nominated by their particular friends. Of the electors chosen in November, 170 voted for Mr. Van Buren ; 78 for Wm. H. Harrison ; 26 for Hugh L. White ; 14 for Daniel Webster ; and 11 for Willie P. Mangum. Of the votes for Vice-President, R. M. Johnson received 144 ; Francis Granger, 77 ; John Tyler, 47 ; Wm. Smith, 23. The votes were said to have been purposely scattered, in the hope of so weakening Mr. Van Buren, as to bring the election into the House of Representatives.

CHAPTER IV.

Administration of Martin Van Buren.

Mr. Van Buren was inaugurated on the 4th of March, 1837. Being first in the confidence of his predecessor, and having been one of his principal advisers, he was almost universally supposed to be committed to his policy. The extreme caution of Mr. Van Buren against the expression of his opinions on public measures, the epithet, "non-committal," was pretty generally applied to him. It had been the policy of Mr. Calhoun, for years before the election, to compel his rivals to "show their hand" on the Slavery question, on which the South felt so very sensitive. Such, especially, had been the case on the subject of the recognition of the independence of Texas, and her annexation to the United States, and also on the questions of prohibiting the transmission of Anti-Slavery papers through the mail, and the abolition of Slavery in the District of Columbia. And Mr. Van Buren had, in answer to questions propounded to him before the election, declared, that, if elected, he "must go into the Presidential Chair the inflexible and uncompromising opponent of every attempt, on the part of Congress, to abolish Slavery in the District of Columbia, against the wishes of the slaveholding States; and also with a determination equally decided to resist the slightest interference with it in the States where it exists." And he declared, in his Inaugural address, that "no bill conflicting with these views can ever receive my constitutional sanction." Mr. Van Buren was generally spoken of as "the Northern man with Southern principles." The declarations above quoted served to confirm his title to this designation. Besides their evidence of his servility to the Slave Power, they were objectionable in *principle*, as an improper interference, on the part of an Executive, with freedom of legislation. The diminished Democratic majorities in the Northern States at the late election, made it apparent that, to be reëlected, he must strengthen himself at the South. These early pledges of favor to the Slave interest were thus accounted for.

The country was suffering under the pressure caused by the issuing of the specie circular, and other acts of war upon the currency—the result of a policy which he was considered as pledged to continue. In May, a general bank explosion occurred. Specie payments were suspended throughout the country, caused, in great part, by the diversion of specie to the West, and in part by the large loans made by the banks having on deposit the surplus revenue, with the expectation that it would remain with them until it was wanted by the Government; but it had been unexpectedly demanded for distribution among the States.

Speculation was suddenly arrested; the inflated prices of property, especially of real estate, were diminished to the smallest point; and the ideal fortunes which had been made, perhaps in a single "operation," vanished. Mercantile failures in the commercial cities were, in number and amount, unprecedented. The revulsion was complete. The President was requested to rescind the specie circular, and to call an extra meeting of Congress. A proclamation was issued for convening Congress on the first Monday in September.

The suspension, probably, more than all other causes, induced the President to make the call. By the laws regulating the deposits, the federal officers were prohibited from receiving or paying out the notes of any but specie-paying banks. And the Deposit Banks, too, had suspended. Hence, no collection or disbursements of public moneys could be made but in violation of law.

Congress met on the 4th of September. The President suggested the entire disuse of banks as fiscal agents of the Government; and recommended the collection, safe-keeping, and disbursement of the public money by officers of the Government, and the use of specie alone in its fiscal operations. The sales of the public lands having fallen off nearly three-fourths during the year, and the revenue from duties on imports having been diminished nearly one-half, while the appropriations had been increased, he recommended that the fourth and last installment of the surplus revenue to be deposited with the States, be withheld for the use of the Government.

Mr. Wright, of N. Y., of the Committee on Finance, reported a bill in conformity with the President's suggestions. It required the officers receiving the moneys to give bonds for their safe-keeping. The same bill was reported to the House of Representatives. It was to establish the *independent treasury*, more frequently called the "sub-treasury."

Five other bills, designed to give temporary relief to the Government, were reported to the Senate: (1.) A bill to postpone the payment of the fourth installment of the deposits with the States. This bill, after an interesting debate, passed the Senate, 28 to 17. Thus the last installment, ($9,367,200,) was withheld, and has never been deposited with the States. (2.) A bill to authorize the issue of Treasury notes. Mr. Clay, in the course of his remarks on this bill, said: "The Government will not receive the paper of the country, and is about to create a paper of its own, which the country is expected to receive! And thus, all the promises which have been made to us of the flowing of gold and silver all over the country, these promises of a better currency result in the issue of ten millions of paper money!" [Ten millions was the amount authorized.] (3.) A bill extending the time for the payment of merchants' bonds, [for duties.] (4.) A bill for adjusting the remaining claims on Deposit Banks. (5.) A bill to authorize merchandise to be deposited in public stores. All these bills passed both Houses and became laws. The deposit of the fourth installment was postponed until the 1st of January, 1839. But, as has been stated, it has never reached the Treasuries of the States. The three installments which had been deposited, amounted to about twenty-eight millions.

The Sub-Treasury bill reported by Mr. Wright was amended, on motion of Mr. Calhoun, so as to require the eventual payment of all Government dues in specie. This amendment was adopted, 24 to 23. Several Democratic Senators and Representatives took ground against the administration on its financial policy, and left the party. Among them was Senator N. P. Tallmadge, of N. Y

Speaking in opposition to the bill, he deprecated this warfare against the whole credit system of the country. He maintained that if the Government itself had not entered into measures destructive of public confidence, this crisis would not have occurred.

In the House, also, were a number who had separated from their Democratic friends on financial questions, and who united with the Whigs. They were called "Conservatives." By this defection from the party, the Sub-Treasury scheme was defeated. The bill was laid on the table, 120 to 107.

Some readers may not know the origin of this financial plan. In February, 1835, a bill passed the Senate to regulate the deposits of the public money. In the House, Mr. Gordon, of Va., who was opposed to the Bank of the United States as unconstitutional, and to all banks as depositories of the public moneys, moved an amendment, similar to one offered by him to a bill at the preceding session. Mr. Gordon had been a Jackson man; but disapproving the President's interference with the public revenues, he had, since the removal of the deposits, voted on this and kindred questions with the opposition. His amendment was rejected: Ayes, 33; noes, 161. Some Whigs, (among whom was Mr. Adams,) being opposed to the President's "pet bank" system, together with some Democrats, voted for Mr. Gordon's proposition, which provided for the appointment of agents of the Treasurer of the United States, to keep and disburse the revenue, giving bonds for the faithful execution of their office. It was loudly denounced by the Democrats, as a ridiculous, odious Whig measure. Yet this same measure was two years later advocated by them as the panacea for the all-pervading financial disease which afflicted the country.

Two days after the defeat of the Sub-Treasury bill, Congress adjourned (October 16) to the 1st Monday in December.

At the next session, the first regular session of Congress under Mr. Van Buren, (December, 1837,) the President again recommended the establishment of the Independent Treasury. A bill was introduced, proposing the gradual collection of revenues in specie. After an able discussion by Messrs. Wright, Benton, and other Senators in its favor, and Messrs. Clay, Webster, Rives, and White in opposition, Mr. Rives offered a substitute, requiring the payment of the revenue in coin and the notes of specie paying banks issuing large bills only.

Messrs. Grundy, of Tenn., Buchanan, of Pa., and Wall, of N. J., all Democrats, were instructed by their respective State Legislatures to vote against the bill. The two first declared their intention to obey, the last declared his intention to disregard instructions.

The bill was amended by striking out the "specie clause," and further, on motion of Mr. Webster, by prohibiting the Secretary of the Treasury from issuing any general order making any discrimination as to the funds or medium in which debts to the United States should be paid. Thus amended, the bill passed the Senate, 27 to 25. In the House, the bill of the Senate was reported the next day, (March 27th,) and laid on the table, 106 to 98.

Mr. Hubbard, of N. H., had, in the debate in the Senate on this bill, read from that part of the President's Message which ascribed the unexpected results of the late State elections (of 1837) to bank influence; and had undertaken to explain the result in New York. [This State had given large Whig majorities. Out of 128 members of the Assembly, 101 opponents of the administration were elected. Great changes had also taken place in other States.]

Mr. Tallmadge, of N. Y., a "conservative," defended the people against the President's charge. He ascribed the results to the principles of the President and his party, taken from the creed of the "Loco-foco" faction which originated in the city of New York, in 1829. [The "faction" here referred to, were dissenters to the proceedings of a meeting of a Democratic nominating committee in Tammany Hall. The committee having abruptly extinguished the gas, it was re-lighted by loco-foco matches; whence the name of Loco-focos.] This faction, said Mr. T., was turned out of Tammany Hall in the pure days of the Democratic Republican party, and held meetings in the open air, whenever it was necessary to take measures *to reduce the price of flour*, or to carry out any other great principle of political economy! [Allusion was made to a mob in the city of New York, in

February, 1837, at a time of high prices. The notice of the meeting, which was to be held in the Park, declared, that "high prices must come down!" Its object was "to inquire into the cause of the present distress, and to devise a suitable remedy." About 5,000 persons assembled; and after some inflammatory speeches, a large body of them proceeded to some flour stores, and destroyed wheat and flour, with other property, to the amount of $10,000.] After their principles had received the countenance of the administration, they returned to the *wigwam*, displaced the ancient sachems, and there they now illustrate their ideas of freedom of speech and free discussion, by the forcible interruption of the assemblages of orderly citizens who happen to entertain opinions on matters of public policy contrary to their own. They are now the leaders of the party, and the prominent candidates for executive favor. The leading features of their creed, said Mr. T., was the destruction of the whole banking system of the country, the repeal of charters, and the abrogation of vested rights. And this was understood by the people to be the policy of the administration.

In reply to the thrust at State Banks for suspending specie payments, and the act of the Legislature of New York authorizing suspension, Mr. T. said, by the law of that State, (the old Safety-fund law,) a bank failing to redeem its notes for ten days, its doors were enjoined to be closed, and a receiver was appointed to collect its dues and pay its debts. The people owed the banks about $70,000,000. The collection of this amount would have caused general distress and ruin. The Legislature being in session, a law was passed, almost unanimously, to suspend for a year the forfeiture of the charters which had been incurred by their failing to redeem. This act had been denounced by public meetings in New York by the friends of the administration; and this denunciation had been reiterated by the Government organ here.

Mr. T. referred to the President's having recommended "a uniform law concerning bankruptcies of corporations and other bankers," as a measure "fully authorized by the Constitution." The effect of such a law would have been, that every bank in the Union would have been handed over to commissioners, and its concerns closed up; for all had suspended: and the result would have been ruin from one extremity of the Union to the other. Fortunately, Congress did not adopt the recommendation. Mr. T. alluded to the fact that, in 1826, Mr. Van Buren had, on that floor, in a discussion of a bankrupt bill, opposed its application to banking incorporations, "as an odious exercise of power not granted by the Constitution;" but in 1837, as President, he proposes such a law and pronounces it constitutional. The people foresaw what would have been the effects of the proposed bankrupt law, and of the Sub-Treasury scheme. They saw by the official organ, after the latter had been defeated at the extra session, that it was to be again forced upon Congress. The people also saw that some of their representatives here, pursuing the straightforward track of principle, refusing to turn about at the word of command, and opposing the measure which the whole party, with Gen. Jackson at their head, opposed in 1834, and which the official organ then pronounced "disorganizing and revolutionary," were *for* this adherence to principle, denounced and proscribed by this same official organ of the administration. They saw established at the seat of Government, by the discipline of party, a despotism, the most perfect on earth—the *despotism of opinion!* These Mr. T. regarded as the causes of the results of the late elections.

Mr. Calhoun, who had, since the removal of the deposits, or during most of the period of the "war upon the currency," coöperated with the Whigs, again united with the administration, and advocated the Sub-Treasury project as a plan for separating the Government from all banks.

A joint resolution virtually repealing the specie circular of July, 1836, was passed, May 31, 1838, by large majorities in both Houses, and became a law. By this act, all payments to the Government might be made either in specie, treasury notes, or the bills of specie paying banks. By acts of April and June, 1836, however, no bank notes for less than $20, nor those of any bank issuing notes or bills for less than $5, were to be received.

The recognition of the independence of Texas at the preceding session, 1836–1837 and the intimation of an attempt to effect her annexation to the United States, was followed by numerous remonstrances, at the present session, against annexation. Resolutions to the same effect were passed by the Legislatures of some States, and by others resolutions in favor of the measure.

In the Senate, Mr. Preston, of S. C., on the 4th of January, 1838, offered a resolution in favor of the "reännexation" of Texas to the territory of the United States, "with the consent of that State previously had, and whenever it can be effected consistently with the faith and treaty stipulations of the United States." Mr. Preston supported his resolution by a long and able speech.

In the House, Mr. Adams, who had presented a large number of memorials against annexation, moved that these and all others, be referred to a Select Committee. Mr. Howard, of Md., having moved their reference to the Committee on Foreign Affairs,

Mr. Adams said he and his colleagues viewed this question as one which involved the integrity of the Union—a question of the most deep, abiding, and vital interest to the whole American nation. "For," said he, "in the face of this House, in the face of Heaven, I avow it as my solemn belief, that the annexation of an independent power to this Government, would, *ipso facto*, be a dissolution of this Union. And is this a subject for the peculiar investigation of your Committee on Foreign Affairs?" Mr. A. said the question involved was, whether a foreign nation, acknowledged as such in a most unprecedented and extraordinary manner, by this Government, a nation "damned to everlasting fame" by the reïnstitution of that detestable system, Slavery, after it had once been abolished within its borders, should be admitted into the Union with a nation of freemen. "For, sir, that name, thank God, is still ours! And is such a question as this to be referred to a Committee on Foreign Affairs?"

Mr. A. continued his speech at considerable length, condemning the conduct of the last and the present administrations in relation to the affairs of Texas; declaring that the nation to be annexed had its origin in violence and fraud; that the territory of the Republic of Mexico had been invaded by the Executive of this Government; and that conspirators had come here and concerted plans of operations with members of our own Government! And yet we had heard the bold and unblushing pretense that the people of Texas were struggling for freedom, and that the wrongs inflicted upon them by Mexico had driven them into insurrection, and had forced them to fight for liberty! Mr. Adams then referred to certain facts to prove the real origin of the insurrection. The motions of reference were laid on the table, on the motion of Mr. Wise, 127 to 68. In October it was officially announced, that, since the proposition submitted by Texas for admission into the Union had been declined, the Texan Minister had communicated the formal and absolute withdrawal of the proposition.

At the next session, (1838–1839,) the famous "gag resolutions" offered by Mr. Atherton, of N. H., were adopted by the House. One of them required, that every petition, memorial, or paper relating in any way to Slavery, should, on presentation, without further action thereon, be laid on the table without being debated, printed or referred. It was passed, 127 to 78. The introduction of resolutions virtually denying the constitutional right of petition, by a Democrat, and passed almost exclusively by the votes of Democratic members, together with numerous other votes on questions involving the interests of Slavery, proves the union between it and Democracy to have been at this time fully formed; or, that Democracy and Slavery were equally expressive of the real character of the party misnamed "Democratic"—a character which it still maintains.

A singular affair occurred in 1839 and 1840, which deserves notice. In August, 1839, a Spanish schooner, named L'Amistad, lying near the coast of Connecticut, was captured by Lieut. Gedney, of the brig Washington. The vessel was bound from Havana to Port Principe with fifty-four blacks and two passengers on board. The latter were owners of the vessel and cargo, and claimed the blacks as their slaves. Four nights after they were out, the blacks rose and murdered the captain and three of the crew; then took possession of the vessel with the intention of returning to Africa. The two passengers were saved to navigate the vessel. But instead of steering for Africa, they navigated in a different direction when they could do so without detection. The slaves had been purchased at Havana soon after their arrival from Africa. Cingues, the leader of the revolt, and thirty-eight others, were committed for trial. A demand was soon after made upon our Government by the acting Spanish Minister in this country, for the surrender of the L'Amistad, cargo, and alleged slaves, to the Spanish authorities.

The contest between the opposing counsel of the parties, the issuing of several writs of habeas corpus, &c., &c., must be passed over. [See American Statesman, pp. 723–726.]

In January, 1840, the decision of Judge Judson, of the District Court of the United States for Connecticut, was given. The blacks who murdered the Captain and others on board the schooner, were set free. The schooner having been proved to have been taken on the "high seas," the jurisdiction of the Court was established. The libel of Gedney and others had been properly filed, and the seizers were entitled to salvage. Ruiz and Montez had established no title to the Africans, who, it was presumed, had been imported from Africa in violation of the laws of Spain. The demand of restoration made by the Spanish Minister that the question might be tried in Cuba, was refused, as by Spanish laws the negroes could not be enslaved; and therefore they could not properly be demanded for trial. One of them, a Creole, and legally a slave, and wishing to be returned to Havana, a restoration would be decreed under the treaty of 1795. These Africans were to be delivered to the President, under the act of 1819, to be transported to Africa.

An appeal was taken to the Circuit Court of the United States, Judge Thompson presiding, who affirmed the decree of the District Court. And the Government of the United States, at the instance of the Spanish Minister, directed an appeal to be taken to the Supreme Court of the United States. That Court affirmed the judgment of the District Court in every respect as to sending the negroes back to Africa: they were discharged as free men.

The course of Mr. Van Buren in this affair was, by many, deemed highly censurable. His lending to the Spanish Minister the name of the Government, after the two adjudications in the lower Courts, to perfect an appeal to the Supreme Court, for the benefit of the Spanish claimants, who were guilty of a gross outrage upon humanity, was regarded as bad statesmanship, and not justified by any recognized principle of comity between friendly nations. And the disposition manifested by him to effect the delivery of the captives to the Spanish authorities at Cuba, to be dealt with according to the laws of Spain, which would have exposed their freedom to imminent peril, evinced a reprehensible indifference to the claims of humanity.

The 26th Congress signalized itself by a most disgraceful act. As parties in the House were known to be nearly equal, great anxiety was felt on both sides in relation to the election of Speaker. Congress assembled on the 2d of December, 1839, on which day every member, except one, was present. The gains of the Whigs had given them hope of a small majority, provided the contested seats, of which there were not less than six, should be awarded to the Whig claimants, all of whom had certificates of election.

At twelve o'clock, the Clerk of the last House, Hugh A. Garland, in conformity with the former practice, commenced calling the roll of the members elect. Having called the members from the New England States and the State of New York, and one of the members, Mr. Randolph, from New Jersey, he paused, and proposed to pass over the names of the five members whose right to seats was to be contested, until members of the remaining States should have been called. A stormy debate of several days ensued. Opposition members contended that, according to custom, the claimants having regular certificates of election, should be admitted to seats until a formal investigation could be had.

Mr. Halsted, of N. J., demanded that his name be called, and he read that section of the law of his State which makes the Governor's certificate the evidence of election, which, he insisted, the Clerk was bound to receive as *prima facie* evidence of his right to sit there. Various motions were made; but the Clerk refused to entertain them. Having been again directed to begin the call, he again attempted to pass over the State of New Jersey.

Mr. Adams now arose amid great confusion, and interrupted the Clerk ; and order was restored. "It was not my intention," said he, "to take any part in these extraordinary proceedings. I had hoped that this House would succeed in organizing itself ; that a Speaker and Clerk would be elected, and that the ordinary business of legislation would be allowed to commence. This is not the time nor place to discuss the merits of the conflicting claimants for seats from New Jersey ; that subject belongs to the House of Representatives, which, by the Constitution, is made the ultimate arbiter of the qualifications of its members. But what a spectacle do we here present? We degrade and disgrace ourselves, our constituents, and the country. We do not, can not organize ; and why? Because the Clerk of this House ; the mere Clerk, whom we create, whom we employ, and whose existence depends on our will, usurps the throne, and sets us, the representatives, the vicegerents of the whole American people, at defiance, and holds us in contempt. And what is this Clerk of yours? Is he to control the destinies of sixteen millions of freemen? Is he to suspend, by his mere negative, the functions of government, and put an end to this Congress? He refuses to call the roll. It is in your power to compel him to call it if he will not do it voluntarily. [Here he was interrupted with a statement that the Clerk would resign, rather than to call New Jersey.] Well, then, let him resign ; and we may possibly discover some way by which we may get along without the aid of his powerful talent, learning, and genius. If we can not organize in any other way, if this Clerk of yours will not consent to our discharging the trusts confided to us by our constituents, then let us imitate the example of Virginia in the House of Burgesses, which, when Dinwiddie ordered it to disperse refused to obey the insulting mandate."

He then moved that the Clerk proceed with the calling of the roll, who again refused to entertain the motion. Several members inquired how the question should be put. Mr. A. replied that he intended to put it himself. Mr. Rhett, of S. C., then moved that Mr. Adams be appointed temporary Chairman. Mr. R. himself put the question, which was carried ; and Mr. Adams took the chair. Having decided that of the members from the State of New Jersey only those who held commissions in conformity with the laws of the State were entitled to vote, Mr. Vanderpoel, of N.Y., appealed from the decision of the Chair; and after a debate of several days, the decision was negatived, (December 10th,) 114 to 108. The next day Mr. Naylor and Mr. Ingersoll, of Pa., were both denied the right to vote.

Passing over several days' proceedings, we come to the election of Speaker, on the 14th of December. The vote was taken *viva voce*. Mr. Adams' name having been called, he answered: "Reserving all my rights of objecting hereafter to this election as unconstitutional and illegal, I vote for *John Bell*." Other Whig members also voted under protest. John W Jones, of Va., received the Democratic votes, 113; Mr. Bell, 102; scattering 20. Five more ballots were taken on that day. On the 16th, the balloting was resumed; and five more ballots were taken; when R. M. T. Hunter, of Va., was, on the 11th ballot, elected Speaker, having received 119 votes; and Mr. Jones, 55. Mr. Hunter had been a Jackson man, but now acted with the Whigs, but was in favor of the Sub-Treasury. A Clerk was chosen on the 21st; and on the 24th, the President's Message was delivered.

The Committee on elections reported on the 5th of March in favor of the five administration members. Representatives were then elected in New Jersey by general ticket. Further proceedings were had in relation to this subject, extending to the 16th of July.

It is questionable whether the history of legislation in this country furnishes many instances of proceedings so dishonorable and unprincipled as those sketched in the preceding pages. Every member who voted against the admission of those who presented legal certificates of election, *knew* that he acted in violation of a rule established by long usage, and sanctioned by reason and common sense. But it was resolved to force upon the people that darling financial scheme which had been twice rejected—the sub-treasury; and without the votes of these contesting Democrats, another defeat was anticipated. Having secured a majority, the Independent Treasury was established at the same session.

A Presidential election was at hand. Gen. Wm. H. Harrison had been nominated by a Whig National Convention at Harrisburg, in December, 1839 ; and John Tyler for Vice-President.

The Democratic Convention, which met at Baltimore in May, 1840, had nominated Mr. Van Buren for reëlection. No candidate for Vice-President was nominated by the Convention.

The Abolitionists, who had hitherto voted according to their former party attachments, now had candidates of their own—James G. Birney for President ; and Francis J. Lamoyne for Vice-President.

The canvass of 1840 was unusually spirited. The general depression in money and business affairs, ascribed to the interference of the Government with the currency, continued in full force. The Bank of the United States had been destroyed ; and, notwithstanding its capital continued to be employed under a charter from the State of Pennsylvania, State bank capital had been tripled or quadrupled. The paper of some of these banks was greatly depreciated ; that of others had become worthless. In Mississippi, there was, in 1830, besides the branch of the United States Bank, but one chartered bank, with a capital of less than one million of dollars ; in 1838, the chartered bank capital of that State had reached upward of *sixty millions*. The excessive issue of bank paper had been followed by its natural result, the suspension of specie payments, which still continued in some States, especially the Western and South-Western. And where specie payments had been resumed, banks were obliged to restrict their issues.

The prevailing public distress was attributable in great part, to the operation of the Compromise Tariff of 1833, which had now almost reached its lowest rates of duties ; and for the want of adequate protection, many branches of manufactures had either greatly declined or been abandoned ; and vast numbers of laborers had been thrown out of employment. These and other causes had wrought a great change in the popular mind. Many, believing a change of administration could not be for the worse, were disposed to try the experiment.

The Whig candidates, Harrison and Tyler, received of the electoral votes 234. Mr. Van Buren received 60; and Richard M. Johnson, for Vice-President, received 48.

CHAPTER V.

Administration of Presidents Harrison and Tyler.

GEN. HARRISON was inaugurated as President on the 4th of March, 1841.

His Inaugural Address was a long one, and embraced many topics. It was, he said, a defect of the Constitution that it does not prohibit the reëlection of a President. This defect might be corrected by his refusing to serve a second term. Being, by fair construction, no part of the Legislative power, he ought to use the veto sparingly. His power "as the sole distributor of all the patronage of the Government," and his assumption of the power to control the public finances, were dangerous. He rejected the idea of an exclusive metallic currency. He deprecated the agitation of the question of Slavery. And among other things, he expressed "a profound reverence for the Christian religion, and a thorough conviction that sound morals, religious liberty, and a just sense of religious responsibility, are essentially connected with all true and lasting happiness."

The state of the currency and the finances being such as seemed to require immediate attention, he issued a proclamation on the 17th of March, convening Congress on the last Monday (31st) of May. He was soon taken ill, and within eight days, died on the 4th of April, at the Executive mansion in the city of Washington. By virtue of a provision of the Constitution to that effect, John Tyler became the President of the United States.

Mr. Tyler's Inaugural was short. In regard to foreign nations, his policy would be both to render and demand justice. He pledged himself to "a complete separation between the sword and the purse." He would not remove faithful and honest officers, except for giving their official influences to the purposes of party. He would observe a rigid economy in public expenditures. War between the Government and the currency should cease. He retained in office the members of the Cabinet appointed by Gen. Harrison.

Congress met in special session on the 31st of May, 1841. The principal subjects of the Message were those of the revenue, and of a fiscal agent capable of adding increased facilities in its collection and disbursement. The Treasury was deficient eleven and a half millions for the year. But in providing for the wants of the Treasury, he advised not to alter the compromise tariff act of 1833. The employment of State Banks as fiscal agents had been abandoned; but he expressed no opinion as to the benefits of a National Bank. The Sub-Treasury had been plainly condemned.

John White, a Whig member from Kentucky, was elected Speaker of the House by 121 votes, to 84 for John W. Jones, of Va. There was in the Senate also a Whig majority.

A bill was passed repealing the Sub-Treasury. It passed the Senate, 29 to 18; the House, 134 to 87. It contained a provision making it a felony for an officer charged with the safe-keeping and disbursement of the revenue, to use or to loan it. This section was designed to prevent defalcations, of which there were so many, and which amounted to so large a sum, during the preceding administration. [The number of defaulters was said to be about forty; and the sum about two millions.]

The Secretary of the Treasury, Mr. Ewing, recommended the establishment of a Bank. The President having signified to some friends a desire that the Secretary should be called on for a plan, a call was made by both Houses, and a plan was reported. To avoid constitutional objections, it was to be incorporated in the District of Columbia, with power to establish branches only with the assent of the States.

In the Senate, a bill was reported by Mr. Clay. It passed that body, 26 to 23; the House, 128 to 97. It was vetoed by the President. A new bill was prepared with a view to make it acceptable to the President; a deputation having been sent to learn what kind of a bill he would sanction. It was reported in the House, and passed, 125 to 94. It passed the Senate, 27 to 22. This bill also was negatived. Having been formed with special reference to his wishes, and after a consultation with him by a majority of the Cabinet, a second veto was received with great surprise. Two days after, (Sept. 11,) all the Cabinet officers, except Mr. Webster, (Secretary of State,) sent in their resignations. Although the disrespect shown to the resigning Secretaries may have justified their course; yet considered as a matter of expediency, it is believed by many to have been ill-judged; as the rupture seriously damaged the party, and was perhaps the cause of its prostration.

The extra session having been called to consider the finances and the currency, Congress adjourned immediately after the Bank question had been determined. Several important laws, however, had been previously passed; one of which was a bankrupt law, rendered necessary, as was supposed, by the numerous failures produced by the late revulsion in the business of the country.

An act was also passed to distribute among the States the proceeds of the sales of public lands; a measure which had for many years been attempted without success. As the distribution might render an increase of duties necessary, the opponents of a high tariff insisted on the insertion of a condition, that if Congress should increase the duties on imports, distribution was to be suspended, until the cause of the suspension should cease.

A bill was also passed, authorizing a loan of twelve millions of dollars, to supply the deficiency in the Treasury.

The President, in his Annual Message at the second (first regular) session of the 27th Congress, (December 7, 1841,) presented another plan of fiscal agency which, he said, was free from constitutional objections, would furnish a sound paper medium, and facilitate the regulating of exchanges. He also called attention to the Tariff. Congress might, in laying duties for revenue, discriminate in favor of articles for the purpose of encouraging their manufacture. But the duties should not be so augmented as to annul the land proceeds distribution act of the extra session.

Several schemes of finance were brought forward, among them a plan for a "National Exchequer;" but none of them was adopted.

A tariff act, however, was, after a tedious contest, passed near the close of a very protracted session, (August 27th, 1842.) Protection had been a Democratic measure, especially had it been the policy of the Democrats of the North. It had also been, until after Gen. Jackson's election, a favorite measure of his, as has been already observed, and as appears from his votes in the Senate, his celebrated letter to Dr. Coleman, his letter to Governor Ray of Indiana, and some of his earlier Annual Messages. But, as in the case of the Slavery question, the fortunes of the party seemed to demand a union with the South upon this question also; and the protective policy, which had, more than any other measure, contributed to our national prosperity, was almost entirely abandoned by the Democrats, except a portion of those of the State of Pennsylvania. In fact, protection had become a leading and distinct party issue.

Two bills were reported in the House; one by the Committee on Manufactures, Mr. Saltonstall, of Mass., Chairman; the other at a later period of the session, by Mr. Fillmore, from the Committee of Ways and Means, being a bill accompanying the report of the Secretary of the Treasury, (Mr. Forward.) The latter was adopted as the basis of action by the House. This was considered as more particularly a *revenue bill.*

The last reduction of duties under the Compromise Act of 1833, it will be recollected, was to take place *after* the 30th of June, that is, *on* the 1st of July, 1842. And the first distribution of land proceeds under the act of the preceding session was also to be made the 1st of July. As there was no prospect of the passage of the tariff bill before the time of the reduction of duties, a bill had been reported, and was taken up the 10th of June, to extend the time for the distribution to the 1st of August, with a proviso, that nothing therein contained should suspend the operation of the distribution law, which suspension, it will also be recollected, was to take place whenever the duties should be raised. This temporary bill was passed by the House, 116 to 103; by the Senate, 24 to 19. It was sent to the President, and returned with his *veto.* This veto caused great rejoicing by Southern members. One of them, (Mr. Holmes, of S. C.,) said it had rescued the country from impending civil war. The veto message was then discussed in the House for several days, when (July 4th,) the question was taken upon the passage of the bill, notwithstanding the veto: Ayes, 114; noes, 91; absent, 31. Rejected; two-thirds not voting in the affirmative.

The next day, the House again took up the tariff or revenue bill, which passed the House, July 16th, 116 to 112. It provided to continue the distribution of the proceeds of the land sales, notwithstanding the increase of duties. It passed the Senate, August 5th, 25 to 23; a party vote. In the House, only one Democrat, Mr. Parmenter, of Mass., voted for the bill. Against it were 16 Whigs, all but one from Southern States. In the Senate, the votes in its favor were all from Whigs; against it were three Whigs, all Southern. This bill also was returned by the President with a *veto*.

On motion of Mr. Adams, the Message was referred to a committee of thirteen, who made a report, written by Mr. A., reviewing the condition of the country, the action of Congress, the frequent application of the veto, and the reasons assigned. It animadverted very severely upon the acts of the President, charging him with having usurped the whole power of legislation. The report concluded with a resolution proposing an amendment to the Constitution, requiring, instead of two-thirds, a majority of the whole number of members of each House to pass a bill against the President's objections. It was signed by ten of the Committee.

Constrained by the necessity of increasing the revenue, a bill, the same as the former, with the distribution clause struck out, and so modified as to admit free of duty tea imported in American vessels from beyond the Cape of Good Hope, and coffee, was a few days after passed by the House, 105 to 103. It was sent to the Senate, where it received some amendments, (in which the House afterward concurred,) and was passed, (August 27th,) 24 to 23; being *saved* by Mr. Wright's voting with the Whigs. Probably Mr. W. did not wish to incur the responsibility of defeating a measure for revenue. He assigned also as a reason, that "this measure would root out the germ of distribution." The bill was approved by the President.

A separate bill was then passed, repealing the proviso of the distribution act, so as to allow the distribution notwithstanding the increase of duties; but the bill was retained in the hands of the President, and thus defeated.

The disastrous effects of Gen. Jackson's boasted "arrangement" for a direct trade with the British West India Islands, has been mentioned, [page 81-4.] Memorials from the State of Maine, praying for relief, were presented at this session, (1841–1842.) Maine had had ten thousand tons of shipping employed in the trade with the British North American Colonies alone. But since the treaty she had been driven out entirely, while the shipping of the Colonies had increased four-fold; and they had a direct and unembarrassed trade with this country. One petition declared that the opening of our ports to Great Britain had been obtained by fraud. She had promised reciprocity, but she would not grant it. The petitioners prayed that the effect of the President's proclamation in 1830, making our ports free to Great Britain, be done away, and that the navigation acts of 1818, 1820, and 1828, be revived. The petitions were received, but no action was taken upon the subject.

The President's connection with the party which elected him seems to have been dissolved; and the South again claimed him as their own. Said Mr. Rhett, of S. C., "He is a Virginian—a name never coupled with dishonor. He is now at the head of the Government, and being in favor of the institutions of the South, he may rest assured of an earnest and substantial support."

The rush of Anti-Slavery petitions to Congress was unabated. Most of them were presented by Mr. Adams and Mr. Giddings. The views of Mr. Adams on the subject of abolishing Slavery in the District of Columbia were for a long time misapprehended. He was not an Abolitionist, in the popular sense of the word. He zealously and faithfully defended the right of petition and free speech, which the slaveholders and their Northern Democratic allies in Congress refused; but he was not in favor of abolition without the consent of, or compensation to, the owners of slaves. In this he differed from Mr. Giddings, who was an unconditional Abolitionist, being in favor of immediate emancipation in the District of Columbia and other United States territory, by Congress, and in the States, by their respective legislatures.

Mr. Adams, at this session, presented a petition from forty-six citizens of Haverhill, Mass., for a peaceable dissolution of the Union, which he moved to a Select Committee, with instructions to report an answer showing reasons why the prayer should not be granted. This excited the indignation of Southern members. Mr. Gilmer, of Va., offered a resolution declaring, that, in presenting a petition for the dissolution of the Union, Mr. Adams had incurred the censure of the House. Mr. Marshall, of Ky., offered as a substitute two resolutions, one charging him with an offense involving, in its consequences, the crime of high treason ; the other declaring him deserving of expulsion ; but, as an act of grace and mercy, they would only inflict upon him "their severest censure, for the maintenance of their own purity and dignity."

This brought on a debate which continued about two weeks. Messrs. Marshall, Wise, and Adams, were for several days the chief participators. Mr. Underwood, of Ky., Mr. Botts, of Va., and Mr. Arnold, of Tenn., defended Mr. Adams, and opposed the resolutions. Mr. Saltonstall, of Mass., gave a history of the rise and progress of the idea of dissolving the Union, beginning with the various threats from the Southern portion of the Union—from those opposed to a tariff, from the nullification party, &c. He was surprised and distressed at such a petition from his own native town ; but eloquently defended Mr. Adams from the charges of Mr. Wise.

Mr. Adams occupied the floor most of the time during several of the last days of the debate, in his defense ; in which he fully confirmed his title to the name of the "old man eloquent." He was unsparing in his denunciations of the Slave Power for its opposition to liberty of speech and of the press, and the right of petition, &c. He gave the nullifiers a scathing rebuke for seeking to punish him for presenting a petition from forty-five of his constituents, whose views on the subject involved accorded with their own. His assailants having become tired of the discussion, the subject was, on motion, laid on the table, 106 to 93 ; and the reception of the petition was refused, 40 to 106.

Mr. Giddings presented a similar petition from upwards of eighty of his constituents, and moved its reference in the same manner as Mr. Adams had moved his. The reception was refused : Ayes, 24 ; noes, 116.

Mr. Giddings also submitted a series of resolutions in relation to the case of the brig Creole, which, in October, 1841, left Richmond for New Orleans with a cargo of tobacco and slaves, about 135 in number, who rose upon the crew, killed a man on board, named Hewell, part owner of the negroes, and severely wounded the captain and two of the crew. Having obtained command of the vessel, they directed her to be taken into the port of Nassau, in the British island of New Providence. Nineteen of the negroes were there imprisoned by the local authorities, on a charge of mutiny and murder. Their surrender to the American Consul to be sent to the United States for trial, was refused until the advice of the English Government could be had. A correspondence between Mr. Webster, Secretary of State, and Lord Palmerston took place. The British Government maintained, that there was no international law by which we could claim, or they give up, the men who had taken possession of the Creole ; and orders were given for their liberation.

On the 21st of March, 1842, Mr. Giddings submitted a series of resolutions, declaring that jurisdiction over Slavery belonged to the States ; that the States had surrendered to the Federal Government jurisdiction over commerce and navigation upon the high seas ; that Slavery, being an abridgment of the natural rights of man, can exist only by force of *positive municipal law*, and is necessarily confined to the territorial jurisdiction of the power creating it ; that when the brig Creole left the territorial jurisdiction of Virginia, the slave laws of that State ceased to have jurisdiction over the persons on board, who became amenable only to the laws of the United States, and who, on resuming their natural rights of personal liberty, violated no law of the United States ; and that all attempts to reënslave the said persons, or to exert our influence in favor of the coastwise slave trade, was subversive of the rights, and injurious to the feelings and interests of the Free States, unauthorized by the Con stitution, and incompatible with our national honor.

Mr. Botts, of Va., offered a resolution declaring the conduct of Mr. Giddings deserving of the condemnation of the people and the House. After an exciting debate of several days, and without affording him an opportunity of defense, the resolution of censure was passed, 125 to 69. Mr. Giddings then resigned, returned home, was reëlected by a majority of about 3,500 votes, and returned to his seat in the House on the 5th of May.

The annexation of Texas, which furnishes a conspicuous chapter in our political history, was clearly a Democratic measure, showing conclusively the identification of Democracy with Slavery, and the design to give strength and security to this "peculiar institution."

About the year 1834, commenced a rapid emigration from the South-Western States to Texas, then a province of Mexico. Although slavery had been abolished by Mexico soon after she had consummated her independence, these emigrants took with them their *slaves* as well as their rifles. From this fact, and from certain declarations of Southerners, it was evident that at least one object of these adventurers was the *reëstablishment of Slavery in Texas.* In aid of the revolution, troops were enlisted in several of the States of the Union. In 1835, she declared her independence; and in 1836, the revolution was completed by the battle of San Jacinto, in which the Mexican Dictator, Santa Anna, was captured, who, while a prisoner, and under restraint, agreed to a peace on the basis of the independence of Texas; a bargain which he had no power, and probably no desire to carry into effect, after his liberation. The hasty recognition of the independence of Texas by our Government, contrary to the advice of President Jackson, her application for admission into the Union, and her withdrawal of the application, have been noticed.

The South, however, had not abandoned the purpose of annexation. It was openly declared in Southern State Legislatures, and by Southern members of Congress, to be their object, by this measure, to give protection to Slavery, which would be furnished by "an equipoise of influence in the halls of Congress." Said Mr. Wise, a confidential friend of President Tyler, on the floor of Congress: "Let one more Northern State be admitted, and the equilibrium is gone—gone forever. Let the South stop at the Sabine, (the Eastern boundary of Texas,) while the North may spread unchecked beyond the Rocky Mountains, and *the Southern scale must kick the beam*."

President Tyler, in his Annual Message, December, 1843, suggested a forcible interposition to put an end to the war between Texas and Mexico. And Texas was again making movements towards annexation. At the same time a secret negotiation was going on between the two Governments for this purpose. Mr. Upshur, Secretary of State, having been killed by the explosion of the gun "Peacemaker," on board the United States ship Princeton, he was immediately succeeded by Mr. Calhoun, who concluded the treaty of annexation with the Texan commissioners, Van Zandt and Henderson, on the 12th of April, 1844. The treaty was hastened by the apprehension that Great Britain was about to enter into a negotiation with the opponents of Slavery in Texas, which contemplated its abolition in Texas. There was, however, no foundation for such apprehension. Mr. Everett, our Minister in London, having been written to on the subject, answered, that he had been told by Lord Aberdeen, that "the suggestion that England had made, or intended to make, the abolition of Slavery the condition of any treaty arrangement with Texas, was wholly without foundation." It was believed that the information which had given a new impulse to the annexation movement, had been manufactured for the occasion.

On taking the question on the ratification of the treaty, (June 8th,) a majority of two-thirds being necessary, only 16 Senators voted in the affirmative, and 25 in the negative. Messrs. Buchanan and Sturgeon, of Pa., Breese, of Ill., and Woodbury, of N. H., all Democrats, voted for the treaty. Of the Democrats from Free States who voted against the treaty, were, Messrs. Fairfield, of Maine; Atherton, of N. H.; Niles, of Con.; Wright, of N. Y.; Allen and Tappan, of Ohio; and Mr. Benton, of Mo., a Slave State. Some of the latter, however, perhaps most or all of them, were not opposed to annexation, considered as an abstract question. But they feared, as the result, a war with Mexico. Texas claiming disputed territory, our

Government would, if Texas should be received, be compelled to defend the claim against Mexico. Annexation was also held, by some of our statesmen, to be unconstitutional.

Mr. Benton spoke on three successive days against the treaty, and in support of his resolutions, which declared :

1st. That the ratification of the treaty would be the adoption of the war with Mexico. 2d. That the treaty-making power does not extend to the power of making war, and that the President and Senate have no right to make war, either by declaration or adoption. 3d. That Texas ought to be reünited to the American Union, as soon as it can be done with the consent of a majority of the people of the United States and of Texas, and when Mexico shall either consent to the same, or acknowledge the independence of Texas, or cease to prosecute the war against her on a scale commensurate with the conquest of the country.

Mr. Benton contended that the treaty proposed to annex much more territory than originally belonged to Texas ; and therefore the proposition for the "*reännexation of Texas*" was a fraud in words. It was not pretended, even by those who used that word, that the *province* of Texas, when it was ceded in 1819 to Spain, extended further than the boundaries included between the Sabine and the Rio del Norte, and the Gulf of Mexico and the Red River ; whilst the *Republic* of Texas, as defined in the treaty, included the whole extent of the Rio del Norte, and embraced portions of the department of New Mexico with its capital, being many hundreds of miles of a neighbor's dominion, with whom we had treaties of friendship and commerce—a territory where no Texan force had ever penetrated, and including towns and villages and custom-houses now in the peaceable possession of Mexico.

After the treaty was rejected, Mr. Benton brought in a bill which authorized and advised the President to open negotiations with Mexico and Texas for adjusting boundaries, and annexing Texas to the United States.

The President's scheme of annexation by treaty having failed, he appealed to the House of Representatives, in a Message, inviting their attention to the subject, urging, as a reason, that annexation would be endangered if some thing were not done at once. He preferred annexation by treaty ; but if Congress should see fit to adopt some other plan, he would yield his prompt coöperation. The Message was communicated at too late a day to be acted upon at this session. And a Presidential election was to take place before the next session, which closed with the official term of Mr. Tyler.

Public sentiment had designated Mr. Van Buren and Mr. Clay as rival candidates for the Presidency. The Whig Convention was to meet at Baltimore on the 1st of May, 1844 ; the Democratic on the 27th, at the same place. Both of these gentlemen had been requested to express their opinions on the question of the annexation of Texas ; and both complied with the request, in letters of great length.

Mr. Clay said : "If, without the loss of national character, without the hazard of foreign war, with the general concurrence of the nation, without any danger to the integrity of the Union, and without giving an unreasonable price for Texas, the question of annexation were presented, it would appear in quite a different light from that in which, I apprehend, it is now to be regarded." He said the revolt had been greatly aided by citizens of the United States, in a manner and to an extent which brought upon us the reproach of an impartial world ; and we ought not to give occasion for the imputation of having instigated or aided the revolution with a view to territorial aggrandizement. He would not involve the country in a war for the acquisition of Texas. He discountenanced the motive of acquiring territory to strengthen one part of the Union against another.

The letter, of course, was not entirely satisfactory to ultra slaveholding Whigs, because it did not sufficiently favor their interests ; nor did it fully express the views of Northern Whigs, because it did not in terms deprecate the extension of Slavery. Yet the latter, because he was opposed to it for other though less weighty reasons, rendered him generally acceptable to his party in the North.

Mr. Van Buren, in his letter, discusses the subject of annexation at great length. He had, as Secretary of State, by direction of President Jackson, instructed our Minister at Mexico to open a negotiation with the Mexican Government for the purchase of the greater part of the then province of Texas. Gen. Jackson's administration had thus renewed an attempt to accomplish the same object which had been made by its predecessor. Mr. Adams, however, had, in 1827, proposed an acquisition of territory as far West as the Rio del Norte, the extreme Western boundary of Texas; whilst the cession asked for by President Jackson extended only as far as the desert or grand prairie, which lies East of the river Nueces. Both authorized agreements for smaller portions of territory; and the payments were modified accordingly.

Mr. Van Buren discussed the constitutional power to annex Texas. Congress only has the power to admit new *States;* hence Texas, if annexed by treaty, must be acquired *as a Territory.* In this way only, if at all, could it be done constitutionally. The acquisition by treaty, palpable as its unconstitutionality had been deemed, had the sanction of precedent in the purchase of Louisiana. Desirable as the acquisition was, yet, being wholly at variance with the spirit of our treaty of amity and commerce with Mexico, and implying a disposition to espouse the quarrel of Texas with Mexico, he could not favor annexation under existing circumstances. Said he: "We shall act under the eye of an intelligent, observing world." And in reference to the probabilities of provoking a war with Mexico by the measure, he said: "Could we hope to stand justified in the eyes of mankind for entering into it; more especially if its commencement is to be preceded by the appropriation to our own use of territory, the sovereignty of which is in dispute between two nations, one of which we are to join in the struggle?" We were liable, said Mr. Van B., to be misled by the fact, that most of the Texans were once our fellow-citizens, and had still their relatives and friends amongst us. Yet, he says: "Nothing is either more true or more extensively known, than that *Texas was wrested from Mexico, and her independence established, through the instrumentality of citizens of the United States.*"

This letter was unpalatable to the South; and movements were soon made in many places to prevent his nomination. In some of the Northern States, the "Democracy" protested against these Southern movements to defeat Mr. Van Buren. But protests were unavailing; and he had himself, for the harmony of the party, authorized the withdrawal of his name, if it should become necessary.

Mr. Clay was nominated without a ballot—by acclamation. Mr. Frelinghuysen was, on the third ballot, nominated for Vice-President.

In the Democratic Convention, Mr. Van Buren received a clear majority on the first ballot; having 146 votes; Mr. Cass, 83; R. M. Johnson, 24; Mr. Calhoun, 6; and 7 for others. Two-thirds were necessary to nominate. On the eighth ballot, Mr. Van Buren received 104; Mr. Cass, 114; James K. Polk, 44. Mr. Van Buren's name having been withdrawn, on the next ballot the vote was unanimous for Mr. Polk. Probably to ease New York, Silas Wright, Senator in Congress from that State, then at Washington, was nominated for Vice-President, of which Mr. W. was informed by telegraph. Declining the nomination, George M. Dallas, of Pennsylvania, was nominated.

Although a considerable portion of the Democratic party had been opposed to the annexation of Texas, and had concurred with their leader, Mr. Van Buren, in the views expressed in his anti-Texas letter; yet, in conformity with an established rule for which that party is noted, they supported Mr. Polk with their wonted zeal. The questions at issue between the parties were: a protective tariff, annexation, and the Oregon question. [For the information of some readers, it may be necessary to state, that there was a dispute between our Government and that of Great Britain, as to the true boundary line between their territorial possessions on the Pacific; the latter claiming South to the 49th degree of North latitude; and ours as far North as 54 degrees and 40 minutes. And the Democratic Convention had, in one of their resolutions, adopted at Baltimore, declared that they would insist on having "the whole of Oregon, or none." Whereas our Government had previously proposed the 49th degree as a boundary.]

Not only were Northern Democrats ready to make full concession to the South on the question of extending Slavery; they were equally ready to surrender the protective policy. To those who were ignorant (if such there were) of the [seven] principles of that party, (the five loaves and two fishes,) it would have seemed strange to see men—statesmen—who had grown grey during a long advocacy of the protection of home industry, now on the rostrum defending the Southern theory of leaving American labor subject to foreign legislation. The Middle and Western States, which had been nearly unanimous in favor of the protective principle, had, since Gen. Jackson's second election, gradually abandoned it; and their leading men were now using the same arguments which John C. Calhoun and his adherents had for many years employed against a policy to which the country was mainly indebted for its prosperity.

We have noticed the general and protracted distress under the operation of President Jackson's currency measures and the non-protecting tariff act of 1833, which reached its lowest point in 1842. And we have mentioned the passage of the act of 1842, designed both for revenue and protection. It had been urged against its passage, that it would fail as a revenue measure, because the increased duties would so diminish importations, as to produce less revenue than the low duties were yielding; and that the high duties would be oppressive to the people, especially the poorer classes, who would be compelled to pay higher prices for the necessaries of life.

But these predictions had signally failed, as they had always failed before. The Secretary of the Treasury had estimated the wants of the Treasury at 26 or 27 millions, and had prepared this bill with that view. Under the last year of the compromise act previous to the operation of the act of 1842, the revenue from imports was only about one-half that amount; whereas, during the first three years after the time of its having gone fully into effect, the average receipts were $26,808,097, being almost the precise sum estimated! And even before it went into effect, preparations for manufacturing, for mining, and other branches of industry, began to revive. Dismissed workmen in all the agricultural and manufacturing portions of the country again found remunerative employment. Let any one refer to the papers of that day, and he will see how remarkably the industry of the country was revived.

Importations, instead of having fallen off as had been predicted, maintained about the average of former years, because the people again had the means of purchasing. And as to prices, they had, within the first year after the act went into effect, fallen much below those which the "poor laborer" had paid when half the time out of employ, or receiving half as high a price for his labor. I have before me a list, prepared by merchants of the city of Richmond, Va., of the prices of staple goods in that city for the years 1841 and 1843, the year before and the year after the passage of the act of 1842, showing a reduction of from 10 to more than 30 per cent. Imports of specie were also largely increased, and the rates of interest greatly reduced. In the face of all these and other facts, Democratic speakers at every meeting declaimed loudly against this "oppressive" tariff, and thus duped multitudes of their hearers, who, at the ensuing election, voted for a President and members of Congress, by whom this policy which had so signally benefitted the country, was overthrown, and a system established which eventually resulted in the "crash" of 1857—a result similar to that produced by every other non-protecting tariff.

In the tariff State of Pennsylvania, a downright swindle was practised upon the friends of protection; a large portion of whom were ignorant of the views of Mr. Polk on this question. He had, in 1842, when a candidate for Governor in Tennessee, written a letter for publication, addressed to the people of that State, in which he said: "I had steadily, during the period I was a Representative in Congress, been *opposed to a protective policy*, as my recorded votes and public speeches prove. Since I retired from Congress, I had held the same opinion. In the present canvass for Governor I had avowed my opposition to the tariff act of the late Whig Congress"—the act of 1842. Yet his friends were now, (1844,) circulating a letter through the Democratic papers of Pennsylvania, written by him to Judge Kane, of that State, representing himself as *in favor of a reasonable protection to home industry*. And to give greater effect to the fraud, the motto inscribed on the party banners in a large portion of the State, was: "Polk, Dallas, and the Tariff of 1842!" The ticket was voted for by the honest but deluded Pennsylvanians ; who gave that State to the Democratic candidate, who, with the help of a Democratic Congress, broke down the policy which they had supposed they were supporting by voting for him. Some Democratic papers even had the effrontery to represent Mr. Clay as being opposed to the protective policy !

Some of Mr. Clay's Southern friends were in favor of annexation, and feared his election would jeopard that measure. In his answer to a letter from that section, he said : "Personally I could have no objection to the annexation of Texas ; but I certainly would be unwilling to see the existing Union dissolved or seriously jeoparded for the sake of acquiring Texas." The Abolitionists, or "third party" men, seized upon the expression, "Personally I could have no objection to annexation," and used it to represent him as favorable to that measure. One-third of the votes given for the Birney electoral ticket, in the State of New York alone, if given for that of the Whigs, would have secured the election of Mr. Clay. Possibly Texas might have been annexed during the next Presidential term, even had Mr. Clay been elected ; but it is certain that the unprovoked, unnecessary, disgraceful, *aggressive war of conquest against Mexico for the benefit of the Slave Power, would not have occurred.*

Of the electors chosen in November, 170 voted for Polk and Dallas ; and 105 for Clay and Frelinghuysen.

The great measure of the next session of Congress, (1844-1845,) was the annexation of Texas. President Tyler again urged it upon Congress. He regarded the recent election as the expression of the will of the people in favor of immediate annexation. In the Senate, Mr. M'Duffie introduced resolutions declaring the rejected treaty to be a "fundamental law of union between the United States and Texas, when the authorities of Texas shall agree to the same." Mr. Benton gave notice of a bill "to provide for the annexation of Texas to the United States," similar to that introduced by him at the preceding session. This bill advised negotiation for the adjustment of boundaries. In the House, C. J. Ingersoll, from the Committee of Foreign Affairs, reported resolutions for annexation, which, after having been amended, were adopted. They provided that questions of boundary that might arise should be laid before Congress. The United States were not to become liable for the debts of Texas ; but she was to retain all the public funds, debts, taxes, and dues owing to the Republic ; and all vacant lands. And new States not exceeding four, in addition to the State of Texas, might be formed out of the territory thereof ; the States to be admitted, with or without Slavery, as the people might desire ; but North of 36 degrees and 30 minutes, Slavery was to be prohibited.

The resolutions were finally passed, 120 to 98. As classified by Niles, of the 120 who voted in the affirmative, 112 were Democrats, 53 from Free, and 59 from Slave States ; the other 8 were Whigs, all from Slave States. Of the 98 who voted in the negative, 28 were Democrats, all from Free States ; and 70 were Whigs, 52 from Free, and 18 from Slave States.

Another classification was as follows : The number of Democrats voting was 140 ; from Free States, 81 ; from Slave States, 59. Of the 81, 53 were for, and 28 against annexation. The number of Whigs voting was 78 ; 52 from Free, and 26 from Slave States. Of the latter, 8 were for, and 18 against the bill. The 59 Democrats from the Slave States, all voted for the bill, and the 52 Whigs from the Free States, all voted against it.

The resolutions adopted by the House were amended in the Senate, by adding a resolution, leaving it to the discretion of the President, either to submit the resolutions as an overture to Texas for admission, or to negotiate a treaty for that purpose. The resolutions were ordered to a third reading, 27 to 25, all the Senators being present. The amendment of the Senate was concurred in by the House, 132 to 76. So the triumph of annexation was complete, as it is not probable that either Mr. Tyler or Mr. Polk would have jeoparded the measure by negotiation. It was said, however, that Messrs. Benton and Bagby without whose votes the resolutions would have been lost, voted for them from their confidence that Mr Polk, upon whom it was supposed the choice would devolve, would elect this mode But Mr. Tyler seized upon the last moment of his official existence, to exercise, himself, the power conferred by the resolutions.

The question of annexation, relieved from all doubt as to its constitutionality, and from all apprehensions of difficulty with Mexico, would probably have received the votes of nearly all the Democrats in both Houses.

CHAPTER VI.

Administration of James K. Polk.

JAMES K. POLK was inaugurated as President, on the 4th of March, 1845. As was naturally expected, the subjects of Slavery and Annexation found a place in his Address. He deprecated interference with certain "domestic institutions" as an "attempt to disturb or destroy the compromises of the Constitution," which must "lead to the most ruinous and disastrous consequences." He regretted, "that in some sections of our country, misguided persons had indulged in schemes and agitations; whose object was the destruction of domestic institutions in other sections." These schemes he, as a true Southerner, was pleased to call "*moral treason*." Respecting the Tariff he said: "Justice and sound policy forbid the Federal Government to foster one branch of industry to the detriment of another, or to cherish the interests of one portion to the injury of another portion of our common country." He congratulated the country on the reünion of Texas to the United States. The annexation was "not to be looked upon as the conquest of a nation seeking to extend her dominions by arms and violence, but as the peaceful acquisition of territory once her own." He also reässerted "our title to the country of the Oregon to be 'clear and unquestionable,'" and pledged himself "to maintain, by all constitutional means, the right of the United States to that portion of our territory."

Mr. Polk chose for his Cabinet: James Buchanan, of Pa., Secretary of State; Robert J. Walker, of Miss., Secretary of the Treasury; Wm. L. Marcy, of N. Y., Secretary of War; George Bancroft, of Mass., Secretary of the Navy; Cave Johnson, of Tenn., Postmaster-General; John Y. Mason, of Va., Attorney-General.

On the 6th of March, six days after the date of the act of annexation, the Mexican Minister protested against the dismemberment of Texas from Mexican territory, and declared the purpose of Mexico to enforce her right to recover the territory ; and he gave notice of the termination of his mission, and asked for his passports. On the arrival of the news of annexation at the city of Mexico, diplomatic relations between the two Governments were there also terminated.

Early in the summer, President Jones, of Texas, laid before the Texan Congress a proposition from the Mexican Government, to acknowledge the independence of Texas, upon three conditions : (1.) Texas not to annex herself or become subject to any other country. (2) Limits and other arrangements to be matters of agreement in the final treaty. (3.) Texas to consent to refer the disputed points with regard to territory and other matters, to the arbitration of umpires. But the proposition was rejected ; and resolutions were adopted accepting the terms of annexation to the United States. This acceptance was, in July, ratified by the people of Texas in Convention.

Mexico considered annexation an act of war, and declared her intention to resent the injury, and to resort to arms. At the request of the Congress and the people of Texas, our Government sent an army into that territory to defend it against invasion. The army was ordered to take position between the Nueces and the Del Norte. A strong squadron was sent to the coast of Mexico, as a precautionary measure.

Several installments of the Mexican indemnity were due ; and claims of more than three millions had been recognized by a treaty, which the Mexican Government had not yet ratified. Mexico having consented to renew diplomatic relations, a Minister, (Mr. Slidell, of Louisiana,) was sent with full power to settle all difficulties. His reception, however, was refused, on the ground of the inadequacy of his special power to treat upon the questions which the Mexican Government intended to make the subject of negotiation. It would recognize him only for the purpose of treating in relation to Texas and the boundary.

Gen. Taylor, having been with his troops at Corpus

Christi from August to January, and no hostile act having been committed by the Mexicans, was ordered, in January, 1846, to the left bank of the Rio Grande, (Rio del Norte,) where he arrived with a company of dragoons, (in advance of the main army,) on the 24th of March. He was met by a deputation of 30 or 40 men, with a message from Gen. Mejia, a Mexican commander, protesting against the invasion. On the approach of the fleet of transports, the custom-house at Point Isabel, and a few other buildings, were burnt by the Mexican commandant. On the 28th, the army of occupation, consisting of about 3,500 men, arrived. About one month thereafter, hostilities commenced.

On the 11th of May, 1846, the President sent to Congress a Message, announcing a state of war, commenced on the part of Mexico, whose Government, he said, "after a long-continued series of menaces, had at last invaded our territory, and shed the blood of our fellow-citizens on our own soil." And he asked Congress to recognize the existence of the war, and to place in the hands of the Executive the means of prosecuting it. A bill to raise the necessary men and $10,000,000 was immediately reported in the House, and passed, 142 to 14. The next morning it passed the Senate with slight amendments, 40 to 2, and was returned to the House the same evening, which repassed it the next day with the Senate's amendments. It was sent to the President, who signed it, and issued the war Proclamation the same day.

The Whig members were in a dilemma. They believed the war to be unjust on the part of our Government, having been caused by the dismemberment of a part of the territory of Mexico. The President's ordering the army into Mexican territory, was an act of war, tantamount to a declaration of war, which the Constitution devolved upon Congress. Many, however, in accordance with the popular sentiment, that, however unjust a war may be, it must be supported, voted for the bill; others, because it would render a man unpopular to vote against a war. But the most objectionable part of it was the preamble, which declared the war to exist *by the act of the Republic of Mexico.* This declaration was positively untrue. Our army was the invader. It was on *Mexican soil* that the blood had been shed, and not on ours, as the President had declared. Hence, to vote for the bill was to vote for what was believed to be false. In the Senate, a motion was made to strike out the preamble; but it was lost, 18 to 28. The Democrats were determined to compel the Whigs to indorse the statement of the President, and thus to cover up the iniquity of the project. Some voted under protest, and others refused to vote at all. Thomas Clayton, of Delaware, and John Davis, of Massachusetts, (often called "honest John Davis,") voted in the negative. The members of the House who voted in the negative, were, Messrs. Adams, Ashmun, Grinnell, Hudson, and King, of Mass.; Severance, of Maine; Cranston, of R. I.; Culver, of N. Y.; Strohm, of Pa.; Giddings, Root, Tilden, and Vance, of Ohio.

On the 4th of August, 1846, the President informed the Senate that he had resolved to propose to open a negotiation with Mexico, and asked of Congress money to enable him to negotiate a peace. The object for which the money was wanted, was to purchase territory, if it should be deemed expedient. A bill appropriating $2,000,000 for this purpose was introduced into the House of Representatives, and promptly put on its passage, when Mr. Wilmot, of Pa., a Democrat, moved a proviso, which was carried, declaring that in any territory acquired from Mexico, Slavery should never be permitted. The bill, with the proviso, passed the House; but for want of time, the Senate came to no conclusion on the subject at this session.

The proviso was carried in Committee of the Whole, by a vote 83 to 64; only 3 members (Democrats) from Free States, it was said, opposing it. [Individual votes are not recorded in Committee of the Whole.] The bill with the proviso, was engrossed for its third reading, 85 to 80.

In his Message to Congress in December, 1846, the President adverted to the wrongs committed by Mexico, and the causes of the war; declared its justice on our part, our disposition to peace, and our right to annex Texas; and again charged Mexico with having invaded our soil—asserting the validity of the claim of Texas to the Rio Grande, in opposition to Messrs. Benton, Wright, Adams, and others.

A bill was again introduced appropriating money,

($3,000,000,) to aid in negotiating a peace with Mexico. It passed the House with the "Wilmot proviso," 115 to 110, after an ineffectual motion of Mr. Douglas to amend by prohibiting Slavery in acquired territory North of 36 deg. 30 min. A similar bill passed the Senate, in which body the proviso had been rejected. This bill was sent to the House, the proviso attached in Committee of the Whole, but afterward rejected in the House, 97 to 102; and the bill finally passed without the proviso.

The debate on this bill in the Senate was deeply interesting as well as animated. Many Senators participated. The collision between Messrs. Benton and Calhoun might be called "rich," were it not for the iniquity which it disclosed. A glimpse at a few facts is all that can be given.

Mr. Calhoun said the objects of the war appeared from the President's Message to be three fold: (1.) To repel invasion; (2.) To establish the Rio del Norte as the Western boundary; (3.) To obtain payment for indemnities due our citizens for claims against Mexico. The President had assumed that war existed, and called upon Congress to recognize its existence. That blood had been shed on American soil, he had assumed on the ground that the Rio del Norte was the Western boundary of Texas. And Congress, in declaring that war had been made by Mexico, had recognized that river as the boundary. Hence, the crossing of that river by the Mexicans was considered invasion, which was to be repelled. These two, repelling invasion and establishing boundary, were primary objects; and being involved in the war, the object of indemnity, though not a sufficient cause of war in itself, might be made one of the objects for which the war might be prosecuted.

Mr. Benton charged the war upon Mr. Calhoun. The causes were further back than the march of the army to the Rio Grande. He referred to Mr. C.'s approval of the treaty, as a member of Mr. Monroe's Cabinet, by which territory had been given away; the blame of which had long been unjustly charged upon Mr. Adams, the negotiator of the treaty. He referred also to Mr. C.'s acts and correspondence relating to the independence of Texas, and his purpose to extend Slavery; and to his inducing Mr. Tyler to adopt the course he did, on the last day of his presidency, which measure had precipitated us into the war.

Mr. B. said: "He now sets up for the character of pacificator; with what justice, let the further fact proclaim which I now expose." He said there were, in the summer of 1844, (while Mr. C. was Secretary of State,) three hundred newspapers in the pay of that department, which spoke its sentiments, and denounced as traitors all who were for peaceable annexation by settling, at the same time, the boundary line of Texas with Mexico. These papers acted under instruction; in proof of which he read from a letter as follows:

"As the conductor of a public journal here, he has requested me to answer it, (your letter,) which request I comply with readily. . . . With regard to the course of your paper, you can take the tone of the administration from the * * * * *. I think, however, and would recommend, that you would confine yourself to attacks upon Benton, showing that he has allied himself with the Whigs on the Texas question. Quote Jackson's letter on Texas, where he denounces all those as traitors to the country who oppose the treaty. Apply it to Benton. Proclaim that Benton, by attacking Tyler and his friends, and driving them from the party, is aiding the election of Mr. Clay; and charge him with doing this to defeat Mr. Polk, and insure himself the succession in 1848; and claim that full justice be done to the acts and motives of John Tyler by the leaders. Harp upon these things. . . . Look out for my leader of to-morrow as an indication, and regard this letter as of the most strict and inviolate confidence of character."

Mr. Clayton said, that, during the debate on the Oregon question, in February, 1846, he had learned that our Government had ordered Gen. Taylor to break up his encampment at Corpus Christi, and march to the Rio Grande. The instant he heard it—the public having no means of knowing the fact—he was alarmed at the apprehension of a war with Mexico; and he had privately told Mr. Calhoun, that unless he should interpose to arrest the tendency of things arising from that order, we should be plunged into a war.

At the same time there was danger of a war with England; that he [Mr. Clayton] as a Whig, could effect nothing; and unless Mr. Calhoun and his friends should move in the matter, the Whigs would be powerless. The gentleman was at that time devoted to the object of preventing a war with England. Said Mr. Clayton: "*While the Houses of Congress remained in ignorance, and those who knew could not move, the President was ordering the army upon the Rio Grande, and taking a step, of which the inevitable consequence proved to be war.* . . . At the time war was announced, I denounced it as *the act of the President.* . . . I believe that the war was brought on by this marching of the army, without any necessity—done, too, while Congress was in session, without one word being communicated, as to the intention of the President, to either House."

The action of Congress upon this subject, gave rise to the question: Is it the duty of the Legislature to provide the means for prosecuting a war made unconstitutionally, or by the exercise of usurped power? If so, the President might at any time plunge the country into a war, without the consent or knowledge of Congress, where the Constitution wisely places the power to declare or make war. Another question naturally arises: Can the Legislature which provides the means avoid the responsibility of the war? The Legislature and the Executive are designed to hold checks upon each other. Can either, then, be justified in refusing to interpose its constitutional power to arrest or to prevent usurpation by the other? If not, the people who have to bear the burdens of war, have no security; and the Government would be virtually a military despotism. Mr. Corwin, Senator from Ohio, took ground on this subject, which it is difficult, indeed, to controvert with success. He, almost alone, contended against the popular notion, that *because* war had been made, "we must fight it out;" and that no distinction is to be made between a war secretly brought upon the country by usurped power, and one that is made by the people through their representatives.

In view of all the facts connected with this measure of annexation—its objects—its inception—its incidents, and the means of its accomplishment—what is the judgment which intelligent and candid minds must award to the projectors and abettors of this stupendous scheme of plunder, as Mr. Benton regarded it? Well did Mr. Van Buren say: "We shall act under the eye of an intelligent, observing world. . . . Could we hope to stand justified in the eyes of mankind?" Yet the entire Democratic North, whose favorite candidate for the Presidency deprecated the act contemplated, went over in a body to the assistance of those who were bent on the perpetration of the iniquitous measure! This, however, is but one of a long succession of bad measures inflicted upon the country under the magic name of "Democracy."

Although Mr. Tyler had snatched from his successor the anticipated honor of consummating the annexation scheme, he left on the hands of the latter the management of the other foreign question, the settlement of the conflicting territorial claims of the United States and Great Britain on the Pacific.

A bill had been introduced in the House at the session of 1844–1845, at which the annexation of Texas was effected, to establish a Territorial Government in Oregon. It embraced, under the proposed government, the whole territory West of the Rocky Mountains, and from latitude 42 degrees to 54 deg. and 40 minutes. But as the proposed measure might break up the negotiation then in progress with Great Britain, and lead to war, an amendment was added, providing that the act should not be so construed as to interfere with the rights which British subjects might have under the existing treaty until after twelve months' notice should have been given. An amendment excluding Slavery was also adopted. The bill passed the House, 140 to 49. A motion to take up the bill was made in the Senate on the last day of the session, (March 3, 1845,) but it did not prevail.

President Polk, in his first Annual Message, December, 1845, alluded to the several negotiations under the administrations of Mr. Monroe and Mr. Adams, which had resulted in provisions for the joint occupancy of the territory by the subjects of the two nations, for the term of ten years from 1818; and in a renewal of the provision for joint occupancy for another term of ten years from 1828, and until the treaty should be annulled, which could be done by either party by giving the other twelve months' previous notice to that effect.

It had been rumored before the meeting of Congress, that our Government had offered to treat on the parallel of the 49th degree as a boundary. The "Union," the official paper, contradicted the rumor, and said the administration would insist on the "*whole of Oregon or none.*" [It was contended by some that Great Britain had no just claim to any part of the territory.] It said: "When that word goes forth from the constituted authorities of the nation, 'Our right to Oregon is clear and unquestionable,' who doubts that it will go the whole length and breadth of the land, and that it will be hailed as it goes, by the Democratic party, with one unanimous Amen! And what then? We answer this, then—*the Democracy of this country will stand to its word. It will not flinch.*" It was apprehended that, if the President should recommend the taking possession of all Oregon, and Congress should carry out the recommendation, war would ensue. But to take possession without having given a year's previous notice in order to terminate the joint occupancy, would be a violation of the treaty. Hence, there were those, among whom was Mr. Adams, who urged the giving of the notice as a means of hastening a settlement of the controversy.

After all the gasconade of "stump orators" and the whole Democratic press during the presidential canvass and after the election, the reader will readily judge of the disappointment and mortification of the Democrats on being informed by the President in his Message, that *he had offered to divide on the 49th degree,* without, however, conceding to Great Britain the free navigation of the Columbia river. This proposition having been rejected, it had been withdrawn, and our title to the whole territory asserted. He recommended the giving of notice of the discontinuance of the joint occupancy, and protection to our citizens in Oregon.

Preparations for war were supposed to be making in England. In Congress several measures were proposed; one of which was a preparation for war. A bill was reported for the organization of two regiments of riflemen.

Mr. Adams opposed the bill as unnecessary, both because a bill for one regiment was in progress in the Senate, and because he saw "*no danger of war* at this time." If there were such danger, the first measure ought to be a notice to Great Britain that we meant to terminate the joint occupancy. Yet it was not a joint occupancy. The treaty acknowledged no occupation of the territory by either party; it was a mere commercial convention for free navigation. Twelve months after such notice, the right would accrue to us to occupy any part of the territory. He hoped it would be given, and followed by a *real occupation of the whole territory.* [This declaration produced great sensation.] Mr. Adams noticed the contrast between the indifference of the Calhoun party in Congress on the Oregon question, and their zeal the year before for the acquisition of Texas, even at the cost of war.

After much debate and numerous propositions in both Houses, a joint resolution was adopted, authorizing the President, at his discretion, to give to the British Government the notice required for the abrogation of the convention (treaty) of 1827.

Mr. Benton took ground against Messrs. Cass, Dix, Dickinson, and others, who claimed title to the line of 54° 40'. He said, "the people had been misled—grossly and widely misled—ignorantly at first, as we were bound to believe; designedly now, as we painfully see. The fifty-four forty line never existed. The treaty proves it; yet its existence is still affirmed to mislead the uninformed, and to save the misleaders from the mortification of exposure."

The resolutions authorizing the notice approved by the President, were sent to England to be delivered in person to Her Majesty Victoria. In the midst of speculation and apprehension, PEACE was announced! A conference had taken place between Mr. Buchanan, Secretary of State, and Mr. Pakenham, which resulted in a treaty concluded the 15th of June. Instead of getting the whole of Oregon to "54 40," we obtained no part of it North of 49, and not all the way quite up to that line. The South had secured their object, the annexation of Texas and the prospective acquisition, from Mexico, of additional territory of indefinite extent; and they were not disposed to favor the extension of our territory Northward, and thus to furnish the North with an "equipoise" to the Slave States which they had in prospect. On the whole, the result may be regarded as another triumph of the Slave Power, by its agent, the Democratic party.

Another important object of this ruling power—an object long sought—was, in the name of Democracy, attained at this session—the destruction of the American Protective System. An attempt had been made for this purpose in 1844, but it did not quite succeed. There being now administration majorities in both Houses, there was little hope of saving the Tariff of 1842, whose beneficial effects were felt in all the Free States, and its unfavorable operation was felt nowhere. A more arduous struggle between the advocates and opponents of protection, has probably never occurred.

The *reduction* of the duties was not the only defect of the act of 1846. On some articles no reduction was made. A material fault of the act was the entire *abolition of specific duties*, and the adoption, in full, of the *ad valorem* system. The effects of these two systems have been stated. Not only does the latter encourage fraud in importations; but also affords a less uniform protection, varying with fluctuations in prices. For example: A duty of 30 per cent. on a tun of iron costing $50 in England, is $15. But if the price of iron should fall to $40, the duty would be only $12; if to $30, the duty would be $9. Hence, if the first duty was merely sufficient for protection, the reduced duty would afford no protection at all.

Specific duties had been recommended by our leading statesmen; and they had, from long experience, been found preferable to *ad valorem* duties. But as the latter would seriously affect the manufacturing interest, which was almost entirely confined to the North, Democracy, which had become the synonym of Slavery, yielded to the demand for the change, to the damage of the free labor of the North. The Democratic members from Pennsylvania, with one exception, remained true to the protective principle, and one-fourth of those from New York; and the opposition to the bill derived considerable strength from the Whigs of the Slave States.

The vote in the Senate stood, Yeas, 28 ; Nays, 27. Only one Whig, (Jarnagin, of Tenn., under instructions,) voted for the bill. Of the Democrats who voted against it, were Cameron and Sturgeon, of Pa., and Niles, of Conn.

In the House, there were, Yeas, 114 : Democrats, 113 ; Whig, 1, (of Alabama.) Nays, 95 : Whigs, 71 ; Democrats, 18 ; Native Americans, 6. Of the 18 Democrats, there were from New York, 4 ; New Jersey, 2 ; Pennsylvania, 11 ; Maryland, 1. Native Americans, New York, 4 ; Pennsylvania, 2.

The unfavorable effects of the new tariff were soon felt. Complaints came from different sections. A large number of Woolen and Iron manufactories were very soon adversely affected. Some were suspended ; others discharged a part of their hands ; and others reduced the wages of operatives. Before two years had elapsed there were indications of another revulsion at no distant period. Fortunately, however, the discovery of California gold, and the rapid increase of coin, increased the circulating medium of the country, and the means of paying for imported goods ; and thus postponed the apprehended calamity. But importations continued to increase beyond all precedent, until, in 1857, they reached the enormous amount of about $360,000,000 ; being nearly *three times the average amount imported for the eight or ten years previous to* 1846 ; when (1857) the deferred "crash" at length came ! A more ruinous one, it is believed, has never been experienced in this country.

The President having recommended a Sub-Treasury, a bill was reported early in the session by the Committee of Ways and Means, and passed the House, April 2d, 1846, by a vote of 123 to 67. It passed the Senate, August 1st, by a strict party vote, 28 to 24. By this law, all receivers and disbursers of the public revenue, including all postmasters, were required to collect and pay out specie only.

At the session of 1847–1848, was established a Government for the territory of Oregon. Mr. Douglas had reported a bill for this purpose in August, 1846, to which an amendment excluding Slavery had been adopted in Committee of the Whole. In the Senate, the bill was read twice, referred, and reported on ; but no further action was taken upon the bill.

At the next session, Mr. Douglas, December 23, 1846, again reported his bill, which was read twice and committed. It was discussed in Committee of the Whole, January 11th, 12th, and 13th. The next day, the bill was taken out of Committee, when Mr. Burt, of S. C., moved the following addition (already voted down in Committee) to the clause forbidding Slavery: "Inasmuch as the whole of said Territory lies North of 36 degrees 30 minutes North latitude, known as the line of the Missouri Compromise."

The object of this evidently was to recognize the Missouri line, not as limited to territory owned at the time that line was established, but as extending to all that had since been, or thereafter should be, acquired, so as *to legalize Slavery thenceforth South of* 36 *deg.* 30 *min.* The amendment was negatived: Yeas, 82; nays, 114. From Free States, 5 voted in the minority. No member from a Slave State voted in the majority. The bill then passed, 134 to 35—nays all Southern. This bill, like that of the preceding session, failed to receive the final action of the Senate.

At the next session, 1847–1848, Mr. C. B. Smith, of Indiana, reported to the House a bill to establish a Government for Oregon, which, after postponements and other delays, came out of Committee, August 1st, that provision having been struck out which required the inhabitants of the Territory to be "subject to all the conditions, and restrictions, and prohibitions in the articles of compact contained in the ordinance for the government of the territory North-West of the river Ohio, passed July 13, 1787." [Anti-Slavery restriction.] The House refused to agree to this amendment: Yeas, 88; Nays, 114. Of those who voted for striking out, 5 were from Free States. The bill was then passed, 128 to 71. This vote was entirely sectional, excepting the vote of Mr. Houston, of Del., who voted in the affirmative. In the Senate, the bill was, on motion of Mr. Douglas, amended so as to extend the Missouri Compromise line to the Pacific Ocean, and engrossed for a third reading, 33 to 22. It was returned to the House, where the amendment of Mr. Douglas was rejected: Yeas, 82; nays, 121. From Free States, 3 voted Yea; otherwise all from Free States Nays; and all from the Slave States Yeas. The Senate receded from its amendments, and passed the bill as it came from the House: Yeas, 29; Nays, 25—all from Slave States.

A bill was reported by Mr. Clayton, in the Senate, for the organization of New Mexico and California into Territories; but it was not acted upon at this session.

At the next session, a bill was introduced into the Senate, December 11, 1848, by Mr. Douglas, for the admission of California as a State, to include all the territory acquired by treaty from Mexico. This bill was silent on the subject of Slavery. Mr. Davis, of Miss., proposed an amendment to annex New Mexico to Texas. This would have legalized Slavery in that part of the acquired territory. The people of New Mexico had petitioned Congress, remonstrating against being annexed to Texas, and praying to be protected against the introduction of Slavery into their territory. The Senate did not come to a vote on the bill.

A bill was reported in the House by Mr. Smith, of Indiana, to establish a Territorial Government for Upper California, with the Anti-Slavery proviso, which passed the House, 126 to 87. But the session closed without any action upon it after its reference.

The popularity acquired by General Taylor as a military commander in the war with Mexico, had, for two years before the approaching Presidential election, pointed him out to shrewd Whig politicians as an "available" candidate. Having spent nearly the whole period of his manhood in the army, and having never, as was said, cast a vote at an election, he was not, of course, a party politician. He seemed, however, to have a leaning toward the Whig party. Being a Southern man, and the Whig party of the North being strongly committed to the Wilmot proviso, or the non-extension of Slavery, it was doubted whether he could obtain a nomination; or if nominated, whether he could be elected. In his replies to numerous interrogatories, he uniformly refused to declare himself a Whig, or to be the exponent of Whig doctrines. He would, if elected, be the President of the nation, and not of a party, and he would make no party pledges.

The Democratic National Convention met at Baltimore, the 22d of May, 1848. As in former Conventions, the two-thirds rule was adopted. On the fourth ballot, General Cass received 179 votes ; Levi Woodbury, 38 ; James Buchanan, 33 ; and Gen. Worth, 3, Gen. Wm. O. Butler, of Ky., was nominated for Vice- President.

The Whig National Convention met at Philadelphia, the 7th of June. On the first ballot, Gen. Taylor received 111 votes ; Mr. Clay, 97 ; Mr. Webster, 21 ; Gen. Scott, 46 ; John M'Lean, 2. After another unsuccessful ballot, further balloting was deferred until the next day, when, on the second ballot of that day, Gen. Taylor received 171 votes ; Mr. Clay, 30 ; Gen. Scott, 63 ; Mr. Webster, 12. Millard Fillmore was nominated for Vice-President. No resolutions, or platform of principles, was adopted.

A National Mass Convention was held in the city of Buffalo, on the 9th of August, composed of disaffected Democrats and Whigs, who were designated "free-soil men." Martin Van Buren was nominated for President ; Charles Francis Adams for Vice-President.

The views of Gen. Cass on the Slavery issue were stated in a letter to A. O. P. Nicholson, of Tennessee. He had been in favor of the Wilmot Proviso ; but had receded from that position, and was opposed to the exercise of any jurisdiction by Congress over Slavery in the Territories ; but he would leave to the people of any territory the right to regulate it for themselves.

The views of Gen. Taylor were expressed in a letter to Captain Allison. He was in favor of exercising the veto power only in cases of clear violation of the Constitution, or manifest haste and want of consideration by Congress. In respect to the tariff, the currency, and internal improvements, the will of the people, as expressed through their representatives, ought to be respected and carried out by the Executive. On Slavery he was silent.

Of the Presidential electors chosen in November, 163 voted for Taylor and Fillmore ; and 127 for Cass and Butler.

CHAPTER VII.

Administration of Zachary Taylor and Millard Fillmore.

GENERAL ZACHARY TAYLOR was inaugurated as President on the 5th of March, 1849. His Address was short, and partook much of the character of his numerous letters written before his election. He selected for his Cabinet officers the following: John M. Clayton, of Delaware, Secretary of State; Wm. M. Meredith, of Pennsylvania, Secretary of the Treasury; Thomas Ewing, of Ohio, Secretary of the Interior; George W. Crawford, of Georgia, Secretary of War; Wm. B. Preston, of Virginia, Secretary of the Navy; Jacob Collamer, of Vermont, Postmaster-General; Reverdy Johnson, of Maryland, Attorney-General.

Congress assembled December 3, 1849. Three weeks were spent in fruitless attempts to elect a speaker, when, in order to terminate the contest, it was agreed by the parties to elect by a *plurality* vote. Howell Cobb, of Georgia, was then elected.

The Message of President Taylor was communicated to Congress the 24th. He recommended the revision of the Tariff to augment the revenue, and the adoption of specific duties. The Sub-Treasury, if continued, needed modification. And a loan was recommended to pay the expenses of the war with Mexico. His policy in regard to the new Territories was, that Congress should await the action of the people themselves in forming Constitutions preparatory to the admission of California and New Mexico. This, he believed, would avoid all causes of uneasiness, and preserve confidence and good feeling. Congress should abstain from the introduction of those exciting topics of a sectional character, which had produced painful apprehensions in the public mind. [He had reference, probably, to the excitement usually produced by the attempts, in forming Territorial Governments, to prohibit Slavery. In *principle*, his plan might be objectionable ; *practically*, it would, in the particular cases then existing, be less liable to objections, as Slavery had been abolished in these Territories by Mexico, and it was not probable that the inhabitants would favor its reëstablishment.]

This session was an eventful one—being distinguished for one of the most liberal concessions ever made to the Slave Power. The proceedings in relation to the new territory and Slavery, occupied a large, if not the larger portion of the session.

Mr. Clay submitted resolutions, eight in number, proposing an "amicable arrangement" of the whole Slavery controversy. Although they were designed as a compromise, they were little else than concession. They were, notwithstanding, unacceptable, as a whole, to the ultra Southerners. In fact, they were opposed by Southern Senators as making no concession to the South—as being no compromise at all ! They objected to the admission of California *as a State*, with a Constitution prohibiting Slavery ; unless, as they had the boldness to say, *another new Slave State could be laid off within the limits of Texas*, so as to keep the present *equiponderance* between the Slave and Free States ; and further, unless all this were done by way of *compromise, and in order to save the Union !*

Mr. Clay's resolutions were debated for nearly two months ; the President having in the meantime communicated to Congress a copy of the Constitution of California. Various propositions having been made by Senators, they were referred to a Select Committee of thirteen, (Mr. Clay Chairman,) who made a report embodying them in a single bill, facetiously termed the "Omnibus bill." It was debated, and part after part eliminated, until it passed the Senate only as "A bill to provide for the Territorial Government of Utah." This dismemberment was called "upsetting the Omnibus." Subsequently the other portions of the bill were passed in separate bills. California was admitted ; a Territorial Government bill for New Mexico was passed ; and a bill establishing the boundary of Texas. By this bill a large portion of New Mexico was annexed to Texas to enlarge the area of Slavery, and $10,000,000 given to Texas to relinquish her claims to New Mexico; or as Mr. Benton remarked: "They give 70,000 square miles to Texas, and offer her ten millions to accept it!" Some land, however, of inferior value, was ceded by Texas to the United States. A law to abolish the *slave trade* in the District of Columbia, and the fugitive slave law, were passed. Of course, no restriction was laid upon Slavery in the Territorial Governments of Utah and New Mexico. The Texas boundary bill and the New Mexico Territorial bill were in the House united, and passed in one bill.

The reader is requested to bear in mind two facts: First, these measures, called the "compromise measures of 1850," were intended as a *final settlement* of the Slavery question, and were repeatedly declared to be so since their enactment. Secondly, there was no intimation, in the long debate on these measures, that their adoption would involve or imply a repeal of the Missouri restriction. We shall soon have occasion to advert to these facts.

While these measures were pending, on the 9th of July, 1850, President Taylor died. On the next day, Mr. Fillmore, Vice-President, took the oath of office, and entered upon the duties of President; and the day following, Wm. R. King, Senator from Alabama, was elected President of the Senate, *pro tem.*

Mr. Fillmore reconstructed the Cabinet. He appointed Daniel Webster Secretary of State; Thomas Corwin, of Ohio, Secretary of the Treasury; Charles M. Conrad, of Louisiana, Secretary of War; Wm. A. Graham, of North Carolina, Secretary of the Navy; Alexander H. H. Stuart, of Va., Secretary of the Interior; Nathan K. Hall, of New York, Postmaster-General; and John J. Crittenden, of Ky., Attorney-General.

Although a state of comparative peace on the subject of Slavery succeeded the excitement which had been produced by the "measures of 1850," certain events connected with and resulting from these measures are deserving of notice. During their pendency in Congress, a material change on the question of Slavery was manifested by some distinguished Whigs. One of these gentlemen was Mr. Webster. No man had been more fully committed against the extension of Slavery than he. He had on this ground opposed the annexation of Texas. In 1847, he made a speech at a Whig State Convention at Springfield, Mass., in which he said of the Wilmot Proviso :

"This is certainly a just sentiment, but it is not a sentiment to found any new party upon. It is not a sentiment on which Massachusetts Whigs differ. There is not a man in this hall who holds to it more firmly than I do, nor one who adheres to it more than another.

"I feel some interest in this matter, Sir. Did not I commit myself in 1838 to the whole doctrine, fully, entirely? And I must be permitted to say, that I can not quite consent that more recent discoverers should take out a patent. I deny the priority of their invention. Allow me to say, Sir, it is not their thunder. * * * We are to use the first, and last, and every occasion which offers, to oppose the extension of the Slave Power."

When, afterwards, legislation became necessary to establish Governments for California and New Mexico, Mr. Webster was *not* in favor of "using this occasion" to apply the Proviso, to which, in 1847, he held so "firmly." He would leave it to the "physical geography of the country"—to a law "superior to the Proviso—the law of nature"—to "exclude African Slavery there. It needed not the application of a proviso. If the question were now before the Senate, he would not vote to add a prohibition—to reäffirm an ordinance of nature, nor reënact the will of God." Mr. Webster also spoke of "Southern grievances"—of the obligations of the North in regard to the returning of fugitive slaves. Northern Legislatures had displeased the South by passing resolutions on the subject of Slavery in the District of Columbia, and sometimes even in regard to its abolition in the States. He denounced Abolition Societies for interfering with the South. Mr. W., however, made allusion also to the grievances of the North. The time had been when, in defending the North, he did not think himself called on to make an offset by bringing in the groundless complaints of the South.

Mr. Fillmore, too, changed his position on this question. He had, in Congress and out of Congress, long occupied high Anti-Slavery ground. But for this fact, it is doubtful whether the Whig candidates would have received so heavy majorities in 1848. Many Anti-Slavery Whigs, notwithstanding their having pledged themselves to support no man for President who was not known to be in favor of the Wilmot Proviso, voted for the party ticket, alleging as a reason, that a thorough Anti-Slavery man was the candidate for Vice-President. These men subsequently condemned the course pursued by their political favorite. He was severely censured for having approved the new Fugitive Slave law with all its repulsive features. They regarded the old law as sufficiently stringent to answer the demands of the Constitution in relation to the reclamation of fugitive slaves. But he had in other respects truckled to the South. He had given the weight of his influence in favor of the whole series of pro-slavery measures enacted by Congress in 1850.

President Taylor had not been long in office before he found himself in the midst of an opposition, which, though not as yet open and avowed, threatened to embarass his administration. Mr. Clay and Mr. Webster had long aspired to the Presidency ; and the success of Gen. Taylor at the last nominating Convention, had probably extinguished all hopes of their ever reaching the Presidential chair, to which, it is conceded, few American statesmen had stronger claims. It is not very strange that these gentlemen and their particular friends did not render a very cordial support to the administration. Mr. Webster had, before the election, declared the nomination of Gen. Taylor to be "a nomination not fit to be made."

President Taylor, however, disappointed, in some measure, the Anti-Slavery Whigs who refused to support him on account of his supposed friendship for Slavery. It was soon ascertained that he was determined the influence of his administration should not be given to the Slave Power. As has been intimated, he desired to avoid the agitation of the subject of Slavery, which would probably be produced by efforts to prohibit it in California and New Mexico ; and, with this view, he favored their admission as States whenever the people should apply for admission, without requiring them to pass through the Territorial condition. Slavery having been abolished by Mexico before the Territory was ceded to the United States, it was presumed the States would come in as Free States. His policy not being sufficiently Southern to please the slaveholders, he met with opposition from both sections of the Union.

It is well known that, among those who first suggested the nomination of Gen. Taylor, was Mr. Seward. It is believed by some that the idea originated with him and his friend, Mr. Weed. Mr. Seward and Gen. Taylor enjoyed in a high degree each other's confidence. The former entered the Senate cotemporaneously with the accession of the latter to the Presidency; and it is not improbable that he may have had some influence in shaping the policy of President Taylor on this question. The support which the President received from the Senator, gave occasion to the representatives of the Slave Power to excite the jealousy of Mr. Webster, Mr. Clay, and Mr. Fillmore and their friends toward Mr. Seward, who was considered, especially by the Vice-President, as a political rival.

The reader probably begins to see the cause of the somerset performed by Mr. Fillmore on the Slavery question. In 1844, these two distinguished New Yorkers stood upon the same political platform, and addressed the same audiences from the same stands. The Whig State Convention of that year, which nominated Mr. Fillmore for Governor; the Convention of 1847, which nominated him for Controller; and the Conventions of 1848, 1849, and 1850, all adopted resolutions indorsing the Wilmot Proviso. In the series of resolutions adopted in 1850, was one expressing thanks to William H. Seward for the ability and fidelity with which he had sustained, in the United States Senate, the principles of public policy so long cherished by the Whigs of the Empire State, expressed in State and County Conventions, as well as in the votes and instructions of the Legislature. To this resolution, the special friends of Mr. Fillmore objected, declaring, if it should pass, the Whig party of New York would be immediately broken up; and that where the dissenters would go would be determined thereafter. The resolution was adopted. The leaders of the minority, among whom was the Chairman of the Convention, Mr. Granger, then retired, followed by most of those who had voted for the obnoxious resolution, to a Hotel, where they resolved to support Mr. Fillmore, and abjured allegiance to the party supporting Mr. Seward. They resolved also to meet with their friends from other parts of the State at Utica in September. A Convention was accordingly held, and a new party organized, called "Silver Gray," having, it was said, been thus named by its presiding officer, Mr. Granger, who had been again elected Chairman.

Additional evidence of the apostacy of Mr. Fillmore is seen in the removal of the Cabinet officers appointed by Gen. Taylor; in effecting the displacement of the editor of the administration paper at Washington by one more pro-slavery; in the withdrawal of nominations to the Senate made by his predecessor and not yet acted upon, and the nomination, in their place, of his own particular friends; and in an alleged bargain, express or implied, with Southern Democratic Senators while he was Vice-President—it being understood that, in case of a *tie* in the Senate on the "Omnibus bill," he was to save the bill by his casting vote, in consideration of which Southern Senators were to vote against the confirmation of certain nominations made by President Taylor at the suggestion, as was supposed, of Mr. Seward. This allegation was made by Senator Foote, of Mississippi, in a public speech, and, as is believed, has not been contradicted.

But for the death of President Taylor, he would probably very soon have been openly assailed by a matured and powerful opposition, embracing many of the old Whig leaders, with the probable result, if not the design, of bringing him into subjection to the Slave Power. His administration had already been declared to be infected with "Sewardism," which was known to be less attractive to Southern Whigs generally than that "Conservatism" to which Mr. Fillmore had just become a convert. The precise object of this Whig opposition to the administration, further than to effect its overthrow, can not be stated with certainty. It was believed by many that it was intended to form a new party more popular at the South than the old Whig party with its strong Anti-Slavery element in the North, and of which new party Mr. Fillmore was to be the head. Others supposed that an alliance with the Democratic party was contemplated. That such a union was designed to take place at some future time appears somewhat probable from the subsequent course of these Whigs. A large portion, if not a majority of them, have since slidden through the avenue of Know-Nothingism into the ranks of the slaveholders, with whom they have, in the last two presidential campaigns, fought valiantly against principles and measures which they had as zealously supported.

But whatever may have been the *ulterior* design of Mr. Fillmore and his friends, the immediate object was evidently a nomination in 1852. And his reward for the abandonment of a noble and long cherished principle, consists in his having been beaten in Convention by Gen. Scott, and thus saved the mortification of a defeat at the polls by such a man as Franklin Pierce; and in the satisfaction of having received the electoral vote of one State, and that a Slave State, in 1856!

The National Democratic Convention met at Baltimore, on the 1st of June, 1852. On the first ballot, Gen. Cass received 117 votes; James Buchanan, 93; Stephen A. Douglas, 20; Wm L. Marcy, 27. Ballotings were continued on two subsequent days, when, on the 49th ballot, Franklin Pierce, of N. H., received the unanimous vote of the Convention. Wm. R. King, of Alabama, was nominated for Vice-President.

The Whig Convention met at the same place on the 16th of June, and, as the other Convention had been, was in session five days. A platform of principles was adopted, 227 to 60, before any attempt at nomination had been made. Mr. Fillmore received on the first ballot, 132 votes; Gen. Scott, 131; Mr. Webster, 29. Balloting was resumed the next day with the 7th ballot; and on the 53d, the result was, for Scott, 159; Fillmore, 112; Webster, 21. Wm. A. Graham, of N. C., was nominated for Vice-President. Scott and Graham were both declared unanimously nominated.

The platforms adopted by the two Conventions were less dissimilar than usual; on the question of Slavery, they were substantially the same. The Democrats resolved to "resist all attempts at renewing, in Congress or out of it, the agitation of the Slavery question, under whatever shape or color the attempt may be made." The Whigs declared, "That the series of acts of the 31st Congress—the act known as the Fugitive Slave Law included—are received and acquiesced in by the Whig party of the United States; . . . and we deprecate all further agitation of the question thus settled, as dangerous to our peace; and will discountenance all efforts to continue or renew such agitation whenever, wherever, and however the attempt may be made; and we will maintain this system as essential to the nationality of the Whig party of the Union."

The adoption of such a platform was the death blow to the Whig party—it was political suicide. The Northern portion of it had been distinguished from their opponents for their advocacy of free speech, free soil, and free labor; and in former National Conventions they had gone no farther than to be silent on the subject of Slavery, as a matter of necessity; but this humiliating bid against the Democrats for Southern votes was more than some Northern Whigs could indorse. Still the contest was spirited, and exhibited a fair vote for their electoral ticket. The abolition vote, however, for Mr. Hale, was more than double that given for Mr. Birney in 1844. Gen. Scott received the electoral votes of Vermont, Massachusetts, Kentucky, and Tennessee, in all 42. Gen. Pierce received the votes of all the other States, 254.

CHAPTER VIII.

Administration of Franklin Pierce.

FRANKLIN PIERCE was inaugurated the 4th of March, 1853. He alluded in his Address to the subject "which had recently agitated the nation." Slavery was recognized by the Constitution; the States where it existed were entitled to efficient remedies to enforce the constitutional provisions; the "compromise measures of 1850" were constitutional, and must be carried into effect; and he said: "I fervently hope that the question is at rest, and that no sectional, or ambitious, or fanatical excitement may again threaten the durability of our institutions, or obscure the light of our prosperity."

The 33d Congress began its 1st session December 5th, 1853. The President, in his Message, again alluded to the late excitement, and spoke of the restoration of "repose and security to the public mind throughout the Confederacy;" and said: "That this repose is to suffer no shock during my official term, if I have power to avert it, those who placed me here may be assured."

On the first day of the session, the day before the delivery of the Message, Senator Dodge, of Iowa, gave notice of a bill to organize the Territory of Nebraska. It was referred to the Committee on Territories, and on the 15th was reported by Mr. Douglas with amendments. Doubts having been expressed whether the amendments repealed the Missouri Compromise, he made a special report on the 4th of January, 1854, so amending the bill as to assert that the said Compromise "was superseded by the principles of the legislation of 1850, commonly called the compromise measures," and to declare the Missouri restriction "inoperative and void."

This declaration was afterwards, on his own motion, struck out, and the following inserted :

"Which, (the Missouri Compromise,) being inconsistent with the principle of non-intervention by Congress with Slavery in the States and Territories, as recognized by the legislation of 1850, (commonly called the Compromise Measures,) is hereby declared inoperative and void ; it being the true intent and meaning of this act, not to legislate Slavery into any Territory or State, nor to exclude it therefrom, but *to leave the people thereof perfectly free to form and regulate their domestic institutions in their own way*, subject only to the Constitution of the United States."

It is not easy to perceive how any one could sincerely maintain that the Missouri Compromise was, or *could* have been, repealed by the acts of 1850. It has been observed already, that no intimation to that effect had been made during the debates on them. Mr. Chase, in a speech on his motion to strike out the assertion for which the above was afterward substituted on Mr. Douglas' own motion, denied the truth of the statement. He said that, during the long discussion of these measures in 1850, it was never suggested that they were to supersede the Missouri prohibition. At the last session, (1852–1853,) a Nebraska bill passed the House, came to the Senate, and was reported on by Mr. Douglas, who made a speech in its favor ; and in all not a word was said about a repeal by supersedure. The Senator from Missouri, (Mr. Atchison,) had also spoken upon the bill, and had distinctly declared, that *the Missouri prohibition was not and could not be repealed.* The same bill was introduced by the Senator from Iowa, at the commencement of the present session. Nor had he, nor any other man here, so far as could be judged from any discussion, or statement, or remark, even then received the notion that the Missouri prohibition had been superseded. Nor had Mr. Douglas' own report, made only thirty days ago, (Jan. 4th,) expressed such opinion. Besides all these, said Mr. Chase, the Committee on Territories themselves declared, that it was not wise, nor prudent, nor right to renew the old controversy, and to rouse agitation ; but they *would abstain from any recommendation of a repeal of the prohibition.*

Now let the candid reader, from these facts, judge of the

honesty of a Senator, who had the hardihood to insert in his bill and to advocate the declaration, that the Missouri restriction had been repealed. And the reader is requested particularly to note the fact above stated, that the Committee would not recommend such repeal, *as the recommendation would "rouse agitation."* And yet, from that day to this, has the Democratic party, from its leaders down to their humblest followers, denounced their opponents as the authors of the agitation! Must not the man be either very dishonest or grossly ignorant, who charges the agitation upon those who have seen fit to resist the long train of flagrant outrages which were for years perpetrated both by our higher "public functionaries" and the "border ruffians," in their attempts to force Slavery into Kansas?

The bill of Mr. Douglas passed the Senate, 37 to 14.

A bill had also been reported in the House, on the same subject, for which the bill of Mr. Douglas was substituted, which passed, 113 to 100. Yeas from the Free States, 44, all Democrats; from the Slave States 69, of whom 12 were Whigs. Nays from Free States, 91, all Whigs, except two or three, who were called Abolitionists; from Slave States, 9—7 Whigs, 2 Democrats. Absent, and not voting, 21.

The Slave Power having now, by the aid of the Democratic party in Congress, headed by a leading Free State Senator, broken down the barrier which had for thirty-four years restricted Slavery below the Compromise line established in 1820, determined to appropriate the Territory to its own use. Meetings were held in various places, some of them attended by leading citizens of Missouri, to devise measures to prevent "abolitionists," (as they termed all the opponents of the extension of Slavery,) from settling in the Territory.

At one of these meetings, the two following resolutions—similar to those passed at other meetings—were adopted:

"That we will afford protection to no abolitionist as a settler in this Territory.

"That we recognize the institution of Slavery as already existing in this Territory, and advise slaveholders to introduce their property as early as possible."

Before any election had been held, a secret society was

formed *in Missouri*, known by different names, as "Social Band," "Blue Lodge," "Sons of the South," whose members were bound together by oaths, and had passwords, signs and grips, by which they were known to each other. They avowed their purpose to be to extend Slavery into Kansas, by organizing and sending men thither to vote at elections. And at the election in November following, (1854,) for electing a Delegate to Congress, as the Congressional Investigating Committee afterwards reported—*more than two-thirds of the votes were cast by non-residents.* Repeatedly did companies of men go from Missouri into the Territory to control the elections. With arms they forced their way to the ballot-box; threatened judges of elections if they did not instantly resign; and thus dispersed the judges, and elected others in their stead. And because the Governor set aside the elections in some of the districts, and ordered new ones, he incurred the displeasure of these lawless desperadoes, who would not attend the elections, at which Free State men were elected.

And what reason was offered for those unlawful acts? Men from Free States, many of them from New England, under the auspices of Emigrant Aid Societies, were settling in the Territories, with the view, as the "ruffians" asserted, *to make Kansas a Free State.* For *such* a reason, these outrages have been either palliated or fully justified by the greater portion of the Democratic party, *including the two Presidents* under whose administration the struggle for Freedom took place!

It is not strange that a Legislature thus elected should enact laws that would cause a savage to blush. Any person writing, printing, or circulating anything that might endanger the rights of the slaveholder, by inducing his slaves to escape, or in any way assisting in such writing, publishing, &c., was made liable to imprisonment not less than five years. For a free person to assert that persons had no right to hold slaves in the Territory, he incurred a penalty of imprisonment at hard labor for two years! By whom were these inhuman acts condemned? Not by the mass of the Democratic party, now so alarmed at what they consider violations of personal liberty and freedom of speech!

A Convention was called, and Delegates chosen by the Free State men, who met at Topeka in October, and formed a State Constitution, which was adopted by the people in December, by a vote of 1,731 to 46 ; the Pro-Slavery party taking no part in the election. And when the Free State Legislature met, the members were dispersed by an armed force.

Congress met in December, 1855. What notice ought the President, in his Message, to have taken of the Kansas outrages ? He should have unequivocally condemned them, and have recommended provision to be made for the protection of the settlers in the enjoyment of their rights, every candid man will readily answer. But instead of this, he charged the Free States with a disregard of their constitutional obligations, by interfering with the domestic institutions of the Slave States, and vindicated the latter from the charge of aggression upon the rights and interests of the former. He also charged the Governor with a want of vigilance, which he assigned as one of the causes for which he had removed him. He had not done enough to prevent or counteract the tendencies to illegality ; notwithstanding the fact that the Governor *had* endeavored to correct these illegalities, by ordering new elections ; and this is the *true* reason why he was regarded as not the right man for the place. This is sufficiently evident from the fact, that every Governor appointed by President Pierce—as also by Buchanan—during the Kansas struggle, whenever he undertook to check *ruffianism*, or to secure fair play to the Free State party, *was dismissed or compelled to resign !*

In the Senate, the subject was referred to the Committee on Territories, whose Chairman, (Mr. Douglas,) reported, *it was no part of the duty of the Committee to examine and review the laws of the Kansas Legislature.* But it seemed rather to be their duty to indorse the Message of the President, which charged the blame upon those who endeavored to establish free institutions in the Territory, and " to prevent the free and natural action of its inhabitants in its internal organization, and thus to anticipate or to force the determination of that question (Slavery) in this inchoate State." And as did the President, so did Mr. Douglas, censure the

Aid Societies for designing to force a Free State into the Union. The Committee uttered not a word of condemnation against the meetings held in the Territory immediately after the passage of the Kansas bill, to preconcert measures to keep Anti-Slavery men out of the State. Border Ruffianism met no rebuke, but was rather justified. The report stated, in substance, that the Missourians were alarmed by the rapid filling up of Kansas by the opponents of Slavery; that this might endanger the institution in that State; and that its citizens might properly resist the formation of an Anti-Slavery State in their neighborhood. *Such* a report was made by men who were among the acknowledged leaders of a party claiming to be Democratic; and that report has received the approval of the party.

In the House a bill was reported by Mr. Grow, of Pa., for the admission of Kansas under the Topeka Constitution as a Free State. This bill finally passed the House, 99 to 97. Mr. Dunn, of Indiana, afterward succeeded in substituting for this bill one of his own, repealing that clause of the Kansas-Nebraska act which declares the Missouri restriction inoperative and void; and allowing the owners of slaves time until the 1st of January, 1858, to remove them from the State. If not permanently removed before that time, the slaves were to be free. This bill passed the House, 88 to 74.

The repeal of the Missouri Compromise by the slaveholders and their Northern allies, very naturally led to the formation of a new party. This aggressive act of the Slave Power was soon followed by organizations in some of the States, composed of the friends of freedom, irrespective of former party connections, to resist the further intrusion of Slavery upon free territory. And in February, 1856, a National Convention was held at Pittsburg to form a national party. Resolutions were adopted containing substantially the principles which subsequently constituted the basis of the Republican party.

The time having arrived for the nomination of a successor to Mr. Pierce, the Democratic National Convention met at Cincinnati on the 2d day of June, 1856. Mr. Buchanan had been a prominent candidate in the Convention of 1852, having received, of the four principle candidates, Cass,

Douglas, Marcy, and himself, on the first 19 ballots, next to Gen. Cass, the highest number of votes. Mr. Pierce received the nomination only because the Convention was unable to agree upon any other candidate.

Mr. Buchanan had bowed as humbly before the Slave Power for twenty years as any Northern man had ever done. And although he had failed in 1852, he did not relinquish the hope of yet attaining the coveted honor of a nomination for the Presidency. He was appointed by Mr. Pierce, as Minister to Great Britain. Before his departure for England, he made one more low *conge* to his Southern master, as if to assure him of his continued loyalty during his absence. Whether *remembered* or not, while abroad, it is certain that *he* did *not forget* his master. A conference was held at Ostend, by himself and our Ministers to France and Spain, Mason and Soule, at which the project was discussed, of acquiring Cuba for annexation to the United States, the price named for the purchase being 150 or 200 millions of dollars. These three gentlemen accordingly issued a Manifesto, in which they said: "After we shall have offered Spain a price for Cuba far beyond its present value, and this shall have been refused, it will then be time to consider the question: Does Cuba, in the possession of Spain, seriously endanger our internal peace, and the existence of our cherished Union? Should this question be answered in the affirmative, then, by every law, human and divine, *we shall be justified in wresting it from Spain, if we have the power.*" Stronger evidence it was hardly possible to give of devotion to Southern interests than had been repeatedly given by him.

Mr. Buchanan resigned his mission in season to return and attend to the great object of his political aspirations. He was successful. On the first ballot, the vote was, for Buchanan, 135; for Pierce, 122; for Douglas, 33; for Cass, 5. After a few ballots, the friends of Pierce gradually transferred their votes to Douglas. On the 16th ballot, Buchanan received 168 votes; Douglas 121; Cass 6. On the next ballot, all the votes, 296, were for Buchanan.

Mr. Pierce had served the slaveholders most faithfully. Whether he was surpassed in his fidelity to their interests by his successor, let the history of the next administration decide.

As a Platform, the Convention adopted the leading principles declared by former Conventions, with numerous additional resolutions, directed against the American party, "which bases its exclusive organization upon religious opinions and accidental birth-place;" and against the Republican party, as "sectional," and "seeking to embroil the States and incite to treason and armed resistance in the Territories." They also adopted, as a principle, "non-interference by Congress with Slavery in the Territories or in the District of Columbia; approved the "Monroe Doctrine;" "sympathized with the efforts of the people of Central America, to regulate that portion of the continent which covers the passage across the inter-oceanic isthmus;" meaning, it is presumed, the attempt of the fillibusterer, Walker, to revolutionize that country; and "expect of the next administration every proper effort to insure our ascendancy in the Gulf of Mexico;" in plain language, to acquire Cuba as plunder from Spain.

The Republican National Convention was held in Philadelphia on the 17th of June. Messrs. Seward, Fremont, Banks, and Judge M'Lean, were candidates. Mr. Seward, as was announced before the balloting commenced, had requested the withdrawal of his name. Col. Fremont was, after several ballots, declared unanimously nominated.

The resolutions adopted as the Republican Platform, "deny the authority of Congress, or of a Territorial Legislature, to give legal existence to Slavery in any Territory;" claim for Congress "sovereign power over the Territories for their government;" charge Pierce's administration with sanctioning violations of the constitutional rights of the people of Kansas, enumerating many of the outrages, murders, &c.; condemned the Ostend Circular as unworthy of American diplomacy, embodying "the highwayman's plea, 'might makes right;'" declare a Railroad to the Pacific to be imperatively demanded; and "appropriations by Congress for the improvement of rivers and harbors of a national character, required for the accommodation and security of existing commerce, to be authorized by the Constitution."

Mr. Buchanan received the electoral votes of all the Slave States, except Maryland, and of New Jersey, Pennsylvania, Indiana, Illinois, and California; in all, 174 votes. Mr. Fillmore, candidate of the American party, received the votes ot the electors of Maryland, 8. Col. John C. Fremont received the votes of all the Free States, except the five before mentioned, 114.

The last session of Congress under Mr. Pierce, met the 1st of December, 1856. The President in noticing the election just past, says, "the people have asserted the constitutional equality of all the States," and "have condemned the idea of organizing more geographical parties." He censured those who "seek to prevent the spread of Slavery into the present or future States of the Union;" says, "they endeavor to prepare the people of the United States for civil war;" that "violent attack from the North" begets "a spirit of angry defiance at the South." He mentions as among "the long series of acts of indirect aggression" upon the South, the "objecting to the admission of Missouri" as a Slave State, and the prohibiting of Slavery in Territories; and he attributes the disturbances in Kansas to the "unjust interference on the part of persons not inhabitants of the Territory." Of course he does not mean by these officious "persons" the Missourians who went thither with the avowed purpose of "interfering" with the elections! Again there is no utterance of condemnation against the violence and the frauds committed by the Missouri intruders or the Pro-Slavery residents, who coöperated with them in their atrocities.

Who can contemplate such servility to the Slave Power as is manifested in the Messages and acts of this President, without disgust and indignation? But he has already received a large installment of deserved retribution. Mr. Pierce and his successor can hardly fail to see, that, by their making common cause with the South against the advocates of freedom in the North, not merely conniving at, but positively aiding in carrying out their flagitious purpose of subjecting Free Territory to the dominion of Slavery, they have encouraged the slaveholders in their insolent demands upon the North for further concessions, the denial of which was made the occasion of the Rebellion, for which they—these Northern Democratic leaders—are to be held in a great measure responsible.

Again Congress failed to pass a law for the benefit of Kansas. Mr. Grow, of Pa., reported to the House a bill, declaring the acts of the Territorial Legislature to be a violation of the organic act, and therefore of no effect, and requiring the Governor to order an election for choosing members of a new Legislature, and providing against unlawful and fraudulent voting. This bill passed the House, 98 to 79. The Yeas, 92 Republicans and 6 Fillmore men, were all from Free States. Of the Nays, 65 were from Slave States, and 14 from Free States; 20 Fillmore Americans, and 59 Democrats.

In the Senate, the bill was laid on the table, 30 to 20. Yeas, from Slave States, 22; from Free States, 8. Nays, from Free States, 18; from Slave States, 2.

Notwithstanding these failures to provide relief for Kansas, its condition had been improved under the administration of Gov. John W. Geary, who had been appointed in July, 1856. It being understood that he intended to side with neither party, the Pro-Slavery leaders published an address, in which they complained that *they had not found in him such a successor as they had asked;* and they feared that "he would prove no more efficient than his predecessors," (Reeder and Shannon.) They therefore hastened to gather an army from Missouri and other Slave States before the arrival of the Governor. Acting-Governor Woodson, by proclamation, declared the Territory in a state of rebellion and insurrection, and called upon the militia and other citizens to aid in putting down and punishing the insurrectionists.

Gov. Geary arrived. He ordered a restoration of property; declared publicly his intentions to do justice to all classes; and advised forbearance on the part of the Free State men, as they could ask the next Legislature to revise the laws. He endeavored also to increase the energy of the judges, whose inefficiency had become notorious.

In January, 1857, the Free State Legislature met at Topeka; but a large portion of its members were arrested by a deputy marshal, and the session was broken up. The Territorial Legislature met the next week at Lecompton; and as the Free State men had taken no part in the election, both bodies were entirely Pro-Slavery. Gov. Geary recommended the repeal of some objectionable acts; but his recommendation was disregarded. An act was passed to provide for electing a Convention to frame a Constitution; the election to be held in June, and the Delegates to meet at Lecompton in September. None were to be allowed to vote who were not in the Territory on or before the 15th of March. This was designed to shut out the votes of the Free State men, who had fled from their homes during the disturbances of the past year, and would be unable to return before that day. Another objection was the Constitution was not to be submitted to the people for their sanction or rejection. The Governor had informed certain members, before its passage, that if this objection should be removed, he would waive other objections, and approve the bill. They replied, that this would defeat the object of the act, which was to secure Kansas to the South as a Slave State. The bill was passed, vetoed, and again passed, and became a law.

Another act was passed for the election of a new Legislature, in October, all persons not in the Territory by the 15th of March, being again excluded.

Gov. Geary, thinking that he was not duly sustained by the Government, resigned his office at the close of Mr. Pierce's administration.

CHAPTER IX.

Administration of James Buchanan.

JAMES BUCHANAN commenced his Presidential term on the 4th of March, 1857.

We come now to a new Chapter in the history of Pro-Slavery Democracy. A new plank is inserted in the Democratic Platform. The time-honored doctrine held and practiced by the political Fathers, that Congress had power over Slavery in the Territories, and that, being against natural right, it could exist only by special, positive enactment, was superseded, in 1848, by a new article in the Democratic creed, introduced by Gen. Cass, known by the now familiar name of "popular," or "squatter sovereignty;" which places the power exclusively in the hands of the people of the Territories. This principle was sought to be carried into effect by Mr. Douglas in his Kansas-Nebraska bill, which proposed "to leave the people free to form and regulate their domestic institutions in their own way."

President Buchanan, in his Inaugural Address, announced, as about to appear, still another improvement in the Pro-Slavery Platform. Slavery in the Territories had been found to be a judicial question, belonging to the Supreme Court of the United States, before whom it was now pending, and would be speedily and finally settled. He did not, however, inform the public what the decision was to be, although he probably knew. He gave it as his opinion that, under the Kansas-Nebraska act, the proper time for the people of a Territory to determine the question would be when the number of residents in the Territory should justify the formation of a Constitution with a view to admission as a State. The non-intervention doctrine of Cass and Douglas had been understood to concede to *the people, represented in their Legislature, full power over Slavery.* But this doctrine was by the Inaugural scattered to the winds. Nobody ever doubted the right of the people to *exclude* Slavery on adopting a Constitution. But if this is THE way to do it, it must be out of the power of the Territorial Legislature.

Mr. Buchanan, however, was wrong in saying that *this* question was now pending in the Supreme Court; that is, *judicially*. The question "legitimately" before the Court was one which involved the right of Dred Scott and his family to freedom. The Court, (according to previous understanding, as some believe,) two days after the Inauguration pronounced judgment, reversing the judgment of the Circuit Court of St. Louis County, and directed the dismissal of the suit for want of jurisdiction. Scott's master had taken him into Illinois and Minnesota, and remained with him in free territory for several years. It had been held, until now, that a Slave taken by his master into a free State, became free. Some readers may desire to know upon what ground Chief Justice Taney based his new decision. It was, that free negroes, whose ancestors were slaves, *could never become citizens*. The Constitution did not recognize them as citizens. He said: "They had for more than a century been regarded as beings of an inferior order, and altogether unfit to associate with the white race, either in moral or political relations; and so far inferior, that *they had no rights which the white man was bound to respect; and the negro might justly and lawfully be reduced to Slavery for his benefit.*" The reader may ask: What relation had this decision to the question of power over Slavery in the Territories? None at all. The "decision" to which the President probably alluded, was a *volunteer opinion* of the Judges, wholly extra-judicial. The doctrine of "popular sovereignty," it was found, was not likely to secure the establishment of Slavery in Kansas; and it might hereafter prove equally ineffectual in other territory. The *people* could not be trusted to settle and regulate "their own institutions." Slaveholders wanted some improvement in the Democratic creed which would authorize them to carry their slaves into all territory "without let or hindrance." Their wish was gratified. The Supreme Court Judges gave it as their opinion, that the Missouri Compromise was unconstitutional; that Congress had no power over Slavery in the Territories; and that slaveholders have the right to take their slaves into any territory as any other property. A few ultra Southern statesmen had been bold enough to assert this doctrine; but it remained for the Judges of the highest judicial tribunal of the Union to come to their help by giving them the benefit of the weight of their opinion. *Judicially* it decides nothing, as there was no case of this kind before them as a Court for decision. *Politically*, it had the effect of encouraging the Pro-Slavery party in their attempts to extend Slavery, as they were assured that the question of their right to hold slaves in the Territories, if such question should ever be tried, would be decided in their favor.

The minority Justices maintained the old doctrine established by the Courts, and held by eminent statesmen, North and South, that "all Slavery has its origin in power, and is against right;" that it requires, as essential to its existence, municipal regulations, which the Constitution has neither made nor provided for. In eight distinct instances, beginning with the first Congress, has Congress excluded Slavery from territory of the United States; and in six distinct instances in which Congress organized governments for territories, has Slavery been recognized and continued, beginning also with the first Congress, and coming down to the year 1822. These acts were severally signed by seven Presidents of the United States, beginning with Gen. Washington, and coming down as far as John Quincy Adams; thus including all who were in public life when the Constitution was adopted. Hence they inferred that, by taking the plaintiff into a State where Slavery was prohibited, he became free.

Mr. Buchanan appointed Robert J. Walker, of Miss., Governor of Kansas, to succeed J. W. Geary; and Frederick P. Stanton, of Tenn., was appointed Secretary. Mr. Stanton, who arrived first in Kansas, as well as Gov. Walker after his arrival, advised the Free State men to take a part in the election of Delegates to the Constitutional Convention, assuring them that there should be a fair election. But they declined. Many, however, were induced to vote at the October Territorial election. Gov. Walker admitted the unfairness of the apportionment, by which some Free State Counties were not allowed a Representative in either branch of the Legislature ; but he promised to protect the polls against illegal voters. The result was, that the Free State Delegate to Congress, nine of the thirteen Councilmen, and twenty-seven of the thirty-nine Representatives, were elected by the Free State party !

The Constitution framed at Lecompton, affirmed the right of slave-owners to hold their slaves in the Territory as other property, and prohibited laws for the emancipating slaves without the consent of their owners, or without payment being made for them. It also prohibited laws to prevent emigrants to the State from bringing with them their slaves.

Prominent among the efforts of the Pro-Slavery party to force Slavery upon the people of Kansas, was the "Lecompton swindle," as it was familiarly termed. The people were not allowed to vote for or against the Constitution. Only the Slavery sections were submitted, and these in such a manner that every person voting must vote *for* the Constitution. The ballots were to be indorsed, "Constitution *with* Slavery," or "Constitution with *no* Slavery." So obnoxious were some of its provisions, that many Democrats were opposed to it, among whom was Mr. Douglas himself, who desired that the people should have a fair opportunity of voting on the question of its adoption. Every voter, if challenged, must take an oath to support the Constitution, if adopted. It was to be in force after its ratification by the people, *before it could receive the sanction of Congress*, and required an election, as soon as possible, for State officers, members of the Legislature, and a Delegate to Congress; the object of which was, *to supersede the Republiean incumbents recently elected.* It also prevented the present Anti-Slavery Legislature from repealing the laws of the old Territorial Legislature. And it prohibited any amendment previous to 1864, until which time Slavery might not be abolished.

Gov. Walker having, in pursuance of instructions from Mr. Buchanan, pledged his efforts to procure its submission to the popular vote, and having failed, the Free State party determined to put their own government into operation, at all events : and the peace of the Territory was seriously threatened. Gov. Walker had gone to Washington to confer with the President upon the subject ; but had found, on his arrival, that Mr. Buchanan had already given the Lecompton scheme his approval ! Before, however, this fact could be communicated to Kansas, Secretary Stanton, (then Acting-Governor,) had (December 3d,) called the new Legislature to meet on the 7th, to provide for a direct vote upon the Constitution on the 21st. The President, on being informed of this act, removed Mr. Stanton, and appointed J. W. Denver in his stead.

The President had said in his instructions to Gov. Walker, that "unless the Convention should submit the Constitution to the vote of all the actual settlers of Kansas, and the election should be fairly conducted, the Constitution ought to be, and, he believed, would be rejected by Congress." But Gov. Walker, finding himself not sustained by the President, resigned his office rather than return to Kansas, and force the President to remove him for disobedience to his instructions. In his letter of resignation, addressed to the State Department, he gave a statement of the unfair apportionment of the Delegates, the omission of many counties from the registry, and the taking of the census in less than one-half of them, &c., &c.

The Free State men not voting, the result was, "For the Lecompton Constitution *with* Slavery," 6,143 ; "For the Lecompton Constitution *without* Slavery," 569. Many votes were alleged to have been illegal. The Territorial Legislature convened by Gov. Stanton, ordered an election two weeks later, (Jan. 4th, 1858,) at which the vote was, "*For* the Constitution *with* Slavery," 138 ; "*For* the Constitution *without* Slavery," 24 ; "*Against* the Constitution," 10,226 !

The election of State officers, &c., provided for by the Constitution, was held on the 4th of January. Only a portion of the Free State party voted. Calhoun, President of the Convention, with men of his own selection, canvassed the election returns, and reported the election of the entire State ticket by an average majority of about 500, and two-thirds of the Legislature. One or more men were arrested for getting up fraudulent returns ; and Calhoun, having refused to appear as witness, and having been arrested on a writ of attachment, escaped to Washington. So gross were the frauds represented to be on the authority of both Mr.

Stanton and Gov. Denver, that certificates of election were granted to Free State candidates.

On the 2d of February, 1858, President Buchanan transmitted a copy of the Lecompton Constitution to Congress. In his accompanying Message, he said a part of the people of Kansas were "in a state of rebellion," and had "done all they could to overthrow the Government established by Congress." And in the face of all the facts, and especially of that most unfair mode of presenting the question of Slavery, which denied the people the privilege of voting against the Constitution at all, he said the election of the 21st of December, had "afforded them opportunities, if in the majority, of making Kansas a Free State according to their own professed desire." And he pronounced the whole movement legal and fair! He said, too, that it had been adjudged by our highest judicial tribunal, that Slavery exists in Kansas by virtue of the Constitution of the United States; and "Kansas is therefore, at this moment, as much a Slave State as Georgia or South Carolina."

The Senate Committee on Territories reported a bill for the admission of Kansas. Mr. Douglas dissented, and made a separate report. He said there was no evidence that the Constitution was the act and deed of the people of Kansas. The only lawful election was that held on the 4th of January, which had rejected it.

Mr. Douglas opposed the admission of Kansas under the Lecompton Constitution, not because it authorized Slavery; for he said he did not care whether it was voted *down* or voted *up;* but because the administration was opposed to his favorite doctrine of popular sovereignty, upon which the administration had come into power.

To overcome the opposition of the people of Kansas to the Lecompton Constitution, Congress made to them a proposition in the nature of a *bribe.* The proposition was, to admit Kansas with her Pro-Slavery Constitution, and to grant to the State large quantities of land for the support of schools and a university, for public buildings, &c.; the salt springs, not exceeding twelve; and five per cent. of the proceeds of the sales of the public lands for making roads and internal improvements. These propositions were to be voted on at an election, each ballot to be indorsed,

"*For* proposition of Congress and admission," or "*Against* proposition of Congress and admission." And as an additional inducement to accept the proposition, the admission was to be immediate; but if the proposition should be rejected, admission was to be deferred until the population should be equal to the ratio of representation, which was then about 93,000, which number might not be reached for years. At the election, (Aug. 2, 1858,) there were, to *accept* the proposition, 1,788 votes; to *reject* it, 11,088.

The President, in his next Annual Message, (December, 1858,) again speaks of the Lecompton Constitution as unexceptionable in its general features, and as having provided for submitting the Slavery question to the people; and charged its opponents with preferring a continuance of Slavery to a surrender of their revolutionary organization. Having twice rejected the Constitution, they should have no authority to form another, until they should have a population equal to the ratio required for a Representative.

The vindictiveness of the President and his friends in Congress towards the people of Kansas, was further evinced by their treatment of the application from Oregon for admission. The population of this Territory was less than that of Kansas; yet this was not made an objection to its admission, while Kansas was to be punished by being kept out of the Union for an indefinite period.

Gov. Denver having resigned, Samuel Medary, of Ohio, was appointed as his successor, and entered upon his duties in December, 1858. The Territorial Legislature met in January, 1859. An act was passed repealing the obnoxious laws of the first Legislature, called the "bogus laws;" also an act for submitting to the people the question of a new Constitutional Convention at an election to be held on the 3d Monday in March; and a bill to abolish and prohibit Slavery, which, however, failed, having been passed at so late a day as to enable the Governor to defeat it, by refusing to sign and return it.

At the election in March, the majority in favor of a Convention was nearly 4,000. Of the Delegates chosen at the election in June, 35 were Republicans, 17 were Democrats. The Convention met at Wyandot on the 5th of July, and adjourned on the 27th, after adopting a Constitution by a vote of 34 to 13. All the Democrats present voted against it, and refused to sign it. It prohibited Slavery. In October, it was ratified by a majority of about 4,000. The Democrats professed to be opposed to making Kansas a Slave State, and to be in favor of Mr. Douglas' Territorial sovereignty doctrine. They desired the annexation to Kansas of that part of Nebraska south of the Platte ; the retaining of the gold region about Pike's Peak ; the exclusion of free negroes from the State, and the prohibition of bank issues ; in all of which they had been defeated.

The President, in his Annual Message, December, 1859, did not recommend the admission of Kansas with her new Constitution, as he had done the year before with a Slavery Constitution. But he again "cordially congratulates" Congress "upon the final settlement, by the Supreme Court, of the question of Slavery in the Territories ;" which gave to every citizen "the right to take his property of any kind, including slaves, into the common Territories, and to have it protected there under the Federal Constitution. Neither Congress nor a Territorial Legislature, nor any human power, has any authority to annul or impair this vested right." *Hereafter*, when a Territory *shall have a sufficient population* to form a State, they may exercise the right of Popular Sovereignty in forming a State Constitution preparatory to admission.

The House passed a bill for the admission of Kansas under the Wyandot Constitution, 134 to 73. In the Senate, Mr. Seward introduced a bill for this purpose, which, after considerable delay, was rejected, 27 to 32. Of the Yeas, 2 were Democrats ; Nays, all Democrats. So Kansas was left still in the condition of a Territory.

For some years past, efforts have been made to keep the Public Lands from going into the hands of monopolists and speculators. Millions of acres have been bought in large tracts on speculation ; and persons wishing to purchase lands in small quantities for actual occupation, have been compelled to pay exorbitant prices, or seek farms in less desirable localities. For the benefit of the poorer class of laboring men, preëmption acts have been passed. Attempts have also been made to procure the passage of a law, granting gratuitously, or for a merely nominal price, to every actual settler, a limited quantity of land as a Homestead. The selling of large tracts to speculators is deemed objectionable as leading to a landed aristocracy. But the division of land into small freeholds is unfavorable to the existence of Slavery. Hence, this policy has been opposed by the South and the Democratic party.

In January, 1859, a bill relating to preëmptions being under consideration in the House, Mr. Grow, of Pa., moved to amend the bill by adding a section, providing, "that no public land shall be exposed to sale by proclamation of the President, unless the same shall have been surveyed, and the return of each survey duly filed in the Land Office, for ten years or more before such sale." The effect of this amendment would be to open these lands to preëmption ten years before they could get into the hands of the speculator; thus giving the industrious settler time to pay for his farm from the products of the soil.

To defeat this amendment, a motion was made to refer the bill and amendment to the Committee of the Whole, where it would probably have been buried for the session. The motion failed: Yeas, 90; Nays, 92. The amendment was then adopted: Yeas, 98; Nays, 81. All the Republicans present voted in the affirmative, together with 18 Democrats. Mr. Blair, of Missouri, Republican, was the only member from a Slave State who voted for the bill. Of the votes from the Slave States, all but 9 were in the negative. The question was then taken upon the passage of the bill, and lost: Yeas, 91; Nays, 95. Of those who voted in the affirmative, 80 were Republicans, 9 Democrats, and 1, (Mr. Davis, of Md.,) American. Of those who voted in the negative, 85 were Democrats, and 10 were Americans; all of the latter being from Slave States. Of the Democrats, 26 were from the Free States. Of the 9 Southern members who had voted for Mr. Grow's amendment, all but Mr. Blair voted against the bill; from which it would appear that they were opposed to the amendment, though they voted for it.

Both of the members from Minnesota, (Cavanaugh and Phelps,) expressed their high displeasure at the vote of their political friends. Mr. C. said:

"With reference to the vote on this bill to-day, with an overwhelming majority of this side of the House voting against my colleague and myself, voting against this bill, I say it frankly, I say it in sorrow, that it was to the Republican side of the House to whom we were compelled to look for support of this just and honorable measure. Gentlemen from the South, who have broad acres and wide plantations, aided here to-day by their votes more to make Republican States in the North, than by any vote which has been cast within the last two years. These gentlemen came here to ask us to support the South ; yet they, to a man almost, vote against the free, independent labor of the North and West.

"I, Sir, have inherited my Democracy ; have been attached to the Democratic party from my boyhood, have believed in the great truths as enunciated by the 'fathers of the faith.' . . . But, Sir, when I see Southern gentlemen come up, as I did to-day, and refuse, by their votes, to aid my constituents, refuse to place the actual tiller of the soil, the honest, industrious laborer, beyond the grasp and avarice of the speculator, I tell you, Sir, I falter, and I hesitate."

A Homestead bill was introduced at the same session, which proposed to give a quarter-section of land to every actual settler continuing to occupy it for five years from the time of entry. The bill passed the House, February 1, 1859, 120 to 76. Of the Yeas, 82 were Republicans, 38 were Democrats. Of the Nays, 75 were Democrats and Southern Americans ; and 1 Republican, Nichols, of Ohio. Of the Democrats who voted for the bill, only three were from Slave States.

In the Senate, where the Democratic majority was larger than in the House, no direct vote was permitted to be taken upon the measure ; Southern Senators having succeeded in obtaining priority to other bills, one of which was the bill for the purchase of Cuba, of the passage of which, not one Senator, probably, had the least expectation. It will be seen that the question was one between Free Labor and Slave Labor, or between the Republican party and the Democratic or Slaveholders' party. This will still more clearly appear from subsequent action upon the subject.

At the next session, on the 6th of March, Mr. Lovejoy, from the Committee on Public Lands, reported a bill, (previously introduced by Mr. Grow,) offering to actual settlers one hundred and sixty acres of land which was subject to preëmption at $1 25 per acre, or eighty acres at $2 50 per acre, on terms similar to those of the bill of the preceding session. On receiving the patent, the settler was to pay $10, which sum was to be considered as a compensation for expense of survey, &c.

The bill was read twice and referred to the Committee of the Whole. On the 12th of March, a motion to reconsider the vote by which the bill had been referred to that Committee, was agreed to, 106 to 67. In the affirmative, 83 Republicans, 23 Democrats—of the latter were 5 Anti-Lecompton Democrats, as they were called from their opposition to the efforts of the administration to force upon the people of Kansas the Constitution formed at Lecompton. In the negative, 52 Democrats, and 15 Southern Americans, who generally coöperated with the Democrats.

The bill being now before the House, Mr. Lovejoy moved that the bill be engrossed and read the third time. Mr. Branch, of N. C., moved to lay it on the table. Lost, 62 to 112; the Yeas being all from the South, except Mr. Montgomery, Democrat, of Pa.; the Nays all from the North, except Mr. Craig, Democrat, of Missouri. The bill was then read a third time and passed: Yeas, 115—Republicans, 86; Democrats, 28; North American, 1. Nays, Democrats, 47; South Americans, 18.

In the Senate, a substitute for the House bill was reported by Mr. Johnson, of Tenn., granting Homesteads at 25 cents an acre, not to include the preëmptors then occupying public lands. Mr. Wade moved to substitute the House bill. Lost, 26 to 31: Yeas, all Republicans, except 3, Douglas, Rice, and Toombs; Nays, all Democrats. On the 10th of May, Johnson's bill was passed, 44 to 8. The House refused to concur; and the Senate refused to recede. A Committee of Conference agreed upon the Senate bill with slight amendments; one of which restricted its benefits to heads of families. The friends of the measure being unable to pass such a bill as they wished, accepted this. The House agreed to the report of the Committee, 115 to 51 ; the Nays all from the Slave States : the Senate, 36 to 2.

The bill was sent to the President, (Buchanan,) who, as if determined to let no opportunity pass without showing his devotion to Southern interests, returned the bill to the Senate, with his veto. He professed to see in it, unconstitutionality, inequality, and injustice to several classes of individuals and to the old States, and a reduction of the revenue. The question was then taken on the passage of the bill against the objections of the President. Yeas, 28 ; Republicans, 19 ; Democrats, 9. Nays, 18, all from the South. So the bill failed for want of a two-thirds majority.

That the Democratic party was then, as it long had been, in fact, *the* Pro-Slavery party, received additional confirmation at this session. Senator Davis, (now Southern President,) submitted a series of resolutions of an extreme Southern character, declaring the intermeddling, by any State or its citizens, with the domestic institutions of other States, on any pretext whatever, political, moral, or religious, to be in violation of the Constitution, insulting to the States, and tended to weaken and destroy the Union ; asserting the right of slaveholders to take their "peculiar" property into the Territories ; denying to Congress or a Territorial Legislature the power either by direct, or by indirect and "unfriendly" legislation, to impair or to annul this right ; declaring that if the Judicial and Executive authority should not possess means to insure adequate protection to these constitutional rights in a Territory, it would be the duty of Congress to supply such deficiency ; that a State should be entitled to admission with or without Slavery ; and that any interference with the rendition of fugitive slaves, was subversive of the Constitution, and revolutionary.

All the resolutions except one, after having been thoroughly debated by such approved Democrats as Davis, Benjamin, and other Senators of the "fire-eating" stamp, were adopted by an almost strict party vote. Even the first and second, which were expressly directed against all discussion of the morality or political expediency of Slavery, were adopted by a vote of 36 to 18 or 20 ! Mr. Harlan, of Iowa, Republican, offered an amendment to the second, as follows :

"But the free discussion of the morality and expediency of Slavery should never be interfered with by the laws of any State or of the United States; and the freedom of speech and of the press, on this and every other subject of domestic and national policy, should be maintained inviolate to all the States."

What would the political Fathers have thought, if such a sentiment had been voted down by any legislative body in their day? So scrupulous on the subject of freedom of speech and of the press were some of the ratifying State Conventions, that they were indisposed to ratify, without submitting to Congress, among other propositions for amendment, a guaranty to this very right; and so proper was it regarded, that it was at once adopted by the States as a part of the Constitution. Yet, in the Senate of the United States, in the year 1860, *a resolution substantially declaring the exercise of this right unconstitutional, and a violation of the most solemn obligations, was adopted by a vote of two to one;* the majority at the same time claiming to be the representatives of American Democracy! Is it strange that Northern Democrats should now manifest such opposition to an administration which is employing the forces of the nation to put down a rebellion instigated and led by the authors and advocates of these resolutions, *which were intended as the creed of the Democratic party*? The general acquiescence of the party and its presses in these resolutions, leaves no doubt, that, had the South remained in the Union, the sentiments of these resolutions would constitute the party Platform in 1864, as they probably will, even if the rebel States shall not have returned.

The country was now entering upon another exciting Presidential campaign. The principles involved in the election of 1860—its incidents—its momentous consequences—render it memorable beyond any that had ever occurred. And it was the Kansas question which, more than any other cause, contributed to give it this distinction. The honors and the emoluments of the Presidential office had for many years been dispensed by the Slave Power. It had, in 1852, erected the Platforms of both the Democratic and Whig parties, and the Democratic Platform in 1856, into which Mr. Buchanan assured the people he had *merged* himself, and which, as the event showed, served the purpose of his election. This platform was essentially the Cass and Douglas doctrine of Non-intervention, or Popular Sovereignty. The latest improvement in Democracy had not then been announced; or the time had not come when it was deemed safe to present it for acceptance to the North. But having been enunciated by the Supreme Court, and the public mind having partially recovered from the shock which its announcement had produced, it was now proclaimed as the true Democratic doctrine.

But, as we have seen, the Southern Democracy committed a fatal mistake in their hasty attempt to force this innovation into the Democratic creed, which has resulted, not only in the division of the party, and the disruption of the Union, but in the infliction of a mortal wound upon itself. To secure Southern favor was the principal motive that prompted the repeal of the Missouri Compromise by the Kansas-Nebraska act, the claims of whose author had not, in previous Conventions, been duly appreciated, and who intended not to be outdone in obsequiousness to the Southern Oligarchy. But the honors in the Presidential game having been awarded to Mr. Buchanan, Mr. Douglas' hope must necessarily be deferred until 1860. But unfortunately his favorite doctrine of Popular Sovereignty had been superseded, and a cloud had somewhat obscured his prospects.

The Democratic National Convention met at Charleston on the 23d of April, 1860. The number of Delegates was 303; and, having adopted the two-thirds rule, 202 votes were necessary to nominate. But the Convention decided to adopt a Platform before proceeding to ballot for a candidate. Having endeavored for seven days in vain to agree upon one, and there being no hope of such a result, (the Platform reported by the Douglas men having been adopted, 165 to 138,) whole delegations of some, and parts of the delegations of others, of the States of Alabama, Mississippi, Florida, Texas, Louisiana, Arkansas, Delaware, South Carolina, and North Carolina, seceded from the Convention; met in another place, and adopted a series of resolutions of the ultra Southern character; and adjourned to meet at Richmond the 11th of June.

The regular Convention proceeded to ballot, 202 votes still

being declared necessary to a choice. After 57 ballots had been taken, in which Mr. Douglas had received on each ballot from 145 to 152 votes against about 100 for all others, the Convention adjourned to meet at Baltimore on the 18th of June.

The Republican National Convention assembled at Chicago the 16th of May. The contest was chiefly between the friends of Mr. Seward and Mr. Lincoln. On the 3d ballot, the latter received a majority of all the votes, and was declared unanimously nominated. Hannibal Hamlin, of Maine, was nominated for Vice-President.

The Democratic seceders met at Richmond on the 11th of June, and the next day adjourned to the 21st. They then reässembled, and adjourned from day to day, awaiting the action of the Convention at Baltimore, which had met on the 18th, pursuant to adjournment. The week was spent by the latter in fruitless endeavors to determine the claims of delegates, when a large portion of them again withdrew from the Convention, leaving few besides the friends of Mr. Douglas, who proceeded to ballot for President, and gave him 181½ votes ; J. C. Breckinridge, 7½ ; Mr. Guthrie, 5½.

The seceders subsequently nominated John C. Breckinridge, of Ky., for President, and Joseph Lane, of Oregon, for Vice President.

A fourth nomination was made by a Convention claiming to be representatives of the "Constitutional Union Party," who met at Baltimore the 9th of May, from twenty States, and nominated John Bell, of Tenn., for President, and Edward Everett, of Mass., for Vice-President. This Convention constructed no party Platform, other than to declare that "platforms adopted by partisan Conventions have the effect to mislead and deceive the people, and to widen the political divisions of the country, by the creation and encouragement of geographical and sectional parties," and to *resolve*, "That it is both the part of patriotism and of duty to recognize no political principle other than *the Constitution of the country, the Union of the States, and the enforcement of the laws, &c.*

The principles of the other parties were more definitely

expressed, so that, however discordant, they were not liable, without doing violence to language, "to mislead and deceive the people."

The Republican Convention reässerted the doctrines of the Declaration of Independence in regard to human Rights, and declared no principle at variance with any previously affirmed. The lapse of time, however, required the introduction of several new subjects. The "new dogma that the Constitution of its own force carries Slavery into the Territories;" the efforts of the administration to keep Kansas out of the Union with a Constitution prohibiting Slavery; and sundry other measures were severely condemned.

The Seceders' or Breckinridge Convention affirmed the Cincinnati Platform of 1856, but, with such explanations as virtually to annul it. It declared, that all citizens have an equal right to settle in the Territories, without having their rights of person or property impaired by Congressional or Territorial legislation; that it is the duty of the Federal Government to protect these rights; and that the right of Sovereignty commences when the people of a Territory, having an adequate population, form a State Constitution. What does this leave of the Popular Sovereignty of 1856?

It was the boast of Mr. Douglas and his party, that they still adhered to that principle. Let their Platform adopted at Baltimore decide. It adopts, as did the other Democratic Convention, the Platform of 1856, adding only certain other resolutions; one of which declares, "That the Democratic party *will abide by the decision of the Supreme Court of the United States over the institution of Slavery within the Territories.*" Another, "That it is the duty of the United States *to afford ample and complete protection* to all its citizens, *at home* or abroad." And another, "That it is in accordance with the true interpretation of the Cincinnati Platform that, during the existence of Territorial Government, the measure of restriction imposed by the Federal Constitution on the powers of the Territorial Legislature over the subject of domestic relations, *as the same has been, or shall hereafter be, finally determined by the Supreme Court,* shall be respected by all good citizens, and *enforced with promptness and fidelity by every branch of the Federal Government.*"

Here we see that the party was pledged to the support of the decision of the Supreme Court in the Dred Scott case. That decision was, that "every citizen has a right to take with him into the Territory any article of property which the Constitution of the United States recognizes as property. The Constitution recognizes slaves as property, and *pledges the Federal Government to protect it.*" And as was asked concerning the other Platform, so we ask concerning this, What does it leave of Popular Sovereignty?

The truth is, Mr. Douglas was in a dilemma. In his efforts to open the way for the spread of Slavery by the repeal of the Missouri Compromise, he had aimed at Southern support for the Presidency. No other man had rendered the South greater service. During the Kansas struggle, prior to the perpetration of the Lecompton swindle, he had sustained the Ruffian atrocities. Not a word of condemnation had escaped his lips. He then, probably, anticipated no repudiation of his cherished non-intervention principle. When, however, the new doctrine was announced by the Supreme Court, he was compelled either to adopt it, or abandon all hope of Southern favor. He chose the former. He publicly declared that he accepted the Dred Scott decision, and then endeavored to reconcile it with the Popular Sovereignty of 1856. He from necessity admitted the right to take slaves into the Territories, and that the owners, if protected at all, must be protected by the Territorial Legislature. These might either refuse to act upon the subject, or might, by "unfriendly action," prohibit Slavery. This could be done by refusing remedies to the slaveholders, or by imposing heavy taxes upon his chattels. But an appeal might be made to the Supreme Court, which might declare these laws unconstitutional. This, however, is unworthy of being called an argument. It is virtually *an abandonment of his original ground.* Yet in his public speeches during the campaign of 1860, he ignored his own party platform, at least in certain latitudes, and declared, as in his speech at Concord, N. H., that "the principle he stood upon was the right of the people to make their own laws, and to establish institutions to suit themselves." It is not easy to reconcile this language either with the Platform or with common honesty.

Of the electors chosen in November, Mr. Lincoln received all the votes of all the Free States, except New Jersey, in which, in consequence of a fusion of the opposition parties, a part of the Lincoln electors was chosen.

For Lincoln and Hamlin: California, 4; Connecticut, 6; Illinois, 11; Indiana, 13; Iowa, 4; Maine, 8; Massachusetts, 13; Michigan, 6; Minnesota, 4; New Hampshire, 5; New Jersey, 4; New York, 35; Oregon, 3; Pennsylvania, 27; Rhode Island, 4; Vermont, 5; Wisconsin, 5; Ohio, 23.—180

For Breckinridge and Lane: Alabama, 9; Arkansas, 4; Delaware, 3; Florida, 3; Georgia, 10; Louisiana, 6; Maryland, 8; Mississippi, 7; North Carolina, 10; South Carolina, 8; Texas, 4.—Total, 72.

For Bell and Everett: Kentucky, 12; Tennessee, 12; Virginia, 15.—Total, 39.

For Douglas and Johnson: New Jersey, 3; Missouri, 9.—Total, 12.

Immediately after the result of the election was known, movements began to be made at the South to carry into effect the long studied purpose of the Secessionists. That this purpose was not first formed *after* the election, there is abundant evidence. In the first place, they had reason to believe, and probably did believe, that the strength of the party, concentrated upon a single candidate, was sufficient to elect him. And Mr. Douglas, having a decided majority of the Delegates in the Charleston Convention, was entitled to the nomination. His services in the cause of the South had been all that could have been reasonably expected from the most loyal Southerner. True, he had, from fear of endangering his prospects at the North, spoken somewhat equivocally on the subjects of non-intervention and the Dred Scott decision; but having gone so far as to declare his acceptance of that decision, the South had no just ground to suspect his loyalty to the Slave Power. The secession from the Charleston Convention, therefore, furnishes, of itself, reasonable evidence of a purpose indirectly to aid the election of Mr. Lincoln, which was to be made the pretext for seceding.

In addition to this evidence of premeditated secession, is

the fact that the Republican party had uniformly disclaimed the intention, and denied to the General Government the power, to interfere with Slavery in the States; and some of the secession members of Congress had the frankness to admit, in the debates at the succeeding session of Congress, that they apprehended, under Mr. Lincoln, no interference with their rights in this respect. Moreover, it had been ascertained that there would be, in both Houses of Congress, Pro-Slavery majorities; which fact, in connection with the declared opinion of the Supreme Court, placed the supremacy of the Slave Power beyond all question, notwithstanding the election of a Republican President.

Much clamor was made in Congress about what were called the "Personal Liberty Acts" of some of the Northern States, and resistance to the recapture of fugitive slaves. This, too, was a mere pretense, intended to deceive, not only the North, but their own constituents, a majority of whom were opposed to secession. The real intention, as both prior and subsequent events and declarations prove, was to establish a great Slave Empire, which was ultimately to include Mexico, Cuba, and several of the South American States, and in which the Republican principle was to be either almost or altogether superseded by a system in which wealth and labor should be separated.

But we have positive testimony to prove the designs of the South. When, in 1850, it was proposed to convene "a Southern Congress" for the initiation of measures looking to the defense of the South, a debate was had on the subject in the Legislature of South Carolina, from which some extracts are here given. In reference to the wrongs inflicted upon the South—

"Mr. Lyles said: The remedy is the union of the South, and *the formation of a Southern Confederacy*. The friends of the Southern movement in the other States *look to the action of South Carolina;* and he would make the issue in a reasonable time, and the only way to do it is by *secession.* There would be no concert among the Southern States *until a blow is struck.*

"Mr. Sullivan . . . denied the right or the power of the General Government to coerce the State in the case of secession. He thought there never would be a union of the South *until this State strikes the blow* and makes the issue.

"Mr. Richardson said there was no remedy for these evils in the Government; we have no alternative left us but *to come out of the Government.*

"Mr. Preston said he was opposed to calling a Convention, because he thought it would *impede the action of this State* on the question before the country. *He thought it would impede our progress towards disunion.* He thought Conventions dangerous things, except when the necessities of the country absolutely demand them. He said he had adopted the course he had taken, simply and entirely *with the view of hastening the dissolution of this Union..*

"Mr. Keitt said he would sustain the bill for electing Delegates to a Southern Congress, because he thought it would *bring about a more speedy dissolution of the Union.*"

In 1856, leading statesmen and editors in the Southern States, as they have since done, avowed their determination, in case of the election of an Anti-Slavery President, to dissolve the Union. Senator Slidell, of Louisiana, said, "if Fremont should be elected, the Union would be dissolved." Toombs, of Georgia, said, "The Union would be dissolved, and ought to be dissolved."

Senator Butler, of South Carolina, said: "When Fremont is elected, we must rely upon what we have—a good State Government. Every Governor of the South should call the Legislature of his State together, and have measures of the South decided upon. If they did not, and submit to the degradation, they would deserve the fate of slaves. *I should advise my Legislature to go at the tap of the drum.*"

Mr. Keitt, of S. C., a member of Congress, said, in a speech at Lynchburg, Va.: "If Fremont is elected, *adherence to the Union is treason to liberty.* (Loud cheers.) I tell you now, that *the Southern man who will submit to his election, is a traitor and a coward.*" (Enthusiastic cheers.)

Preston S. Brooks, at a festival made by his constituents, and intended as a compliment for his attempted assassination of Senator Sumner, said: "We have the issue upon us now; and how are we to meet it? I tell you, fellow citizens, from the bottom of my heart, the only mode which I think available for meeting it, *is just to tear the Constitution of the United States, trample it under foot, and form a Southern Confederacy, every State of which will be a slaveholding State.* (Loud and prolonged cheers.) I believe it, as I stand in the face of my Maker ; I believe it, on my responsibility to you as your honored representative, that *the only hope of the South is in the South,* and that the only available means of making that hope effective, *is to cut asunder the bonds that tie us together, and take our separate position among the family of nations.* These are my opinions. They have always been my opinions. *I have been a disunionist from the time I could think.*"

"If I was a commander of an army, *I would never post a sentinel who would not swear that Slavery is right.*"

"If Fremont be elected President of the United States, I am for the people in their majesty rising above the law and leaders, taking the power into their own hands, going by concert, or not by concert, and *laying the strong arm of Southern freemen upon the Treasury and archives of the Government.*" (Applause.)

The Charleston Mercury, the chief organ of South Carolina Democracy, said : "*Upon the policy of dividing the Union,* of separating the South from her Northern enemies, and establishing a Southern Confederacy, *parties, presses, politicians, and people, are a unit. There is not a single public man in her limits, not one of her present Senators or Representatives in Congress, who is not pledged to the lips in favor of disunion.*"

Gov. Wise, of Virginia, in 1856, said : "To tell me we should submit to the election of a Black Republican, is to tell me that Virginia and the fourteen Slave States are already subjugated and degraded, (cheers ;) that the Southern people are without spirit and without purpose to defend the rights they know and dare not maintain."

Said a writer from Washington in a New Orleans paper : "It is already arranged, in the event of Fremont's election, or a failure to elect by the people, to call the Legislatures of Virginia, South Carolina, and Georgia to concert measures to withdraw from the Union before Fremont can get possession of the army and navy and the purse-strings of the Government. Gov. Wise is actively at work already in the matter *The South can rely on the President in the emergency contemplated.*"

Judge Daily, at a meeting held at Knoxville, Tenn., since the election of 1856, said: "During the Presidential contest, Gov. Wise had addressed letters to all the Southern Governors, and that the one to the Governor of Florida had been shown him, *in which Gov. Wise said he had an army in readiness to prevent Fremont from taking his seat if elected,* and asking the coöperation of those to whom he wrote."

Charles J. Faulkner, formerly a Congressman from Virginia, and Minister to France under Buchanan, said at a public meeting in Virginia: "Should William H. Seward be elected in 1860, where is the man in our midst who would not call for the impeachment of a Governor of Virginia, who would silently suffer that armory (at Harper's Ferry) to pass under the control of such an Executive head?"

The Richmond Enquirer, an acknowledged exponent of Southern Democracy, said in reference to the assault on Sumner: "Sumner and Sumner's friends must be punished and silenced. Either such wretches must be hung, or put in the penitentiary, or the South should prepare at once to quit the Union.

"If Fremont is elected, the Union will not last an hour after Mr. Pierce's term expires. . . . It will be the duty of the South to dissolve the Union, and form a Southern Confederacy.

"Let the South present a compact and individual front. Let her, if possible, detach Pennsylvania, Southern Ohio, Southern Indiana, and Southern Illinois, from the North, and make the highlands between the Ohio and the lakes the dividing line. Let the South treat with California; and, if necessary, ally herself with Russia, with Cuba, and Brazil."

Senator Iverson, of Georgia, addressing his constituents before his departure for Washington, in 1860, said: "*Slavery must be maintained—in the Union, if possible; out of it, if necessary: peaceably, if we may, forcibly, if we must.*

"In a confederated government of their own, the Southern States would enjoy sources of wealth, prosperity, and power, unsurpassed by any nation on earth. No neutrality laws would restrain our adventurous sons. Our expanding policy would stretch far beyond present limits. Central America would join her destiny to ours, and so would Cuba, now withheld from us by the voice and votes of Abolition enemies."

Jefferson Davis, U. S. Senator from Mississippi, in a speech to the people of that State, in 1859, said: "For myself, I say, as I said on a former occasion, in the contingency of the election of a President on the platform of Mr. Seward's Rochester speech, let the Union be dissolved. Let the great, but not the greatest of evils, come."

A volume of similar expressions might be collected from the speeches and writings of Southern men, showing their hatred of the Union, and their intention of quitting it whenever the Government should pass out of the hands of the Pro-Slavery Democratic party. And, it may here be asked, From what prominent Northern Democrat now in good standing in the party, has such language ever met with deserved rebuke? Instead of this, these Disunionists have received the caresses and enjoyed the confidence of their Northern friends down to the time of the Secession, and *have retained their sympathies to the present day.*

In the debates on the passage of the ordinance of secession, and other proceedings of the Convention of South Carolina, are the following:

"Mr. Parker—It is no spasmodic effort that has come suddenly upon us, but *it has been gradually culminating for a long series of years*, until at last it has come to that point when we may say *the matter is entirely right.*

"Mr. Inglis—As to delay for the purpose of a discussion, I for one am opposed to it. As my friend Mr. Parker has said, most of us have had this matter under consideration for the last twenty years, and I presume we have by this time arrived at a decision upon the subject.

"Mr. Keitt—Sir, we are performing a great act, which involves not only the stirring present, but embraces the whole great future of ages to come. *I have been engaged in this movement ever since I entered political life.* We have carried the body of this Union to its last resting place, and now we will drop the flag over its grave. After that is done, I am ready to adjourn and leave the remaining ceremonies for to-morrow.

"Mr. Rhett—*The secession of South Carolina is not the event of a day. It is not anything produced by Mr. Lincoln's election, or by non-execution of the Fugitive Slave law. It has been a matter which has been gathering head for thirty years.* . . In regard to the Fugitive Slave law, I myself doubt its constitutionality, and I doubted it on the floor of the Senate when I was a member of that body. The States, acting in their sovereign capacity, should be responsible for the rendition of fugitive slaves. That was our best security."

From these and other evidences of the determination of the more Southern Slave States to secede, how unnecessary were all attempts, by compromise and concession, to arrest the progress of secession! *Coercion* was the only preventive; and had President Buchanan had the honesty and the moral courage to take the necessary measures to reënforce the forts near Charleston, and enforced the collection of revenue in the Southern ports, the Rebellion with its tremendous consequences might have been prevented. He was importuned by his friends to act in the matter; but, either from sympathy with the seceders, or from timidity, he persisted in leaving them to carry their designs into effect. *Such* a responsibility no other public functionary in this country ever incurred. The decision of the President not to send additional troops to strengthen the Charleston forts on the urgent call of Major Anderson, then in command of Fort Moultrie, induced Gen. Cass, Secretary of State, to resign; he having contended, it is said, that such reënforcement was necessary to insure peace, and to protect the public property, which was the duty of the Government.

Gen. Scott, as early as October 29, 1860, wrote to the President: "It is my solemn conviction that there is some danger of an early act of rashness preliminary to secession, viz., the seizure of some of the following forts:" naming some eight or ten, including Moultrie and Sumter, most of them without garrisons or with insufficient ones, and recommended their being guarded "against surprises." He said also: "With the army faithful to its allegiance, and the navy probably equally so, and with a Federal Executive, for the next twelve months, of firmness and moderation, which the country has a right to expect—*moderation* being an element of power not less than *firmness*—there is good reason to hope that the danger of secession may be made to pass away without one conflict of arms, one execution, or one arrest for treason." But the President continued inactive ; his Secretaries plundering the Treasury, plotting treason, placing the national arms at the disposal of the traitors, and scattering the navy ; and the Government was betrayed, powerless, into the hands of its enemies.

One act of service to the slaveholders remained to Mr. Buchanan. Having another Annual Message to prepare, he took occasion to give the "Northern agitators" one more thrust before his retirement. It was in his view a serious offense, that, for five and twenty years, they had presumed to express their dislike of Slavery, without the fear of Southern lordlings before their eyes. The old patriots and statesmen spoke of Slavery as a moral and political evil—a "*curse*"—and of slaveholders as "*despots*"—terms quite as severe as are used by the Phillipses and Garrisons of the present day. Now, a man can not, without incurring the strongest censure of the Democrats, so much as say to a slaveholder, "Why do you thus ?"

Mr. Buchanan said "the Slavery question could be easily settled, and peace and harmony restored. All for which the Slave States have ever contended, is to be let alone." True, Mr. President. Had the slaveholders been permitted to do just as they pleased—to spread the curse of Slavery over an empire, to be divided, as fast as might be necessary to keep up the desired "equilibrium," and formed into States inhabited mainly by an unpaid, ignorant, mixed, and degraded population, dwelling in rude and filthy cabins, instead of being peopled by industrious free laborers, whose thrift, intelligence, and high social position, are evinced by the convenient dwellings, by churches, and school-houses, and manufactories which overspread the country ; could these petty "despots," as Jefferson called them, have continued to lord it over their fellow men, and to riot upon their unrequited labor, without extracting from the friends of humanity an expression of sympathy for their suffering brethren, or an effort for their relief; and could they have extorted from the people one more concession—*à constitutional guaranty of the right to govern, by the lash and the chain, all the territory now owned, and hereafter to be acquired, by the United States*, and enactments prohibiting the discussion of the morality of the "peculiar institution," and the transmission, by mail, of all obnoxious papers, as Mr. Buchanan and his Democratic associates in Congress attempted to do in 1836; in short, could only the people of the North have been compelled *to let the slaveholders alone*;—then, indeed, "peace and harmony" might have been preserved. *Such* guaranties would doubtless, even now, appease the traitors, and bring back every Rebel State into the Union. And could Mr. Buchanan be invested with plenary power to settle this question, "peace and harmony" would be speedily "restored."

The President denied the constitutional right of Secession; but he told the country he had no authority to enforce the obedience of a State; and so he *let the traitors alone*, and, in utter disregard of the importunities of loyal Democrats, refused to reënforce the forts which were too feebly garrisoned for effectual resistance or protection, or to make any other provision for the execution of the laws. What could have been more encouraging to the Rebels?

The message also directs a missile at "geographical" or "sectional parties," intended, of course, for the party which had elected Mr. Lincoln. The general hue and cry about "sectionalism," kept up for years to the eve of the Rebellion, and the repetition of the denunciation of "sectional parties" by the President, indorsed by the party throughout the North, tended to confirm the hope of the traitors that any efforts of the new administration to enforce the laws against them would be resisted by their Northern friends.

The reader will pardon a digression here to notice this accusation of "sectionalism." Why is a party formed *to oppose* the extension of Slavery more sectional than one whose object is *to promote* its extension? *Slavery* is a *sectional* institution. *Freedom* is *national:* to secure its blessings to THE WHOLE NATION is the object of the Constitution. A party, therefore, organized to effect this object, is not, in the true sense of the word, a sectional party. Is not rather a party whose business it is *to support* a sectional interest, a sectional party? As, however, it is the grand object of the Democratic party to *nationalize* Slavery, I am not disposed to dispute its claim to nationality. But admitting that a party opposed to Slavery, because its voters are limited to one-half of the States, is really sectional: Is that fact a valid objection to such a party? *Its claims to support are to be determined by the nature of its objects;* and it is immaterial whether all its members reside in one State, or are scattered through all the States. Every measure of political or moral reform has a local beginning. It is discussed; the sentiments of its advocates are proclaimed; the judgment of men is every where addressed through the public Press and otherwise. The friends of the measure depend upon its merits to commend it to the public support; and by free discussion and the dissemination of correct information, it soon finds supporters in every community. But the slaveholders dread discussion, and deny freedom of speech and of the Press. Restore this constitutional right; admit light into the benighted South; and a stronger Anti-Slavery party would soon be found there than there has ever been or now is in the North; and the cry of "sectionalism" would be silenced.

The sentiment that, because Slavery is confined to a portion of the Union, it does not concern the people in other portions, has no foundation either in morals or in logic. It is in perfect accordance with that of Cain: "Am I my brother's keeper?" or with that of a man who should refuse to rescue a fellow man from the hands of a robber. The law of humanity—the law of nature, which is the law of God—*demands* interference, by all moral and lawful means, in behalf of the oppressed and the suffering.

But another reason—*political expediency*—justifies opposition to Slavery by the people of the Free States. The evils of Slavery are not altogether local; *it affects the whole nation.* That it paralyzes the industry and retards the prosperity of a State, has been a thousand times confessed by slaveholders themselves, and may be seen on the slightest comparison between the Free and the Slave States. Slavery closes the doors against the free laborers of other States. It creates an antagonistic *sectional interest;* gives to slaveholders a disproportionate influence in the Government; and, as the event shows, endangers the Union.

To this it will be replied, that the holding of slaves is a constitutional right. True; and being such, it is not to be infringed. But all due respect for this right does not forbid the use of all legal and constitutional means to remove or abate the evil. The *necessity* which compelled acquiescence in the reservation of this right, does not make Slavery just or expedient; nor does it rightfully preclude attempts by any man or party to effect its restriction or abolition.

Slavery also affects the *honor* of the nation: it is a *national disgrace,* for which the North as well as the South is responsible. But for the countenance and support which Slavery has received from the people of the Free States, it would long since have been on a rapid decline, if not on the point of extinction. The Rebellion and its awful consequences would have been avoided; and we should need no advice from Mr. Buchanan or any other Northern abettor of treason as to the means of *restoring* "peace and harmony to a distracted country." Its peace and harmony would never have been disturbed. Could a tithe of all that has been said and done by Northern "doughface" politicians be at once presented to the minds of candid men, they would not wonder that the nation has been brought into its present perilous condition. What, for example, can be imagined to be more likely to produce such a result than the sentiments expressed by Ex-President Fillmore in his highly applauded speech at Albany, in 1856? Forgetting all his anti-slavery acts and speeches, he said:

"We see a political party presenting candidates for the Presidency and Vice-Presidency, selected for the first time from the Free States alone. . . . Can it be possible that those who are engaged in such a measure can have seriously reflected upon *the consequences which must inevitably follow,* in case of success? *Can they have the madness or the folly to believe that our Southern brethren would submit to be governed by such a Chief Magistrate?*"

If such language is not treasonable, it is very nearly so. Did the speaker mean to intimate that Gen. Fremont, or Mr. Dayton, Mr. Fillmore's old Whig brother, had they been elected, would have violated their official oaths by infringing the constitutional rights of the South? The legitimate inference from his language is, that "our Southern brethren" *would have just cause for refusing to submit to the laws of the Union.* No wonder if, after the utterance of such sentiments by a thousand presses and ten thousand tongues in the Free States for more than twenty years, the slaveholders had, in the supposed contingency, refused, or that, four years later, they did refuse, to "submit to be governed by such a Chief Magistrate?" Who believes that "our Southern brethren," if they had been plainly told from the beginning, that all demands for anything more than to be "let alone" within their States would be denied, would ever have rebelled against their Government? But they were spoiled by the "sugar plum" policy. What they could not readily obtain by teazing, they extorted by threats of running away. And the time having come when no further concessions were expected, they turned, and kicked the hand by which they had been fed to surfeiting. And now, both the North and the South, the latter as principal, the former as accessory, are, for the giant sin of oppression, writhing under the inflictions of a righteous Providence, who has declared concerning the wicked, "Though hand join in hand, he shall not go unpunished."

South Carolina seceded the latter part of December, and immediately took measures to obtain possession of the national forts within the State. Major Anderson, commander of the forts in the Charleston harbor, aware that Fort Moultrie, in which the garrison then was, was unable to resist the land forces, quietly withdrew on the night of the 28th of December, and took possession of Fort Sumter. Other States followed the example of South Carolina, not only in the act of secession, but in robbing the Government, taking possession of United States' forts, arsenals, and other property within their borders. Louisiana seized the United States Mint and the Sub-Treasury at New Orleans with half a million of dollars. The traitor Secretaries, Cobb, of the Treasury; Floyd, of War, and Thompson, of the Interior, resigned their offices; and Senators and Representatives gradually withdrew from Congress, though some of them remained for a time after the purpose of their States was known, in order, probably, to influence the public mind in their favor, or to alarm the Government into submission.

The President appointed John A. Dix, of New York, Secretary of the Treasury, and Joseph Holt, of Kentucky, Secretary of War. These proved to be faithful and efficient officers, who checked, in some measure, the downward course of the Government.

One of the most atrocious acts of treachery was perpetrated by Gen. Twiggs, commander of the United States forces for the department of Texas, who surrendered the military posts and other property under his charge to the State authorities.

Several propositions were offered in Congress in the hope of pacifying the South, or at least of preventing the secession of the border Slave States. The most prominent one was that of Mr. Crittenden, of Kentucky, a Union man, who had been elected by the American party. He proposed the restoration of the Missouri Compromise, and an amendment of the Constitution, guarantying Slavery South of the established line, not only in the territory now belonging to the Union, but *in all that might hereafter be acquired.* This proposition was introduced before many States had seceded, and while the Southern representation was nearly full. Before the purpose of secession had been fully formed, so liberal a concession would, it is presumed, have been promptly accepted by the South. But it was highly objectionable to the North. The requests of the slaveholders had from an early period been granted by the generous North. Having by indulgence grown exacting, and demanding what once they would hardly have presumed to ask as a favor, these demands also, sometimes enforced by threats of disunion, were conceded by the pliant North. The South having at length broken her faith by the repeal of the Missouri Compromise, and destroyed the confidence of the North in her pledges, any further concession, especially one of such magnitude as that now asked, and that, too, under threats of breaking up the Union, would have been dishonorable and humiliating in the extreme. It would also tend to encourage the resistance, in future, of factious minorities to the will of majorities, however fairly and clearly that will may have been expressed.

The concession asked was moreover unreasonable. Slavery was aggressive, and never satisfied. Its life depends upon extension. In time, its allotted territory would be too small; and some pretext would again be conceived for another invasion of Mexico, or of some other neighboring State, with a view to further acquisitions of territory for the extension of the Slave Dominion. And what rendered the proposition peculiarly objectionable was, that the contemplated concession being secured by a *constitutional provision*, however injuriously it might affect the North, relief would be impossible. Slavery is inexorable; and the redress of any grievance dependent upon a constitutional amendment requiring the ratification of three-fourths of the States, would be hopeless. These reasons, (more might be given,) are sufficient to justify the North in rejecting the proposition of Mr. Crittenden. It would have been an *entire surrender to Slave Power for all time*, with no probable benefit to the Union.

Fixed in the purpose of a separation from the North, State after State seceded; and before the inauguration of Mr. Lincoln, a Southern Confederacy was formed, and a provisional Government established at Montgomery, Alabama.

One important fact connected with this rebellion—and one which inspires the hope of a more ready return of the seceded States to the Union than many are looking for—is, that Secession has never been sanctioned by the people of those States. The question has never been fairly submitted to them. It is believed that, if a deliberate and unbiased expression of the will of the people had been given, large majorities in all but two or three of the seceding States would have voted against Secession. And hence there is good reason to believe, that, when the authority of the General Government shall have been so far established in any of those States as to insure protection to its inhabitants, the majority of them will cheerfully return to their allegiance.

Great anxiety was felt in regard to the probable course of the border Slave States, especially Virginia, as her action would be likely to influence that of other States. In the latter part of January, the Legislature of this State adopted resolutions proposing a meeting of Commissioners from all such States as were willing to unite with Virginia in an effort to adjust the existing controversy, so as to afford to the people of the slaveholding States adequate security to their rights. These resolutions were sent by Ex-President Tyler to the President, by whom they were communicated to Congress.

In pursuance of this invitation, a "Peace Convention" met at Washington on the 4th of February, 1861, and adjourned on the 27th. Twenty-one States were represented: Maine, New Hampshire, Vermont, Massachusetts, Rhode Island, Connecticut, New York, New Jersey, Pennsylvania, Delaware, Maryland, Virginia, North Carolina, Kentucky, Tennessee, Missouri, Illinois, Indiana, Ohio, Iowa, and Kansas. The Convention adopted a series of propositions to constitute Article 13 of Amendments to the Constitution, with seven sections. (1.) Slavery was prohibited North of the parallel of 36 deg. 30 min., and secured South of that line. (2.) No future acquisitions of territory, except by discovery and for national uses, without the concurrence of a majority of all the Senators from the slaveholding States, and a majority of all the Senators of the non-slaveholding States, and in case of acquisition by treaty, two-thirds of each class of States must concur. (3.) Congress was to have no power to control Slavery in any State or Territory, nor to interfere with or abolish it in the District of Columbia, without the consent of Maryland and the owners of slaves, nor without compensation to their owners. Sundry other privileges were guarantied to slave owners in this Section. (4.) States were to have the right to pass laws for enforcing the delivery of fugitive slaves to legal claimants. (5.) The foreign slave trade was prohibited. (6.) The provisions in the Constitution relating to Slavery, and the first, third, fifth, and sixth sections of these Amendments, were not to be altered or abolished without the consent of all the States. (7.) Congress was required to provide by law that the United States should pay the owner of a fugitive slave the full value of the slave, if rescued by violence or intimidation from mobs, &c.; and Congress was required to pass a law for securing to the citizens of each State the privileges and immunities of citizens in the several States.

The result of the deliberations of the Convention was communicated to Congress on the 27th of February; but Congress failing to submit the proposed amendment to the States for ratification, the Convention, as was expected, proved a failure. This, however, was little to be regretted. Virginia had, through her leading citizens, declared her determination, if force were employed against the rebel States, to join the Confederacy; and as these were determined on a separation at all events; and as coercive measures could not have been deferred until the States could have acted upon the proposed amendments, neither Virginia nor any other of the subsequently seceding States would have been retained. Nor was it at all probable that the propositions of the Convention would have been ratified by three-fourths of the adhering States.

A few days after the adjournment of the "Peace Convention," Mr. Buchanan's administration expired. President Buchanan came into office at a time and under circumstances which enabled him, with ordinary prudence and honesty of purpose, to make his administration a popular one. But it gained notoriety by its imbecility and corruption, and the incalculable amount of mischief which it wrought. A more faithful servant the Slave Power never had in that office. One good, however, has been ascribed to him, for which he is especially entitled to the gratitude of his immediate predecessor: He made the unpopular administration of Franklin Pierce appear respectable! Probably no man ever carried from the Presidential chair into retirement so little public respect and such a weight of popular odium, as James Buchanan. Well had it been for his own honor as well as for the honor and good of his country, if he had retired to private life before his election to the Presidency.

CHAPTER X.

Administration of Abraham Lincoln.

ABRAHAM LINCOLN entered upon the duties of his office as President of the United States, on the 4th of March, 1861.

Mr. Lincoln's Inaugural Address gave great satisfaction. He assured the people of the Southern States that "their property, their peace and personal security would not be endangered;" that he had "no purpose to interfere with the institution of Slavery in the States where it exists;" and declared that he had no right nor inclination to do so. He acknowledged the binding force of the constitutional provision for reclaiming fugitive slaves. A law designed to carry this provision into effect, ought to guard effectually against the surrender of free men as slaves; and he suggested that it would, at the same time, be well to provide by law to enforce that clause of the Constitution which guaranties, that "the citizens of each State shall be entitled to all the privileges and immunities of citizens in the several States."

The Constitution, he said, "contemplates the Union to be perpetual;" "no State, upon its own mere motion, can lawfully get out of the Union;" and "acts of violence within any State against the authority of the United States are insurrectionary or revolutionary." He considered that, "in view of the Constitution and the laws, the Union was unbroken, and to the extent of his ability, he should take care that the laws of the Union were faithfully executed in all the States." The mails, unless repelled, would continue to be furnished in all parts of the Union.

In respect to "the position assumed by some, that constitutional questions are to be decided by the Supreme Court," he said he did "not deny that such decision must be binding in any case upon the parties to a suit, as to the object of that suit, while it is also entitled to very high respect and consideration in all parallel cases by all other departments of the Government."

Mr. Lincoln appointed, as members of his Cabinet, William H. Seward, of New York, Secretary of State ; Salmon P. Chase, of Ohio, Secretary of the Treasury ; Simon Cameron, of Pennsylvania, Secretary of War ; Gideon Welles, of Connecticut, Secretary of the Navy ; Caleb B. Smith, of Indiana, Secretary of the Interior ; Edward Bates, of Missouri, Attorney-General ; and Montgomery Blair, of Maryland, Postmaster-General.

Although the President had declared his intention to see the laws faithfully executed, he deferred the employment of force until an overt act of war had been committed by the State of South Carolina. On the 12th of April, the assault upon Fort Sumter was made. Long before this, however, an act of war had been committed, by firing into the Star of the West, which had been sent to reënforce Fort Sumter, but was compelled to return without accomplishing the purpose for which she had been sent. On the 15th of April, President Lincoln issued his Proclamation, declaring that the laws were opposed and their execution obstructed, in the States of South Carolina, Georgia, Alabama, Florida, Mississippi, Louisiana, and Texas, and calling for 75,000 troops "to cause the laws to be duly executed," and "to repossess the forts, places, and property which had been seized from the Union." And before midsummer, the nation was in the midst of one of the most sanguinary and desolating civil wars recorded in history. The Proclamation also summoned Congress to meet on the 4th of July.

The call for troops was promptly responded to in all the Northern States ; and money was liberally pledged for the volunteers and their families. Legislatures also made appropriations in aid of the General Government. The call on the Slave States still in the Union met with a very different response. The Governors of all these States, except Delaware and Maryland, positively refused to obey the requisition. Some were unwilling to aid the Government in subduing their sister States ; others doubted the constitutionality of the call. Gov. Hicks, of Maryland, would raise troops only for the defense of Washington. Delaware promptly took her stand with the loyal States.

The Proclamation of President Lincoln was soon followed by a similar one on the part of President Davis, calling on the Southern States for volunteers. The latter also offered liberal inducements for persons to take out letters of marque and reprisal as privateers.

Virginia had long been in a state of indecision. Intimation had been given that, if the Government should employ force against the rebel States, she would join the Confederacy. Immediately after the issuing of the Proclamation, her Convention declared the State out of the Union. As the election at which the delegates to the Convention had been chosen indicated a majority against Secession, the act is presumed to have been effected by menace or fraud. The States of Tennessee, North Carolina, and Arkansas, also soon after joined the Confederacy, which was then composed of eleven States. Four Slave States only remained in the Union; and three of these contained a strong secession element, which rendered their adherence to the Union for a time doubtful.

Early in May, the President issued a proclamation calling for 42,000 additional volunteers, and directed an increase of the regular army and of the navy. In and about Washington were many secret traitors and spies, who did great mischief. Not a few of them were men employed in the public offices. Numerous arrests were made; and some of the persons seized got released by means of the writ of *habeas corpus*; which induced the President, as a measure of safety, to suspend the privilege of this writ. The calling out of the troops, and the summary arrest and imprisonment of persons on suspicion of their being traitors, and the suspension of this writ, have caused much discussion. It is held by some that the powers exercised by the Executive in these acts belong to, or can be authorized, only by Congress. Others maintain that the powers exercised by the Executive are, by a just and liberal construction of the Constitution, implied in the powers conferred upon the Executive; and that, according to any other interpretation, the Government might, in certain emergencies, be overthrown. It is also held, that, in a case of imminent peril to the life of the nation, for which no adequate provision has been made, an Executive would be justified in acting without the authority of a positive law. Upon what ground the President justified his acts, will soon appear from some extracts from his Message to Congress at the extra session in July.

Congress met in special session on the 4th of July, 1861.

The Message of President Lincoln was calm in tone and temper, and firm in purpose to preserve the Union. In speaking of the state of the nation as it was at the time of his Inauguration, he said, among other things :

" A disproportionate share of the Federal muskets and rifles had somehow found their way into these (Southern) States, and had been seized to be used against the Government. Accumulations of the public revenue, lying within them, had been seized for the same object. The navy was scattered in distant seas, leaving but a very small part of it within the immediate reach of the Government. Officers of the Federal army and navy had resigned in great numbers, and of those resigning a large proportion had taken up arms against the Government. Simultaneously and in connection with all this, the purpose to sever the Federal Union was openly avowed ; . . and the Confederate States were already invoking recognition, aid, and intervention from foreign Powers.

" Finding this condition of things, and believing it to be an imperative duty upon the incoming Executive, to prevent, if possible, the consummation of such attempt to destroy the Federal Union, a choice of means to that end became indispensable. This choice was made, and was declared in the Inaugural Address. The policy chosen looked to the exhaustion of all peaceful measures before a resort to any stronger ones. It sought only to hold all the public places and property not already wrested from the Government, and to collect the revenue, relying for the rest on time, discussion, and the ballot-box. It promised a continuance of the mails, at Government expense, to the very people who were resisting the Government ; and it gave repeated pledges against any disturbances to any of the people or any of their rights."

The President recommended provisions for raising 400,000 men and $400,000,000.

In relation to the exercise of the disputed powers just alluded to, after mentioning the call for 75,000 men, and the proclamation ordering the closing of the Southern ports by blockade, all of which was believed to be strictly legal, he proceeds to say:

"At this point the insurrectionists announced their purpose to enter upon the practice of privateering.

"Other calls were made for volunteers to serve for three years, and also for large additions to the regular army and navy. These measures, whether strictly legal or not, were ventured upon under what appeared to be a popular demand and a public necessity, trusting then, as now, that Congress would readily ratify them.

"It is believed that nothing has been done beyond the constitutional competency of Congress. Soon after the first call for militia, it was considered a duty to authorize the Commanding-General, in proper cases, according to his discretion, to suspend the privilege of the writ of *habeas corpus*, or in other words, to arrest and detain, without resort to the ordinary processes and forms of law, such individuals as he might deem dangerous to the public safety. This authority has purposely been exercised but very sparingly. Nevertheless, the legality and propriety of what has been done under it are questioned; and the attention of the country has been called to the proposition, that one who has sworn to take care that the laws be faithfully executed should not himself violate them. Of course, some consideration was given to the questions of power and propriety before this matter was acted upon. The whole of the laws which were required to be faithfully executed, were being resisted and failing of execution in nearly one-third of the States. Must they be allowed to fail of execution, even had it been perfectly clear that, by the use of the means necessary to their execution, some single law made in such extreme tenderness to the citizen's liberty, that, practically, it relieves more of the guilty than the innocent, should to a very limited extent, be violated? To state the question more directly, are all the laws but one to go unexecuted, and the Government itself go to pieces, lest that one be violated?

"Even in such case, would not the official oath be broken, if the Government should be overthrown, when it was believed that disregarding the single law would tend to preserve it? But it was not believed that this question was presented. It was not believed that any law was violated. The provision of the Constitution that the privilege of the writ of *habeas corpus* shall not be suspended, unless when, in cases of rebellion or invasion, the public safety may require it, is equivalent to a provision—is a provision—that such privilege *may be* suspended, when, in cases of rebellion or invasion, the public safety does require it.

"It is insisted that Congress, and not the Executive, is vested with this power. But the Constitution itself is silent as to which or who shall exercise the power; and as the provision was plainly made for a dangerous emergency, it can not be that the framers of the instrument intended that in every case the danger should run its course until Congress could be called together, the very assembling of which might be prevented, as was intended in this case by the rebellion."

Quotations of such length from the Message have been given, that the reader may fully understand the reasons of the President for the exercise of powers which his political opponents allege to have been unauthorized.

Congress adjourned on the 6th of August. The session was remarkable for the unanimity of its proceedings. Party distinctions were scarcely visible. All parties seemed united in a hearty effort to rescue the Republic from the conspiracy which was striking at its existence. Grants of men and means were voted; and authority to meet the emergency was conferred upon the Executive.

To increase the revenue, a Tariff and Direct Tax bill was passed, by which the Tariff of March was modified; and a direct tax of $20,000,000 annually was authorized to be levied upon the property and income of the people of the States and Territories, *including the seceded States.*

As the powers exercised by President Lincoln in his early measures for the suppression of the Rebellion had been questioned, Congress passed "An Act further to provide for the Collection of Duties on Imports and for other purposes," which enables the President, in similar cases, to take the necessary measures to execute the revenue laws. It provides that, if the duties can not be collected in the ordinary way, and in the obstructed ports, they may be collected at other ports in the collection district, or on board of vessels; and such force as shall be deemed necessary may be employed to carry the law into effect. The act also authorizes the prohibition of all commercial intercourse between a rebelling State and other States.

A confiscation act was also passed, by which all property employed or used in aiding an insurrection is to be confiscated. And all slaves required or permitted by their masters to take up arms against the United States, or to work in or upon forts, intrenchments, navy-yards, ships, &c., against the Government, are to be free.

It was doubtless, from the beginning, the hope of the rebel leaders to obtain an early recognition of their Confederacy by Foreign Powers; and especially did they desire such acknowledgment by France and England. In November Mason and Slidell were sent to represent the Confederacy at the Governments of these two countries. Our Government having been informed of their escape from Charleston, dispatched a steamer in pursuit of them. They proceeded, however, to Havana, where they took passage in the English mail packet Trent for England. Captain Wilkes, on his return from the African coast, having heard of it, waylaid the Trent, brought her to, seized these gentlemen with their Secretary, Eustace, and brought them in his own ship to the United States. The announcement of their capture caused great rejoicing, until it became known that England considered the seizure of these men an insult to her flag. Mason and Slidell were confined in Fort Warren, near Boston, awaiting the action of the two Governments. A demand was at length made by England for their release, which was granted by our Government. Secretary Seward, in reply to this demand, assigns as a reason for the surrender of the prisoners, that Captain Wilkes had not, as required by the law of nations, in arresting a vessel of a neutral nation suspected of car rying contraband articles, brought her into a neutral port for trial.

Congress met on the 2d of December, 1861. President Lincoln the next day transmitted to both Houses his first Annual Message, this being the first regular session of the 37th Congress. In reference to the attitude which the nation should maintain with regard to slaves and Slavery, he said:

"In considering the policy to be adopted for suppressing the insurrection, I have been anxious and careful that the inevitable conflict for this purpose shall not degenerate into a violent and remorseless revolutionary struggle. I have, therefore, in every case, thought it proper to keep the integrity of the Union prominent as the primary object of the contest on our part, leaving all questions which are not of vital military importance to the more deliberate action of the Legislature. In the exercise of my best discretion, I have adhered to the blockade of the ports held by the insurgents, instead of putting in force by proclamation the law of Congress enacted at the late session for closing those ports. So also, obeying the dictates of prudence as well as the obligations of law, instead of transcending, I have adhered to the act of Congress to confiscate property used for insurrectionary purposes. If a new law upon the same subject shall be proposed, its propriety will be duly considered. The Union must be preserved; and hence all indispensable means must be employed. We should not be in haste to determine that radical and extreme measures, which may reach the loyal as well as the disloyal, are indispensable."

He here alludes to the Confiscation Act passed at the extra session in July. He signed that act with great reluctance; but his doubts of its policy and justice seem to have been removed. He had become convinced—and the public mind was rapidly coming to the conclusion—that, as the Rebellion in a great measure derived its support from Slavery, and that, as the labor of the slaves was scarcely less serviceable than the same number of soldiers, the latter subsisting on the products of that labor; it was just and proper that, instead of remanding to their owners slaves that came to our side of the lines, they should be retained, and employed on our works of defense.

An act was passed at this session prohibiting Slavery in all present and future Territories of the United States.

Another act was passed, petitions for which had so long agitated Congress and the country, but which had many years ago ceased to be prayed for—the abolition of Slavery in the District of Columbia. This act contains a provision which requires compensation to be made by the Government to the owners of the slaves.

In July, 1862, the President issued a Proclamation by which he confiscated the property of all persons who, at the end of sixty days, should still continue in rebellion against the Government. And on the 22d of September he issued the Proclamation of Emancipation, declaring that, on the 1st day of January, all slaves in any rebel State should thereafter be FOREVER FREE ; the States then in rebellion to be designated by proclamation of the President. And he calls attention to the Confiscation Act, and the act of March, 1862, which makes an additional article of war, forbidding the forcible returning of fugitives to their masters, and enjoins obedience to the requirements of these acts.

The policy of proclaiming freedom to the slaves in the rebellious States, had for some time been suggested as a measure of safety to the nation. It was, however, deemed by many as of doubtful expediency as well as constitutionality. Mr. Lincoln, whatever may have been his opinion, prudently deferred action until public sentiment seemed to call for the measure. It was condemned, however, by the mass of the Democratic party ; and not a few of Mr. Lincoln's political friends deemed it impolitic, as it would tend to alienate many Union men in the Southern States, and essentially weaken the Union cause without effecting its intended object. It is believed that comparatively few of the friends of the administration, or of others who do not sympathize with the slaveholders, now regret the measure.

The idea of this mode of emancipation was not conceived since the commencement of the Rebellion. Many years ago, in a debate on a resolution affirming the exclusive right of the Slave States to abolish Slavery, John Quincy Adams said :

"When your country is actually in war, whether it be a war of invasion or a war of insurrection, Congress has power to carry on the war, and must carry it on according to the laws of war; and *by the laws of war an invaded country has all its laws and municipal institutions swept by the board*, and martial law takes the place of them. This power in Congress has perhaps never been called into exercise under the present Constitution of the United States. But when the laws of war are in force, what, I ask, is one of those laws? It is this: that when a country is invaded, and two hostile armies are set in martial array, the commanders of both armies have power to emancipate all the slaves in the invaded territory. Nor is this a mere theoretic statement. The history of South America shows that the doctrine has been carried into practical execution within the last thirty years. Slavery was abolished in Colombia, first by the Spanish General Morillo, and secondly by the American General Bolivar. It was abolished by virtue of a military command given at the head of the army, and its abolition continues to be law to this day. It was abolished by the laws of war, and not by municipal enactments. * * *

"I might furnish a thousand proofs to show that the pretensions of gentlemen to the sanctity of their municipal institutions, under a state of actual invasion and of actual war, whether servile, civil, or foreign, are wholly unfounded, and that the laws of war do, in all such cases, take the precedence. I lay this down as the law of nations. I say that the military authority takes, for the time, the place of all municipal institutions, *Slavery among the rest.* Under that state of things, so far from its being true that the States where Slavery exists have the exclusive management of the subject, *not only the President of the United States, but the Commander of the Army, has power to order the universal emancipation of the slaves.*"

Nor did this doctrine originate with Mr. Adams. In the Virginia Convention which ratified the Constitution, Patrick Henry opposed the ratification on the ground that it gave to Congress the power, under certain circumstances, to abolish Slavery. He said:

"One of the great objects of Government is the national

defense. The Constitution gives power to the General Government to provide for the *general defense*, and the means must be commensurate to the end. All the means in the possession of the people must be given to the Government which is intrusted with the public defense. May Congress not say *every black man must fight?* In the war of the Revolution, Virginia passed an act of Assembly, that every slave who would join the army should be free. At some future time, Congress will search the Constitution to see if they have not the power of manumission. And have they not, sir? Have they not the power to provide for the general defense and welfare? May they not think that these call for the abolition of slavery? May they not pronounce all slaves free? and will they not be warranted by that power? The paper speaks to the point; they have the power in clear, unequivocal terms, and will clearly and certainly exercise it."

In the latter part of September, a meeting of the Governors of the loyal States was held at Altoona, Pa., to consult on the interests of the nation. About one half of them were present, and some of those absent were represented by men of their choice. They united in a memorial approving the President's Emancipation Proclamation, and resolved, by every proper and lawful means, to strengthen the hands of the Government in the struggle against the Rebellion.

Congress assembled on the 1st of December, 1862. The President, in his Message, recommended to Congress 'a plan of Emancipation, to be embodied in articles, and proposed to the State Legislatures or to State Conventions for ratification. The propositions were substantially as follows:

1. Any State abolishing Slavery prior to the 1st of January, 1900, should receive for each slave emancipated a certain compensation.

2. Slaves having "enjoyed freedom by the chances of the war," to be forever free; loyal owners to be compensated.

3. Congress might provide for colonizing free colored persons, with their own consent, beyond the limits of the United States.

These propositions of the President were by some erroneously considered as inconsistent with, or an abandonment of, his Emancipation policy. The project embodied in the Message, however, had respect to loyal States and those which should become such, and was designed as a measure of conciliation and peace. The Proclamation was a war measure, and intended to operate only on Rebels, to weaken their power.

The first of January, 1863, was approaching, and a deep interest was felt in regard to the promised Proclamation of the President. The opinion had been expressed that he would recede from the position he had taken in the Proclamation of September, which declared that "all persons held as slaves within any State or designated part of a State, *the people whereof shall then be in rebellion against the United States*, shall be then, henceforth, and FOREVER FREE."

In the last Proclamation, he designates, as being in rebellion, all the seceded States, except Tennessee, (which is not named,) the forty-eight counties designated as West Virginia, and seven counties, including the Cities of Norfolk and Portsmouth, in the Eastern part of Virginia; and thirteen parishes, (counties,) including the City of New Orleans, in Louisiana. The State and the parts of States exempted from the effect of the Proclamation, were considered as having been recovered to the Union. The people declared free are enjoined to abstain from all violence; and advised to labor faithfully for reasonable wages; and they are informed that they will be received into the armed service of the United States. The repugnance to the employment of colored men in the army, which long prevailed, has been nearly overcome; and about 25,000 of these former aiders of the Rebellion have already been added to the force of the Union.

About the time of the issuing of this last Proclamation, West Virginia was, by an act of Congress, admitted into the Union. The measure had met with much opposition both in and out of Congress, but was carried by heavy votes. The President was said to have taken the written opinions of all the members of his Cabinet before he gave the bill his signature.

CHAPTER XI.

Present Parties contrasted. The Democratic Party the Party of the Rebellion.

Although there are in the Free States few who in express terms justify the Rebellion, no fact is more clear than that a majority of those who now compose the Democratic party, either sympathize with those who are in arms against the Government, or palliate the treason. In almost every official document relating to the subject, in the proceedings of party Conventions, in speeches, and in private conversation, Democrats have charged those who have opposed the extension of Slavery, with being the criminal authors of our present national troubles. On the other hand, scarcely a sentiment uttered, or an act performed, or a public measure demanded, by the slaveholders, in favor of Slavery, has been condemned or opposed by the mass of that party. Certain it is, that many of the most flagitious outrages upon individual rights, murder not excepted, have been palliated or tacitly approved, and *not one has been generally and heartily condemned.* Some facts sustaining these assertions have been given in preceding Chapters ; to these others will be added. It is designed also to defend the opponents of the Pro-Slavery Democracy against the slanders and censures of their adversaries, and vindicate their principles and their policy. They entertain or propagate no new sentiments on the subject of Slavery--none that were not avowed and inculcated by the Fathers long before and long after the organization of the Government. Their first and leading principle is that self-evident truth asserted in the Declaration of Independence—*the political equality of mankind.* Modern Democrats, North as well as South, deny that Jefferson and his compatriots meant to include in the words, " all men," the African race. This is a wanton slander upon their reputation—a modern invention. To prove it such, we have only to show that they condemned Slavery. The enslavement of the African race is sought to be justified on the ground that they are naturally incapable of taking care of or governing themselves, and consequently were designed by the Creator to be the *chattels* of the more highly endowed races. Our Fathers condemned Slavery, and advocated the manumission of the slaves. This they could not consistently do if they had not believed them entitled to the "*inalienable rights*" which they claimed for themselves. Hear what they said on this subject:

"*It is shocking to human nature that any race of mankind and their posterity should be sentenced to perpetual Slavery;* nor in justice can we think otherwise of it, than that *they are thrown amongst us to be our scourge one day or other for our sins;* and as freedom must be as dear to them as to us, what a scene of horror must it bring about! And the longer it is unexecuted, the bloody scene must be the greater."—*Memorial of Citizens of New Inverness, Georgia, to Gen. Oglethorpe,* 1739.

"There is not a man living who wishes more sincerely than I do *to see a plan adopted for the abolition of it,* (Slavery;) but there is only one proper and effectual mode in which it can be accomplished, and that is by legislative authority; and this so far as my suffrage will go, shall never be wanting."—*Washington to Robert Morris.*

"I never mean, unless some particular circumstance should compel me to it, to possess another slave by purchase, *it being among my first wishes* to see some plan adopted by which Slavery in this country may be abolished by law."—*Same to John F. Mercer.*

Jefferson, supposing the case of the slaves rising some day for freedom, said: "The Almighty has no attribute which can take sides with us in such a contest."—*Notes on Virginia.*

"The whole commerce between master and slave is a continual exercise of *the most unremitting despotism on the one part,* and degrading submission on the other." * * * "With what *execration* should the statesman be loaded who, permitting one half of the citizens thus to trample on the rights of the other, transforms those into *despots,* and these into enemies, *destroys the morals of the one part,* and the *amor patriæ* of the other! Can the liberties of the nation be thought secure when we have removed their only firm basis—a conviction in the minds of the people that these liberties are the gift of God? That they are not violated but by his wrath? Indeed, *I tremble for my country when I reflect that God is just, and his justice can not sleep forever.*"—*Notes on Virginia.*

"My sentiments [in favor of the abolition of Slavery] have been forty years before the public. Had I repeated them forty times, they would only become more stale and threadbare. Although I shall not live to see them consummated, *they will not die with me;* but living or dying, they will ever be in my most fervent prayers."—*Letter to James Heaton,* 1826.

For language far more mild than that here employed by Jefferson against Slavery, men have since his day suffered death in this *land of liberty!*

"I think it wrong to admit into the Constitution the idea that a man may have property in man."—*James Madison in Cons. Conv.*

"*The augmentation of slaves weakens the States; and such a trade is diabolical in itself, and disgraceful to mankind.* As much as I value a union of these States, I would not admit the Southern States [South Carolina and Georgia] into the Union, unless they agree to a discontinuance of this disgraceful trade."—*George Mason, of Virginia, in Cons. Conv.*

"By the eternal principles of justice, no master in the State has a right to hold his slave in bondage for a single hour." * * * "In the name of Heaven, with what face can we call ourselves the friends of equal freedom and the inherent rights of our species, when we pass laws inimical to each; when we reject every opportunity of destroying, by silent and imperceptible degrees, *the horrid fabric of individual bondage reared by the mercenary hands of those from whom the sacred flame of Liberty received no devotion.*"—*Wm. Pinkney to the Maryland Legislature, June,* 1789.

"Never will your country be productive, never will its agriculture, its commerce, or its manufactures flourish, so long as they depend on reluctant bondmen for their progress. 'Even the very earth,' says Montesquieu, 'which beams with profusion under the cultivating hand of the free-born laborer, shrinks into barrenness from the contaminating sweat of a slave.' This sentiment is not more figuratively beautiful than it is just."—*Same to same, November*, 1789.

Volumes might be filled with quotations from our old patriots and statesmen, similar to the foregoing. To utter or publish such sentiments within the present revolting States would subject him who uttered them to the halter, without judge or jury, or "the benefit of the clergy." The mere *suspicion* that men have entertained opinions unfavorable to Slavery, has made them the victims of fiendish mobs, instigated by men in high social position, and in politics allied with Northern Democrats in *hunting down*, and denouncing as "aggressors upon Southern rights," all who dare question the morality of "the institution," or its right to unlimited extension. Where is the man, however orthodox in every other respect, yet manifesting the least disposition to weaken the Slave Power, or in any way to oppose its taking possession of our free territory, who has, for many years past, been knowingly nominated and elected to any important office by the Democratic party, or who has been appointed to such office by a Democratic Executive? There may have been such instances; but they are believed to be very rare. *Sympathy and coöperation with slaveholders have been, and are still made by the party, an indispensable qualification for office.* The right of the Slave Power to appropriate to its use all the territorial possessions of the United States, is the very "corner stone" of the Democratic Platform.

Not only do the opponents of the Democratic party agree with the political Fathers in respect to *the immorality and injustice of Slavery*, but also in *the political expediency and constitutionality of its restriction.* By a Georgia Colonial Congress, in 1775, Slavery was pronounced "dangerous to our liberties as well as lives; debasing part of our fellow creatures below men, and corrupting the virtue and morals of the rest; and which *is laying the basis of that liberty we contend for*, and which we pray the Almighty to continue to the latest posterity, *upon a very wrong foundation.*" Jefferson said, it "transforms men into despots, and *endangers our liberties.*" Mason said, it "*weakens the States.*" Pinkney said, it was "*injurious to agriculture, commerce, and manufactures.*" This is proved by a comparison of the Slave States with the Free States. The expediency of restricting and abolishing Slavery, was not generally questioned at that time ; nor is it now by the opponents of the Democratic party.

So also do they hold to the old established doctrine of *the power of Congress over Slavery in the Territories.* This power was exercised by the first Congress under the present Constitution, in an act recognizing and enforcing the Ordinance of 1787, which prohibited Slavery in the Territory North-West of the Ohio. In this Congress were sixteen of the framers of the Constitution, one of whom reported the bill for this act, which was signed by Washington, also one of the framers of the Constitution. No one, so far as the record shows, expressed a doubt of its constitutionality. Subsequently North Carolina and Georgia ceded to the General Government the territory now constituting the States of Tennessee, Mississippi, and Alabama. In the deeds of cession was a condition that Congress should not prohibit Slavery in the territory ; implying that Congress had the power. But, though Congress did not *prohibit* Slavery, it did *interfere* with and contract it to some extent. The act of 1798 organizing the Territory of Mississippi, prohibited, by fine, the bringing of slaves into it from any place without the United States ; and slaves so brought were to be free. In this Congress also were several who had been members of the Constitutional Convention. A still more marked restriction of Slavery was incorporated into the act organizing, in 1804, the Territory of Orleans, now the State of Louisiana. In this Congress were two of those who had framed the Constitution. In passing the Missouri Compromise act, power over Slavery was again exercised by Congress, in prohibiting its extension North of latitude 36 deg. 30 min. In numerous other acts has the power been exercised, without objection on constitutional grounds, even from Southern members. The doctrine in question has been tacitly acknowledged or expressly declared by leading politicians, statesmen, and jurists, North and South, some of whom are now prominent in the Democratic party ; also by Democratic State Legislatures.

In 1848, the Legislature of Wisconsin, (Democratic,) with only three dissenting votes in the Senate, and five in the House, declared Slavery to be "an evil of the first magnitude, morally and politically," and instructed the Senators and requested the Representatives of that State in Congress, to use their influence in favor of inserting in the act organizing any new Territory, a provision against the introduction of Slavery into it.

In 1849, a Convention of the Democratic party of Maine, declared Slavery to be "at variance with the theory of our Government, abhorrent to the common sentiments of mankind, and fraught with danger to all who come within the sphere of its influence; and that *the Federal Government possesses adequate power to inhibit its existence in the Territories of this Union;*" and they enjoined the Senators and Representatives to "employ all their influence to procure the passage of a law forever excluding Slavery from the Territories of California and New-Mexico."

In 1847, the Legislature of Delaware, while the United States were at war with Mexico, declared the war to have been "occasioned by the annexation of Texas, with a view to the addition of Slave Territory to our country, and the extending of the Slave Power in our Union;" declared such "acquisitions to be hostile to the spirit of our free institutions, and contrary to sound morality;" and instructed their members of Congress "to vote against the annexation of any territory to our Union, which shall not thereafter be forever free from Slavery."

In the Legislature of New York, January, 1847, Samuel Young, a Democratic Senator, introduced a resolution to the effect, that, if any territory should be thereafter acquired, the act by which it should be acquired or annexed, should contain a provision whereby Slavery should be forever excluded therefrom.

Similar resolutions have been several times passed by the Legislature of New York by votes nearly unanimous, Democrats voting with their Whig opponents in the affirmative. The resolutions of 1849 were presented in the Senate of the United States, and supported in an able speech, by Hon. John A. Dix, a distinguished Democrat. In his speech he said:

"With a single exception, all the non-slaveholding and one of the slaveholding States, have declared themselves opposed to the extension of Slavery into territory now free. Sir, I fully concur in the propriety of this declaration. I believe that Congress has the power to prohibit Slavery in California and New-Mexico ; that it is our duty to exercise the power, and that it should be exercised now."

At a Democratic meeting in the city of New York, in October, 1848, at which those prominent Democrats, S. J. Tilden, John Van Buren, and John Cochrane made speeches, Mr. Cochrane introduced resolutions strongly denouncing Slavery and its extension to new territory ; and they were adopted.

In 1848, Greene C. Bronson, Chief Justice of the State of New York, then and now a Democrat, in a letter declining an invitation to a political meeting, wrote :

"Slavery can not exist where there is no positive law to uphold it. *It is not necessary that it should be forbidden ; it is enough that it is not specially authorized.* If the owner of slaves removes with or sends them into any country, State, or Territory, where Slavery does not exist by law, they will from that moment become free men ; and they will have as good a right to command the master, as he will have to command them. Entertaining no doubt upon that question, I can see no occasion for asking Congress to legislate against the extension of Slavery into free territory ; and as a question of policy, I think it had better be let alone." * * * "But if our Southern brethren should make the question, we shall have no choice but to meet it ; and then, whatever consequences may follow, I trust the people of the Free States will give a united voice against allowing Slavery on a single foot of soil where it is not now authorized by law."

Declarations similar to the foregoing have been made by many other prominent Democratic statesmen ; and resolutions in favor of prohibiting Slavery in the Territories have been passed by other Democratic Legislatures than those which have been mentioned.

In view of all this, why has the Republican party been represented as sectional, ultra, radical, and even revolutionary, when the truth is, it is THE CONSERVATIVE PARTY OF

THE UNION—*standing upon the Platform built by the founders of our Government*, and holding the same doctrines which were until recently avowed by some of the very men who now stigmatize the party as sectional, radical, aggressive, &c., &c. Among these men are Cushing and others, of Massachusetts; Fillmore, Hunt, Granger, the Brookses, and a large number of others, of New York; and a greater or less number in other States.

Passing over the affirmative answers of Mr. Fillmore to the "radical" questions of the Abolitionists in 1838, when he was a candidate for Congress, what sentiments did he utter in his elaborate speech delivered in many places during the Presidential campaign of 1844? The principal issues between the Whig and Democratic parties were the Tariff, Oregon, and Texas questions. Having disposed of the others, and come to the last, he remarked, in substance: "Important as are those questions upon which I have spoken, *compared with this great question of the extension of Slavery, they dwindle into insignificance!*" He stated the fact that the South had furnished Presidents for forty-four out of the fifty-six years since the organization of the Government, and was now presenting still another candidate! He told his hearers also how much more than a due proportion of the time other important offices had been filled by the South. Earnestly did he urge the duty of Congress to prohibit the extension of Slave Territory; such prohibition being then, of all others, *the* object of the Whig party of the North. Of the questions which divided the two great parties in 1844, the two which may be considered as not now permanently disposed of or settled, and which are likely to arise again, are the Tariff and Slavery Restrictions, on both of which the Republican party stands precisely where Mr. Fillmore and his associates stood until 1850, when they *repudiated* this great principle which they had declared more important than all others. Will these old Whig leaders, or any of their bolting friends, mention one important particular in which the Republicans differ in principle from the Northern Whigs of 1844? Or, will they show why the epithets "sectional," "radical," and the like, which they apply so profusely to the opponents of slave extension, were not equally applicable to themselves?

Or, will they give the public a reason for deserting those with whom they labored so arduously for the restriction of Slavery, and uniting with their opponents who have advanced from their former pro-slavery position to an extreme not then dreamed of, and which is nothing less than the *nationalizing of Slavery*? I repeat the declaration, that the party which proposes to prohibit the extension of Slavery by acts of Congress, is THE TRUE CONSERVATIVE PARTY; and they who represent this party as having introduced into its creed or platform any anti-slavery principles not in accordance with those maintained by our most eminent statesmen, from the time of the organization of the Government, down to a comparatively recent period, either know not whereof they affirm, or are guilty of an attempt to deceive.

Let us now examine the principles and character of the Democratic party. To bring them more distinctly to view, I will, after stating a few facts of a general nature, briefly recapitulate some of the more prominent acts of the party which have marked its singular career. Its leading object has been *power*—POLITICAL SUPREMACY. For power, it has not only trampled upon the principles of the political Fathers, but abandoned its own, as occasion required. POWER, not political reform, was the object of its organization. It was founded in corruption. As was stated in the beginning of its history, Mr. Adams' administration was to be "put down though pure as the angels," &c. A purer or more enlightened administration there has not been. Yet, by misrepresentation, fraud, and other malign influences, it was "brought down."

Next to its false accusation of Adams and Clay, the first great fraud of this party, and that from which it has derived its greatest and most permanent advantage, is the assumption of its deceptive title, "The Democratic Party." In its name and the popularity of its first chosen leader, its strength mainly consisted. With little experience in civil life, the prestige of the well earned title of "Hero of New Orleans," more than counterbalanced that deficiency. Though he had been extensively denounced as a "Federalist," and a "Dictator," and utterly "unfit to be the President of a Republican people," he was adopted by his detractors, and christened "Democrat." This covered all his past political errors, transformed him into a statesman of the highest rank, and drew to his support that large class of electors who are incapable of distinguishing between the name and the principle of Democracy. Such were nine-tenths of all foreigners. Having from experience learned to hate tyrannical governments, and sought in this country the blessings of free institutions, they were easily inveigled into the Democratic net; the *name* being presumed to indicate the *principles* of the party, as distinguished from those of their opponents, which, it was no less natural for these uninformed strangers to presume to be Anti-Republican. The number of foreigners and of the scarcely less ignorant of our native citizens thus deceived, has at all times exceeded the Democratic majorities. Add to these the large numbers whom the leaders have always managed to rally from the dram-shops and other haunts of the idle and the vicious, and it is easy to account for the predominance which Sham-Democracy has maintained, with the exception of a few brief intervals, for more than thirty years.

Look for a moment at the composition of the party. It is readily conceded that a large portion of its members are men of intelligence, high moral worth, and Christian character. But it will hardly be denied by persons of ordinary observation, that more than two out of every three of the more uninformed, the intemperate and vicious portion of most communities belong to that party. Witness, for example, the contrast between the Northern and Southern parts of Illinois. The latter, which from the mental and moral darkness so generally prevalent there, has acquired the very significant sobriquet of "Egypt," rolls up immense majorities for the Democratic ticket—nearly equal, in some townships, to the whole number of votes cast; while the former, whose population is distinguished for its high civilization, and its moral and intellectual culture, gives nearly as large majorities against the Democracy. Again, contrast the more rural, or more sparsely settled counties, whose electors are composed mainly of the industrious laboring classes, and where churches and school-houses abound, with the cities, large numbers of whose population grow up in the hot-beds of vice; and it will generally be found that the Democratic party receives its greatest support in the latter. The same, or even a greater difference exists between the Sixth Ward of the City of New York, which includes that famed spot called "Five Points," and those wards of the same city, which are peopled by industrious, thrifty, and intelligent mechanics and other business men. It is in the former, and others most nearly resembling it, that the Democratic party usually obtains its majorities of tens of thousands in that city.

It is not contended that correctness of political sentiment in every community is in exact proportion to the measure of its morality and general intelligence. But if, as a *general rule*, the virtuous and well informed portion of our citizens are not more likely to form right opinions on matters of public concern, or are not safer depositaries of political power, than the ignorant and vicious, then there is no truth in the old maxim, that "Virtue and intelligence are the only safeguards of liberty;" and our fathers were fools.

The expediency of laws for the encouragement and protection of home industry against foreign competition, was a favorite doctrine with those who instituted our Government. The want of a power in the General Government to effect this object was the immediate cause of calling the Convention that framed the Constitution, in which this power was inserted. And the first act of a general nature, and the second on record passed under the Constitution, declares, in a preamble, one of its objects to be, "the encouragement and protection of domestic manufactures, by duties on goods, wares and merchandises imported." The policy of protection was generally admitted, and scarcely opposed in Congress, except by representatives of the Northern shipping and importing, and the Southern planting interests, until after the organization of the Democratic party and the election of Gen. Jackson. Nor was the power to protect *for the sake of protection* to any considerable extent denied: and not until years after the formation of this party was protection made a party question.

Although laws designed more or less for protection had previously been enacted, protection as a permanent system adapted to a state of peace, was not commenced until 1816; the wars of Europe, from the time of the organization of our present Government to the peace of 1815, having furnished a market for surplus American bread-stuffs And although the protection afforded to most articles by the first few acts was inadequate, the policy was continued, and its efficiency from time to time increased, until the reëlection of Gen. Jackson. The South having contributed, in the greater proportion, to the strength of the Democratic party, it has dictated and prescribed the policy of the party, which has been the mere instrument or agent of the slaveholders, through which they have given law to the nation. Democratic protectionists, one after another, abandoned their long cherished principles which they had learned from Washington and Jefferson and Madison and other statesmen of their time, and adopted the teachings of Southern free traders and nullifiers. Even the President, who had carried the protective principle further than many of its advocates, began to descend from the high position he had occupied, and continued his descent, until he well nigh reached the free trade level. From 1833, to the time of the secession, excepting the four years from 1842 to 1846, the industrial interests of the country have been compelled to struggle against the unfriendly legislation dictated by the enemies of protection. Within this period, the country has been several times visited with those commercial revulsions and financial embarrassments, attended with bank suspensions and the general depression of the national industry, which the non-protective policy has never failed to produce.

To serve the slaveholders has been the leading object of the Democratic party. Whatever they have demanded, it has yielded ; and some things have been granted unsolicited. Hence Democracy has long been the synonym of Slavery ; and the Democratic party is *de facto* the Slavery party. Let us see whether the acts of Democrats and of the Democratic party do not sustain these declarations.

No one will deny that the abandonment of the protective policy, just mentioned, was a concession to the slaveholders, and intended as such ; for Mr. Clay, the author of the measure, himself declared one object of it to be the *pacification of the nullifiers.*

In 1837, Mr. Van Buren, in his Inaugural Address, announced his predetermination to approve no bill for the abolition of Slavery in the District of Columbia ; though he stands on the record as conceding to Congress the constitutional right to do so.

For many years the people petitioned Congress to exercise this power ; but the Democratic party in Congress virtually denied the right of petition, and suppressed freedom of speech in Congress on the subject of Slavery.

Emigrants, chiefly from the Slave States, settled in Texas with a view to the revolutionizing of that Mexican province, the reëstablishing of Slavery therein, and its annexation to the United States. The Democratic party, the faithful servant of the slaveholders, promptly carried the scheme of annexation into effect, adding to its territory, as Mr. Benton and other prominent Democrats declared, many thousands of square miles, and securing, by a provision in the act, the right to divide the State into four Slave States.

Not satisfied with this enormous plunder from a weak nation incapable of resistance or retaliation, the project was conceived of extending our territorial acquisitions indefinitely toward the Pacific. The President, a Democrat and slaveholder, concealing his iniquitous design, ordered our amy into Mexican territory to provoke a war. The object was accomplished. Hostilities were commenced, and the war was prosecuted until Mexico was glad to make peace by the relinquishment of a large portion of her territory, a part of which has been consigned to Slavery. It was in view of this acquisition that Mr. Wilmot moved his proviso to keep Slavery out of the territory that might be acquired. But it was rejected by the Democratic party in Congress. And when, in 1850, governments were to be instituted for the different portions of this territory, California applied for admission as a State into the Union, the Democratic party refused the admission of California as a Free State, unless New Mexico and Utah were left open to Slavery, and unless to this concession were added an enactment that Slavery should not be abolished in the District of Columbia ; and another providing more effectually for the recapture of fugitive slaves. With all these advantages, the slaveholders, it was natural to suppose, would be contented ; and for aught that appeared, they were contented; for it was understood, in 1850, that the Slavery question should not be again agitated in Congress.

But, after a brief period of peace, (a little more than three years,) a Northern Senator, whose claims to the Presidency, presented in National Convention, had not been duly recognized, in order to strengthen these claims, unsolicited, so far as the record shows, *tenders* to the slaveholders his efforts to effect the repeal of the Missouri Compromise, by which alone Slavery had for more than thirty years been kept within a certain boundary line. Southern members of Congress had, in the debates on the measures of 1850, which were to settle this question for all time, admitted the sacredness and binding force of that Compromise, which was not to be disturbed. And Mr. Douglas himself had a few years previously said, in a public speech: "It has received the sanction of all parties in every section of the Union. It had its origin in the hearts of all patriotic men who desired to preserve and perpetuate the blessings of our glorious Union. . . . All the evidences of public opinion seem to indicate that this Compromise has become canonized in the hearts of the American people *as a sacred thing, which no ruthless hand would be reckless enough to disturb.*" After so strong an asseveration, what motive but that to which the act has just been ascribed, could have impelled the "ruthless hand" of that Senator to the perpetration of the "reckless" deed? A different motive, however, must be invented. It now occurs to the Senator that the restrictive act is unconstitutional, and that, by the measures of 1850, it has been rendered "inoperative and void." The slaveholders, though even they had not been "reckless enough" to ask such a favor, would not refuse what the Democratic party, "with superserviceable liberality," (as one aptly expresses it,) "forced on their acceptance."

The efforts of the party to force Slavery into Kansas, are still fresh in the recollection of the reader. So successful were these efforts, that Kansas was kept out of the Union until the Senators from the seceding States had retired, and left in the Senate a Republican majority.

Nor is this all. To secure entire and perpetual supremacy to the Slave Power, a decree was procured from a party Ju diciary, declaring that slaveholders have a right, under the Constitution, to take their slaves into every Territory of the United States, and to hold them there, any law of the Territorial Legislature or of Congress to the contrary notwithstanding.

After so long a term of faithful service rendered the slaveholders by the Democratic party, and with such apparent alacrity; and after so many expressions of sympathy from the Northern branch of the party for the "abused South;" the slaveholders had no reason to apprehend from their Northern allies any opposition to their meditated secession. By none had more been done to encourage them in their wicked purpose, than by the last two Presidents. In nearly every Annual Message, they had severely belabored those who resisted the aggressions of the Slave Power, or questioned its right to appropriate all the national territory, but administered not the slightest rebuke to their Southern friends.

Nor was the zeal of Northern champions for "Southern rights" materially abated by the Secession. Only two or three weeks after South Carolina had formally seceded from the Union, and was fortifying herself by taking possession of the national forts and the custom-house and the revenue in and about Charleston, a great Democratic Mass Convention was held in the city of New York to forestall coercive measures to put down the Rebellion. The Convention was attended by leading Democrats, and by them addressed in language befitting actual Secessionists.

Two weeks later, (Jan. 31, 1861,) in an early stage of the Secession, a large Democratic State Convention was held in the city of Albany. Ex-Governor (now Governor) Seymour, whose political orthodoxy is universally acknowledged by his party, addressed the Convention in a speech, then enthusiastically applauded, and republished by the State Committee as a campaign electioneering document in 1862, when he was again a candidate for Governor. He spoke as follows:

"The condition of our affairs forces upon us the alternative of compromise or civil war. Let us contemplate the latter alternative. We are advised by the conservative States of Virginia and Kentucky, that if force is to be used, it must be exerted against the united South. It would be an act of folly and madness, in entering upon this contest, to underrate our opponents, and thus subject ourselves to the disgrace of defeat in an inglorious warfare. *Let us also see if successful coercion by the North is less revolutionary than successful secession by the South.* Shall we prevent revolution by *being foremost in overthrowing the principles of our Government*, and all that makes it valuable to our people, and distinguishes it among the nations of the earth? Upon whom are we to wage war? Our own countrymen, whose white population is three-fold that of the whole country in the time of the Revolution. Their courage has never been questioned in any contest in which we have been engaged. They battled by our side with equal valor in the Revolutionary struggle, in the last war with Great Britain, and in the Mexican conflict. Virginia sent her sons under the command of Washington to the relief of beleaguered Boston. Alone, the South defeated the last and most desperate effort of British power to divide our country, at the battle of New Orleans. From the days of Washington till this time they have furnished the full proportion of soldiers for the field, of statesmen for the cabinet, and of wise and patriotic Senators for our Legislative halls.

"It is only bigoted ignorance that denies the equality of their public men to those of the North. To assume that our brethren in fifteen States lack the capacity to understand, and the ability to protect their own interests, is to assume that our Government is a failure, and ought to be overturned. It is to declare that nearly one-half of our people are incapable of self-government. * * *

"In what way is this warfare to be conducted? None have been mad enough to propose to muster armies to occupy their territory. Great Britain tried that in the Revolution, when the population of the South was less than 2,000,000. She attempted invasion again in the late war, when their numbers were less than 3,500,000. * * *

"But some have suggested with complacent air, that the South could easily be subjugated by blockading their ports with a few ships of war. * * * But assuming the success of this measure, who are to be the sufferers? Are we waging war upon the South, or upon the North? Upon the Southern planter, or upon the Northern merchant, manufacturer, and mechanic? * * *

"But let us leave these pecuniary considerations for others

more weighty with every patriot. Upon what field shall this contest be waged? Upon what spot shall Americans shed American blood? Where, on this broad continent, shall we find the arena where every association and memory of the past will not forbid this fratricidal contest? Or, when unnatural war shall have brought upon our people its ruin, and upon our nation its shame, to what ground shall we be brought at last? To that we should have accepted at the outset"

What is there in all this but an encomium on Southern patriotism, Southern valor, Southern statesmanship, and Southern invincibility, on the one hand; while on the other, the attempt to suppress the Rebellion would be an "inglorious warfare;" in which success would be no less revolutionary than Secession. To propose to muster armies to occupy their territory would be "madness;" and to defend the Union against its enemies, would be to incur the guilt and the "shame" of waging an "unnatural war," and of engaging in a "fratricidal contest."

The reader will note particularly the concluding sentence of the above extracts from the Governor's speech, in answer to the question, To what ground shall we be brought at last? "*To that we should have accepted at the outset.*" In other words, after having waged an "unnatural," a "fratricidal," an "inglorious," and an unsuccessful war upon the South, we shall be compelled to make terms with the slaveholders by a surrender of the rights of free speech, free labor, all the free territory acquired and to be acquired, and *the right of the majority of the people to govern.* Will the reader who has read the secession speeches of Davis, and Benjamin, and Iverson, and Breckinridge, in the Senate of the United States as they were about taking leave of that body, point out any essential difference between them and the paragraphs quoted from the speech of this "Northern man with Southern principles?" True, he did not—he *durst* not—advocate the right of Secession; but the language is purely Southern, and the speech would find an appropriate place among the reported speeches of these secessionists in Congress.

Another popular Democratic speaker, James S. Thayer, in the same Convention, amid general applause, spoke as follows:

"We can, at least, by discussion, enlighten, settle, and concentrate the public sentiment in the State of New York upon this question, and save it from that fearful current that circuitously, but certainly, sweeps madly on through the narrow gorge of 'the enforcement of the laws,' to the shoreless ocean of civil war. [Cheers.] *Against this, under all circumstances, in every place and form, we must now, and at all times, oppose a resolute and unfaltering resistance.* The public mind will bear the avowal, and let us make it—*that if a revolution of force is to begin, it shall be inaugurated at home.* [Cheers.] And if the incoming administration shall attempt to carry out the line of policy that has been foreshadowed, we announce that when the hand of Black Republicanism turns to blood-red, and seeks from the fragments of the Constitution to construct a scaffolding for coercion—another name for execution—we will reverse the order of the French Revolution, and save the blood of the people by making those who would inaugurate a reign of terror the first victims of a national guillotine. [Enthusiastic applause.]

"The Democratic and Union party at the North made the issue at the last election with the Republican party, that in the event of their success, and the establishment of their policy, the Southern States not only would go out of the Union, *but would have adequate cause for doing so.* [Applause]

"This is the position I took with 313,000 voters in the State of New York, on the 6th of November last. I shall not recede from it, having admitted that, in a certain contingency, *the Slave States would have adequate cause for separation!* Now that the contingency has happened, I shall not withdraw that admission because they have been unwise or unreasonable in the 'time, mode, and measure of redress.' [Applause.]

"What person, what right of property, what domestic right or privilege, what franchise, what security to life or liberty is infringed by the rupture of the Federal relation between the States? [Applause.]

"But it is announced that the Republican administration will enforce the laws against and in all the seceding States. A nice discrimination must be made in the performance of this duty, not a hair's breadth outside of the mark. You remember the story of William Tell, who, when the condition was imposed upon him to shoot an apple from the head of his own child, after he had performed the task, let fall an arrow. 'For what is that?' said Gesler. To 'kill thee, tyrant, had I slain my boy!' [Cheers.] *Let one arrow winged by the Federal bow strike the heart of an American citizen, and who can number the avenging darts that will cloud the heavens in the conflict that will ensue?* [Prolonged applause.] What, then, is the duty of the State of New York? What shall we say to the people when we come to meet this state of facts? That the Union must be preserved. But if this can not be, what then? PEACEABLE SEPARATION. [Applause.]"

Here is an effusion of pure, unalloyed Secessionism, without attempt at concealment, indorsed by the chosen representatives of the Democracy of the State.

When the proceedings of this Albany Tweddle Hall Convention reached Washington, Lawrence M. Keitt, member of Congress from South Carolina, an avowed Disunionist, exultingly proclaimed: "*There will be more men in New York alone to fight for us than the whole North can put down!*" So testifies Hon. R. Conkling, member of Congress from the Utica District, N. Y.

A meeting was held about the same time in Philadelphia, in which Pennsylvania Democracy gave vent to the same treasonable sentiments. One of the resolutions adopted at the meeting declares,

"That in the deliberate judgment of the Democracy of Philadelphia, and, so far as we know it, of Pennsylvania, the dissolution of the Union by the separation of the whole South —a result we shall most sincerely lament—may release the Commonwealth, to a large extent, from the bonds which now connect her with the Confederacy, except so far as for temporary convenience she chooses to submit to them, and would authorize and require her citizens, through a Convention to be assembled for that purpose, to determine *with whom her lot should be cast; whether with the North and East, whose fanaticism has precipitated this misery upon us, or our brethren of the South, whose wrongs we feel as our own;* or whether Pennsylvania should stand by herself, as a distinct community, ready when occasion offers to bind together the broken Union, and resume her place of loyalty and devotion."

And more of the same kind, had we room, could be given from leading Democrats and presses in that State.

From these and a thousand other expressions of Northern sentiment, condemning in advance a resort to coercive measures to suppress the Rebellion, had not the South reason to expect a *divided North*, rendering the incoming administration powerless against the traitors?

War at length came. Sumter fell by the hands of the Rebels. The indignation of the North was aroused. Party seemed to be for a while forgotten. Men of all parties contributed liberally of their means for the defense of the nation. And among the evidences of the encouragement which had been given to the Rebellion by these declarations of Northern Democratic Conventions and presses against coercion, is the surprise expressed by Rebels on learning the unanimity of the North in providing for the defense of the Union. Northern men who were at that time in the South, state, that the intelligence of the Union war meetings here, after the fall of Fort Sumter, struck the Rebel leaders with astonishment. They had been led to hope that their Northern friends would cripple the arm of the administration if raised to strike at the Rebellion. Without such expectation, it is not improbable that the Secession, if any had occurred, would have been confined to two or three States—perhaps, as in 1832, to South Carolina alone.

It was hoped, for a time, that party warfare would be suspended until the war for the Union should be successfully closed. But this hope was soon disappointed. After a few professions of loyalty—a few expressions of displeasure or regret at the conduct of their "Southern brethren" in not "submitting to be governed by such a Chief Magistrate" as they were not pleased to vote for; the forces of the party were again rallied, and their batteries directed against the administration. An offensive war has been kept up, without intermission, for the last two years, during which time ten ponderous blows have been inflicted, with deadly intent, upon Mr. Lincoln and his associates in the Government, for every gentle rap administered to Jefferson Davis and his Rebel confederates.

Scarcely had the excitement caused by the capture of Sumter subsided, before the Democrats of Maine, in State Convention,

"*Resolved*, That the present civil war which Abraham Lincoln is waging upon sovereign States, is alike unconstitutional, inhuman, and unjust, and, unless speedily checked, must end in the complete overthrow of liberty, and in the establishment of a military despotism."

Not having at hand the entire proceedings of this Convention, I can not say whether any resolution was adopted expressing an opinion of "the present civil war which *Jefferson Davis* is waging upon sovereign States." The participators in a Convention within the borders of his "Confederacy," who should pass the above resolution with the name of Jefferson Davis substituted for that of Abraham Lincoln, would learn, by sad experience, that there are on that side of the line, an "inhumanity," an "injustice," and a "despotism," which differ very materially from the distinguishing characteristics of an administration at home, which leaves them in the full enjoyment of the abused constitutional right of freedom of speech!

What but the same spirit of disloyalty induced the nomination of the notorious Vallandigham as the Democratic candidate for Governor of Ohio? Self-respect may deter some Democrats from giving him their votes; but it is believed that, if no other Democratic candidate should be nominated, he will be voted for by the great body of his party.

Modern Democracy is of the same character in all parts of the Union. Governor Seymour, of New York, from whose Tweddle Hall speech we have quoted, is not the only Governor Seymour who is skilled in the use of Southern language. Connecticut furnishes in her Ex-Governor Seymour, a man whose proficiency in that indispensable acquisition of a genuine Northern Democrat—the slaveholders' dialect—is scarcely inferior to that of his distinguished neighbor of the Empire State. While a candidate for Governor in 1862, he held correspondence with one Captain Gladding, a Rebel officer paroled and sent from the city of New York to Hilton Head for exchange, but arrested there as a Confederate spy, upon whose person was found a letter from this Democratic candidate for Chief Magistrate of a Free State, in which he writes thus to his Southern friend:

"DEAR SIR: Your obliging favor of the 28th inst. [July] has been received and read with pleasure. Though you state that you are a stranger to me, I feel myself already introduced to you by the friendly words breathed through your letter. Since the appearance of a letter of mine, to which you so kindly allude, I have had the satisfaction of learning from quite a number of persons, at home and abroad, that they approve of its contents. * * *

"Your allusion to 'constitutional liberty' suggests painful reflections. Since the inauguration of this war, the men in power at Washington have been robbing us of our rights. The great safeguards of the citizen, protecting him against illegal arrests and false imprisonments, have been struck down by ignorant or wicked rulers. * * * *

"I abhor the whole scheme of Southern invasion, with all its horrible consequences of rapine and plunder. You can not help but see, Sir, what thousands of us are beginning to see, that there can be no Union got in this way. The war might have been avoided, and the Union saved. And it would have been avoided but for a fanatic set of men besieging the President, and who wanted blood and plunder. They have got both, and humanity weeps over the wrecks of body and soul. Those who drive the car of war at this time, have no more idea of saving the Union by their bloody sacrifices of this sort, than they have of changing the course of nature. Still they go on. * * *

"Depend upon it, Heaven will frown on such a cause as this; it can not and will not come to good. Where you find me, in lamenting or exposing this iniquity, you will find me to the end of the chapter. I would rather have the good opinion of fellow-citizens who, like yourself, have given me their sympathy in a time of some considerable trial of one's faith, than to be first among the slayers of kindred, or wear the bloody laurels they may gather in a fratricidal war. I doubt if the Union can be restored at all—things have gone so far now that the only possible chance will be by the adoption of a Christian policy very different from that which prevails at Washington at the present time.

"Though I only know you, Sir, by your very kind letter, I shall not soon forget that it was written, or by whom.

"Accept, I pray you, my best wishes, and believe me, dear Sir, respectfully yours."

Is it difficult to tell whether Loyalists or Rebels share

more largely in the sympathies of the writer of this letter? Its importance would be no equivalent for the space it occupies, but for the fact that its author is the representative of the Democracy of his State. The same sentiments were reïterated by him in public speeches during the campaign, and indorsed by a full party vote at the ensuing election.

But it is needless to adduce additional evidence to prove the prevalence of a disloyal spirit among Democrats. The fact is apparent to every person of ordinary discernment who has any considerable acquaintance with men of that party.

"To save the Union" has been with them professedly an object of the deepest solicitude. For this purpose, the constitutional rights of freedom of speech and of the press have been denied; and Southern laws, in direct violation of the Constitution, the mobbing and flogging and hanging of peaceable Northern men without legal trial:—all must be endured without complaint, lest the slaveholders should break the Union into pieces. Now, when the long meditated work of destruction is in progress, the Executive can not exercise a power, or perform an act, for which there is not an express "thus saith the Constitution," even *to save the nation's life*, without throwing these sensitive Democrats into spasms from fear that a line or a letter of the Constitution has been violated. The arrest and confinement of men under the strongest suspicions of being spies and traitors, and refusing to allow them, under bail, to run at large while awaiting trial at some distant day, with opportunity to continue their services to the Rebels, have been condemned as an unconstitutional suspension of the privilege of the writ of *habeas corpus*, and as tyrannical in the extreme. And the Emancipation Proclamation, which is designed to deprive the Rebels of one of their principal means of carrying on the war against the Union, is also, in their view, a shocking violation of the Constitution, and apparently as distasteful to them as to the Confederate Government itself.

Attempts have been made to weaken the Government by misrepresentation and falsehood. The Democratic presses and politicians call the war an "abolition war," and declare it to be waged for the benefit of the negro. They charge Mr. Lincoln with having, by issuing the Proclamation, violated the Constitthtion and the rights of the States, which, in his Inaugural, he had pledged himself to maintain. They have represented the soldiers as feeling themselves to have been duped in being forced to fight to free the negroes, and as being indignant at their having been induced to enlist under false pretenses. Various other arts and devices have been resorted to in order to disaffect soldiers in the service, and to prevent others from enlisting, and thus to weaken the army.

Resolutions were introduced into the Democratic Legislature of Illinois, which "condemn and denounce the flagrant usurpations of the Administration;" charge the Government with the intention of acknowledging the independence of the Confederacy; declaring that the great North-West shall never be separated from the Southern States of the Mississippi Valley; and, among other things, recommended an armistice, or suspension of hostilities professedly to enable the contending parties to meet in Convention to "reason" each other into terms of peace! which would have given the Rebels—which they just then much needed—time to strengthen themselves for a renewal of the conflict. Similar resolutions were introduced in the Legislature of Indiana. But while the resolutions were pending in these Legislatures, expressions of indignation came thundering up the Mississippi from the soldiers from these States in the South-Western army; and remonstrances against their adoption were received, it is said; from leading Democrats in other States, who began to be alarmed at their effect upon *the party:* and thus their passage was prevented. Their suppression, however, could not conceal the sympathy of their authors for their "Southern brethren," nor the object of their introduction.

While our armies were wholly dependent upon volunteers, Democrats discouraged enlistments. Since the passage of the law for enrolling and drafting, efforts are making in various ways—even mob violence has been resorted to—to prevent the Draft. This opposition to the execution of the law has been greatly encouraged by Democrats in high places, who have endeavored to render the law odious by pronouncing it unconstitutional and oppressive.

Nor does the late destructive and sanguinary insurrection

in the City of New York fail to furnish evidence of Northern sympathy and coöperation with the traitors. Facts have been disclosed which justify the belief, that the instigators of this grand riot, and those who participated in it, were in the interest of the South, and that their object was to spread the Rebellion into the Free States. And it is believed, that, if our army had been defeated at Gettysburg, the Rebel flag would have been raised in New York, as the beginning of a Northern Rebellion.

On the night before the 4th of July, there was extensively circulated through the city, a Manifesto, denouncing the Government in the bitterest terms; declaring "the Southern people" to be justly "fighting for their liberties," and that "a Confederate army, whether on our borders or in our midst, we would hail as friends and deliverers," charging "Abraham Lincoln and the men of his council with a violation of their oaths, the Constitution, and the laws, destroying the Union," &c., &c. This was issued at the time of the battle at Gettysburg. The wild and desperate adventure of Lee so far North, countenances the idea that it had reference to some Northern movement. The breaking out of a formidable insurrection which should divert the attention of the Government and a portion of our military strength to the North, might encourage Lee to march upon Washington, or some other important place. This outbreak had been threatened from the South months before it occurred. The most notorious leader was a Virginian, with whom other Southerners were associated. Men in the city openly rejoiced at the escape of Lee and his army, and at his having "out-generaled Meade." Others were heard to laud Fernando Wood and Governor Seymour, and to cheer Jeff. Davis. The Draft, which was in progress, was used to excite the people; but it was probably the least of the motives to the riot. While the Colored Orphan Asylum was burning, a carriage drove up and two men jumped out, who urged on the mob in the work of destruction. The object of these men may be conjectured from a remark of one of the rioters, that *this would compensate Jeff. Davis for the loss of Vicksburg!*

Now, in all this wanton destruction of property to the amount of millions, in the murders committed, in the vile imprecations of vengeance upon the "niggers," the "abolitionists," the President, and others, and in the plaudits bestowed upon Seymour, Wood, and Davis, how many are supposed to have participated who were not politically connected with the Democratic party, or who would not vote for either of these men as the next President, if he should receive a regular party nomination?

The Draft was suspended for several weeks. Gen. Dix having been appointed to the Department of the East, he addressed to Gov. Seymour a letter inquiring whether the military power of the State might be relied on to enforce the execution of the law in case of resistance to it, and expressing his reluctance to call on the War Department for troops which were needed in the army. Instead of giving a direct affirmative answer, he informs the General that he had written to the President, whose answer, he believed, would relieve both "from the painful questions growing out of the enforcement of the Conscription law;" and that after receiving the President's answer, he would write the General again. General Dix, in his reply, expresses his regret that the Governor had characterized the act as the "Conscription law," which, he says, is "a phrase borrowed from a foreign system of enrollment, with odious features, from which ours is wholly free, and originally applied to the law in question by those who desire to bring it into reproach and defeat its execution."

Not receiving the promised answer in due season, Gen. Dix applied to the War Department for the necessary force, which was promptly furnished. Three days after the troops had been ordered, he received a letter from the Governor, expressing his regret that the President had declined to comply with his request to give up the Draft, and to continue to rely on voluntary enlistments! Could the Governor have believed that the President would comply with such a request? What, then, was his object in causing delay? The reason assigned was, that he had received no notice of the time when the Draft was to be made.

Having been repeatedly pressed to declare his purpose, he tells the General that the "State authorities, under no circumstances, can perform duties expressly confided to others; nor can they undertake to relieve others from their proper responsibilities:" as if he had said, it was not his business to enforce the laws of the Union. But as any disturbances of the peace would be "*infractions of the laws of the State*," the military would, if necessary, be called into requisition.

The letters of the Governor are far from being creditable to him. They manifest that spirit of opposition to the administration and the war which is indulged by a large portion of the Democratic party, especially by its leaders, who find it extremely difficult to conceal their sympathy with the traitors.

Here I had intended to close this history of Modern Democracy. But since the last paragraph was written, a letter from Ex-President Pierce to Jefferson Davis made its appearance in the public prints, which is too valuable a contribution to the history of the Rebellion to be withheld. It was found among the papers of Davis which were recently captured by our army at Jackson, Mississippi.

"CLARENDON HOTEL, Jan. 6, 1860.

"MY DEAR FRIEND: I wrote you an unsatisfactory note a day or two since. I have just had a pleasant interview with Mr. Shepley, whose courage and fidelity are equal to his learning and talents. He says he would rather fight the battle with you as standard bearer, in 1860, than under the auspices of any other leader. The feeling and judgment of Mr. S. in this relation is, I am confident, rapidly gaining ground in New England. Our people are looking for "the Coming Man." One who is raised by all the elements of his character above the atmosphere ordinarily breathed by politicians. A man really fitted for this emergency by his ability, courage, broad statesmanship and patriotism. Col. Seymour (Thos. H.) arrived here this morning, and expressed his views in this relation in almost the identical language used by Mr. Shepley. It is true that in the present state of things at Washington, and throughout the country, no man can predict what changes two or three months may bring forth. Let me suggest that in the morning debates of Congress, full justice seems to me not to have been done to the Democracy of the North. I do not believe that our friends at the South have any just idea of the state of feeling hurrying at this moment to the pitch of intense exasperation between those who respect their political obligations, and those who have apparently no impelling power but that which fanatical passion on the subject of Slavery imparts. *Without discussing the question of right—of abstract power* TO SECEDE, *I have never believed that actual disruption of the Union can occur without blood; and if through the madness of Northern Abolitionists that dire calamity must come, the fighting will not be along Mason and Dixon's line merely.* IT WILL BE WITHIN OUR OWN BORDERS, IN OUR OWN STREETS, BETWEEN THE TWO CLASSES OF CITIZENS TO WHOM I HAVE REFERRED. *Those who defy law and scout constitutional obligations, will, if we ever reach the arbitrament of arms,* FIND OCCUPATION ENOUGH AT HOME.

Nothing but the state of Mrs. Pierce's health could induce me to leave the country now, although it is quite likely that my presence at home would be of little service. I have tried to impress upon our people, especially in N. H. and Connecticut, where the only elections are to take place during the coming Spring, that while all our Union meetings are in the right direction and well enough for the present, they will not be worth the paper upon which their resolutions are written, unless we can overthrow political Abolitionism at the polls, and repeal the unconstitutional and obnoxious laws which in the cause of "Personal Liberty" have been placed upon our Statute books. I shall look with deep interest, and not without hope, for a decided change in this relation.

Ever and truly your friend,

"FRANKLIN PIERCE.

"Hon. JEFF. DAVIS, Washington, D. C."

The papers of Davis furnish additional evidence of the truth of what is said on a preceding page in respect to the service rendered the slaveholders by the last two Democratic Presidents. Mr. Buchanan, in a letter dated some years earlier, and also found among these papers, claimed the honor of having, in a certain instance, gone further in support of Slavery than Southerners themselves; or, as he expressed it, in "out-Heroding Herod." But Mr. Pierce goes a large stride further, and assures his Southern brother, that if war should come, their Anti-Slavery opponents would "find occupation enough at home!" If this letter does not prove the writer, before an impartial public, to be an accessory to treason, what language could convict a man of that crime? Could all the correspondence between Northern and Southern Democrats be brought to light, it would astonish the world, and would remove all doubt from the minds of the most skeptical, that, without the encouragement received from the representatives of the Northern Democracy, Secession would never have been attempted, and that the Rebellion is the act of the Democratic party.

CONCLUSION.

My history of the Democratic party is written. Whether the task has been well or ill performed, is submitted to the judgment of an intelligent and impartial public. It has been my sincere endeavor to make my "Mirror" reflect a true picture of that party. I have not selected for animadversion a few of its most unpopular acts, which are liable to unfavorable criticism; nor have I condemned indiscriminately the measures of any Democratic administration. I have noticed such of the principal measures of all parties as were deemed necessary to enable the reader to form a correct opinion of their general character and policy.

With the Democratic leaders, Power has been the ruling motive. This was the object of the organization of the party; and to perpetuate their ill-gotten power, has been the steady aim of a majority of its leaders. With this view was formed their alliance with the Slave Power, based on Slavery as the cardinal principle of union. On this platform the party achieved several victories. Elated with its successes, it became rampant. It broke down the long-standing barrier to the spread of Slavery; and, having carried its aggressions upon Freedom beyond the point of Northern endurance, it met a repulse in 1860; and its ruling spirits *ruled* one-third of the States out of the Union! This left the party in a minority, without any hope of regaining its ascendency, unless by a reünion with the Slave Power upon the old basis. To this object the efforts of its leaders have been directed ever since the Rebellion commenced. They opposed coercion; they advocated a reconstruction of the Union, with a view to further concessions to the slaveholders; and they have in various ways opposed the administration in its efforts to suppress the Rebellion.

They profess an earnest desire for peace; but they want a peace which shall restore the unity of the party. Hence their opposition to the Emancipation Proclamation. Slavery abolished, all hope of a restoration of the entirety of the party vanishes for ever. They desire peace; but they want to negotiate it themselves; and for this privilege, they would be willing that the war should be protracted until after the 4th of March, 1865. This is a fair inference from both their language and their conduct. After having, in conjunction with their former allies, involved the nation in a desolating war, these Northern Democrats have the assurance to ask for a restoration to power, alleging as a reason, that the Democratic party alone is competent to bring the war to a successful termination! In other words, the present administration is unwilling to prostrate itself at the footstool of the Slave Power, and beg a peace on such terms as His Majesty may be pleased to prescribe. Into such a humiliating posture is this party endeavoring to bring our Government. And to this humbled condition it will be brought, if this party should retrieve its lost power before the Rebellion shall have been suppressed. Do not then the honor and the permanent welfare of the nation demand the efforts of every patriot to put down and exterminate a party under whose despotic misrule Constitutional Liberty has been placed in imminent peril, and which hopes, after an interregnum of four years, to be reinstalled in power, and to resume its "reign of terror?"

Let the friends of the Union not forget, that they have a foe to contend with on this side as well as one on the other side of Mason and Dixon's line. In the war with Sham-Democracy, no weapon is so effective as LIGHT. The Democratic masses are honest and patriotic. But they have long been the victims of an inveterate prejudice. They have been taught to look with suspicion upon everything that was not labeled "Democracy." Thousands are beginning to see that profession is not principle; that they have been beguiled into the service of Slavery by men with Democracy on their tongues while allied in heart and purpose with the enemies of Freedom. Expose fully the evil designs and artifices of their leaders, and they will dissolve their present party connection, and join the party of the Union.

One of the most auspicious "signs of the times" is the growing sentiment, that permanent peace can be secured only by the overthrow of Slavery; and that in the present "irrepressible conflict" between Freedom and Slavery, the latter must yield. That Slavery and the Rebellion will end together, is not to be expected. Many years may elapse before the last vestige of the giant curse—the parent of the present gigantic Rebellion—shall disappear. But we rejoice in the hope, that, in the war which it has waged with Freedom, it will receive, if it has not already received, a wound which shall deprive it of its controlling power in the Government, and hasten its extinction.

Lamentable as the immediate consequences of the Rebellion are, our grief is made tolerable by anticipations of its ultimate happy results. We can not repress the hope, that, when Slavery, which has made us a divided people, shall cease to exist, the two hostile sections will,

"Like kindred drops, be mingled into one;"

will become one in feeling and one in interest. And it is confidently believed that the South will have the greater cause for rejoicing. She will wonder at her folly in having clung with such tenacity to her "peculiar institution," when she shall have found its loss compensated ten-fold by those other institutions which have made the North an object of envy to her less prosperous rival. Northern enterprise and Northern capital will be no longer circumscribed by sectional boundaries, but will find a new and inviting field beyond the Potomac. An extensive and mutually profitable commercial intercourse between the two sections will be established. Churches and school-houses will be multiplied, and diffuse their salutary influence through every Southern community; Southern and Northern society will be assimilated; and the different parts of our great Republic will be united in indissoluble bonds of fraternal affection. Let Slavery and the Rebellion die together, and all these things will be fulfilled before this generation shall have passed away.

INDEX.

ERRATA

Page 42, in the title to the Chapter, for "John Quincy Adams," read *Mr. Monroe.*
" 45, line 16 from bottom, after "one," insert *from.*
" 85, line 9 from bottom, for "33," read 34.
" 98, line 13 from top, for "Moses," read *Amos.*
" 214, line 12 from bottom, for "28," read 26.

www.ingramcontent.com/pod-product-compliance
Lightning Source LLC
LaVergne TN
LVHW010235110826
845151LV00004B/1296

* 9 7 8 1 4 2 5 5 2 4 9 1 3 *